MW00830413

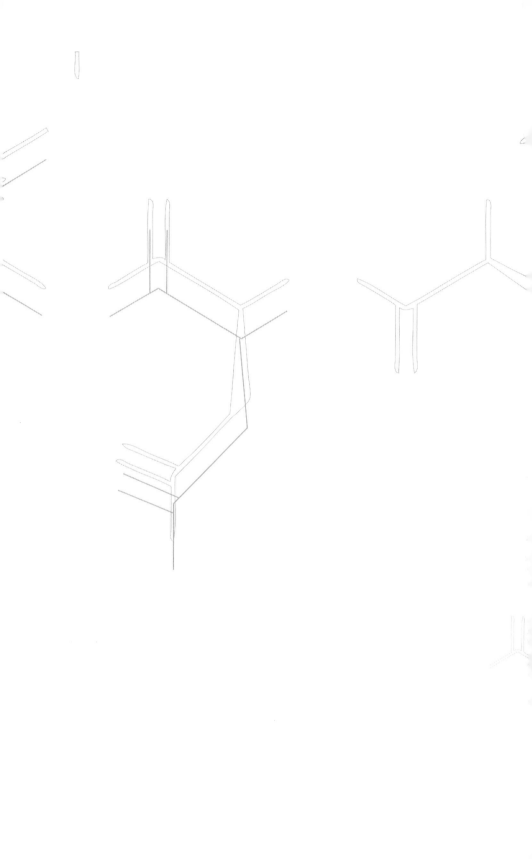

life
before
birth

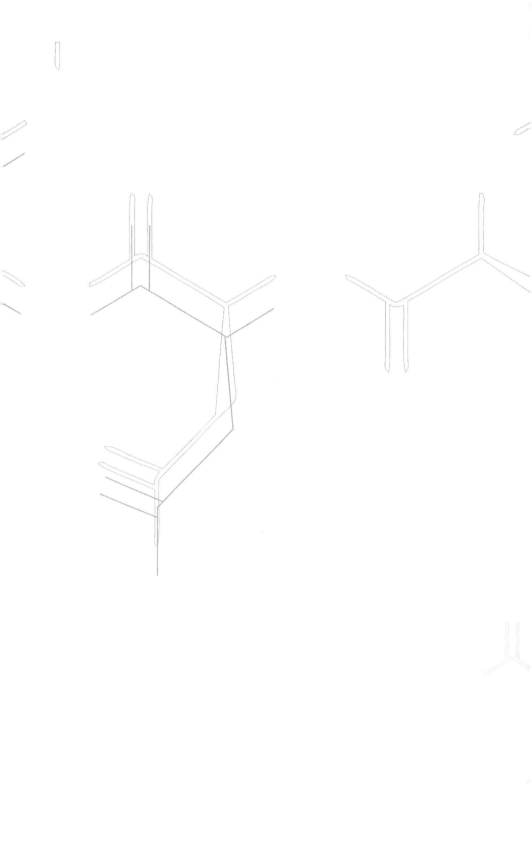

life
before
birth

THE HIDDEN SCRIPT
THAT RULES OUR LIVES

ARTHUR JANOV, PHD

NTI UPSTREAM **nti**_upstream_ CHICAGO

© 2011 by NTI Upstream
All rights reserved. Except as permitted under the U.S. Copyright Act of 1976, no part of this publication may be reproduced, distributed, or transmitted in any form or by any means, or stored in a database or retrieval system, without the prior written permission of the publisher.

NTI Upstream
180 N. Michigan Avenue, Ste. 700
Chicago, Illinois 60601
Visit our website at www.ntiupstream.com

NTI Upstream books may be purchased for educational, business, or sales promotional use. For more information about special discounts for bulk purchases or to book a live event, please contact NTI Upstream Special Sales at 1-312-423-5680.

Cover and interior design by Annie Heckman
Author photo by France D. Janov
Edited by Jeff Link

ISBN: 978-0-9836396-0-2
Printed in the United States of America
Library of Congress Control Number 2011933743

To my wife France, clinical director of training at the Janov Primal Center, and to my staff who have labored in the trenches these many years to help perfect the technique and theory of primal therapy. France has done heroic work to refine the training and practice of primal therapy and so has changed how we at the Primal Center practice therapy. She has spent years putting together the Legacy Project which will be available soon on DVD, detailing the process and practice of primal therapy.

contents

acknowledgments

There are five people who helped make this book possible: my two research associates, Brian Wilson, a medical and science writer, and Peter Prontzos, an instructor at Langara College in Vancouver who sent me a constant flow of new research articles and corrected some of my ideas; my editor, Mary Strobel, who labored for years on the manuscript; my agent, Kimberley Cameron, who manages to get my books to the public; and finally, my wife, France, who read every word and corrected constantly. There is no book without their help.

introduction

In more than one hundred years of psychotherapy very little has changed, except cosmetically. It is still the fifty-minute hour, the sit-up, face-to-face talk, with insight contained in the dulcet tones of a concerned therapist. There is still the horror of the unconscious as a place of ill-defined demons to be avoided at all costs. No one says it, but it is implied in how we carefully steer the patient into the present and away from the past. The Freudians now call it ego-psychology but it is really psychoanalysis with a slightly different focus. Sadly, in the name of progress, more and more therapists have moved away from the past into a present-focused approach; this is particularly true for the cognitive behavior therapies. There is an apotheosis of the present, of the here-and-now, and a move away from the one thing that is curative: history. We are historic beings, imprinted neurophysiologically with our past. Any proper treatment must address that history.

More sadly, for one hundred years we have been talking to the wrong brain. It is that verbal, "talking" brain that prevents any hope of a cure for emotional illness. Communicating with the brain that talks was fine a century ago but now we know so much more about the brain and what it contains; we know that damage done to us is imprinted on lower levels of consciousness far below where words live. Further, we know much more about how early memory is imprinted and how it affects our lives.

A bit immodestly, I have known and seen this now for decades. When I first wrote about how the birth trauma and prenatal experience affect adult behavior, in the 1970s, my ideas were considered "new agey." Now, there are literally hundreds of studies verifying this proposition. There seems to be little question in the scientific community that a pregnant woman's mood and physiology can produce long-term effects on the offspring. If we want to ensure the health and mental stability of future generations, we need a paradigm change in psychology and psychotherapy. We need to push back the envelope from childhood to infancy and gestation. For there is where the most good and harm is done to our offspring. And there is where many of our later ailments and personality traits get their start.

As we move forward, I trust you'll see the enormity of the influence of our life in the womb; the most unexpected effects of womb-life on later heart disease, blood pressure, migraine, epilepsy and personality deviations. While we live inside our mothers we are responding to an environment—her—and the life that unfolds after birth is, in some ways, just a continuation of that maturation inside mother. Think of it: she is the only world the baby knows. He is already developing a personality during these critical nine months of life—growing up in an isolated world where there is only one source of input. He can be born neurotic and prone to disease (or carefree and healthy), not simply because of heredity but also because of experience during womb-life.

Understanding this, what we now must do is fashion a therapy commensurate with our knowledge. Continuing to approach treatment by zeroing in on the talking brain prevents any hope of cure for emotional illness. Instead therapists must traverse the bridge between knowing and feeling. They must adopt an emotional, experiential approach rather than a cognitive one. That is not an easy task.

We need to learn a new language—that of the unconscious—a language with no words, just feelings and sensations. I submit that psychotherapy has not changed radically in nearly the last century because we've always believed that words could help us make profound change in patients; and, in fact, words often are our defense against feeling. But as psychotherapists our goal is to produce feeling human beings, not mental giants. I have stressed for years that access to feelings begins with the right brain, and several studies have demonstrated that addressing the right brain may help penetrate repressed feelings. So long as we focus on the left frontal, thinking brain progress will be limited to this area, not the region where feelings are stored. We will be loaded with insights that mask feelings rather than expand them. Progress will be limited to the psyche and not the whole system.

Now why is that so important? Why should the language of feelings take precedence to thoughts we can verbalize? Because, quite simply, we can only heal where we were wounded. We know that emotional wounds lie deep in the brain, out of range of consciousness. Although the lower brain "talks" to us all of the time, we have never learned how to talk to it. Hypoxia, for instance, a pathological condition in which the body is deprived of oxygen, speaks to us every day. The problem is we do not have the language to talk back, to create a dialogue with higher levels of the brain, such as the prefrontal cortex, and make meaningful changes. The lower brain talks to us in other ways, as well: in our nightmares and colitis, in our high blood pressure and migraines, in our sexual difficulties and interpersonal conflicts. Indeed, our history is asserting itself in our every waking moment; yet, time and again, we go to psychotherapists who want to concentrate solely on the here and now; who want to use the left brain exclusively, coaxing patients to think they are better rather than actually making them better. Worse, these methods often lack the sort of neurophysiologic measurements that are needed for a proper psychotherapy.

At the Primal Center in Santa Monica, California, we treat patients experiencing pain due to repressed childhood trauma. Every patient, every day, has his or her vital signs (heart rate, body temperature, blood pressure) measured before and after sessions, and we have found dramatic changes in our patients after just one year of therapy. For a long time we made brainwave studies of our patients until it got too expensive. As we'll see later in the book, these vital signs and brainwaves may indicate a good deal about our personality and mood, as well as why primal therapy may help to normalize them.

We are walking archives, living in the imprint of our past. For too long we have focused on the present and words, because these are the easiest to access and take no great effort. On top of that, we have not known how to access our neonatal and early childhood history. We do now. To get better, we need to take the emotional trip to our history and undo the damage. We need to relive the repressed pain of early trauma through what I call a "Primal."

The time we return to during a Primal, our fetal life and infancy, is when and where our problems begin and resolution resides. Not only is this time key to the mental health of adults, but it is also profoundly important for expectant mothers who, while carrying their children in the womb, are shaping their destiny. In the course of this book, I hope to clarify what happens to the fetus and baby when the mother feels or acts in a certain way, and what the mother can do to help her child.

Skeptics scoffed when I first described, in the 1970s, the capacity of the fetus to absorb his mother's reality through a neurophysiologic connection. "Where was the research?" they asked. Now the research is catching up. Fifty years ago who would have dreamed that a heart attack at the age of sixty is, in part, caused by things that happened to us sixty years earlier? Who would have guessed a migraine at age thirty has its start before we set foot on this planet? But, as you will see, there is mounting evidence that this is the case. What the mother does, how she feels, what she eats and drinks—all of these are structuring a new life on this planet.

How do I know that the past is engraved in our brains for a life-time? How do I know that reliving our traumatic past helps us heal? That is the subject of this book.

PART ONE:
WOMB-LIFE,
A NEW PARADIGM

1

how love sculpts the brain

During pregnancy and the first critical months of the baby's life, the mother is downloading a good deal of her neurochemistry into the fetus. Her state of being produces alterations in hormone output that will affect the baby, perhaps for a lifetime. If the mother is depressed, hormones change; if the mother is anxious, hormones change; and the expectation of the fetus is that it will meet the same kind of environment after birth as before. The fetus's whole physiology and neurology changes to adapt to the mother's alterations; inside the womb, the baby is reacting to an environment that is possibly the most important one in his or her life. That is why the loving bond between the mother and child is so important.

In my theory, love between the parent and child takes many forms, but essentially it means fulfilling the needs of the baby, including the need for oxygen and proper nutrients while being carried. Lack of love for the fetus deprives him of essential nutrients for his development. This deprivation may assume many patterns and changes as he develops, but, in all cases, it is the subsoil on which later personality is built. Unless we believe that intrauterine life doesn't count, which is to dismiss the considerable evidence that has amassed in the last decade, we must not ignore this time. The child will have emotional needs after birth and still later there will be intellectual needs. Needs have a timetable for when they appear and when they must be fulfilled. This is a basic biologic law, which means that any attempt to fulfill needs out of that timetable will not be effective and will leave the child deprived.

Though he may spend a lifetime trying to fulfill that need, it will always be symbolic rather than real fulfillment because the critical window has passed. I must add one proviso here: later love can and does ameliorate the early imprinted pain but cannot erase it. Only reliving can ultimately get rid of it.

A newborn needs physical contact. When the desire for touch goes unmet early on, any caress or touch at age ten will be helpful but not biologically fulfilling. The early need has been repressed, and, in this sense, love is no longer viable. In order to recover it we will need to unearth basic need in our therapy, so that adults exposed to early trauma will, once again, be emotionally healthy and able to achieve fulfillment. Need is basic and must form the linchpin of any proper psychotherapy. When needs are not fulfilled neurosis steps in, and neurotic behavior follows suit. We've discovered, for instance, that it is very early deprivation that is behind so much of serious drug addiction; the earlier the need the more essential for survival and, hence, the more painful. Pain is commensurate with the urgency for fulfillment. That is why womb needs are almost always a matter of life-and-death.

Love means having a proper birth, without heavy anesthetics to shut down the oxygen supply to the newborn. Most important, it means a mother fairly free of anguish and depression; for her physiologic and emotional state is more or less the offspring's state, not just momentarily, but for a lifetime. And it is not strictly hereditary; it is experience layered on top of genetics, what fetal researchers refer to as epigenetics. In fact, when we see the documentation we discover that how we've been nurtured in the womb and our first years is at least as important, if not more so, than heredity.

As it turns out, love is not as ephemeral as we might have thought. There are enduring physical consequences when it is not there. And therein lies the rub; we are dealing with errors of omission, an absence not a presence—which is why it is so hard to pin down. Research shows us, however, that it is the right side of the brain, in a kind of synchrony, that is sculpting the feeling centers of the baby. When the mother is not loving, not soft and warm and caressing, she is shaping a different kind of feeling structure in the baby's brain. This is particularly true of the right brain, where the very early imprints take place. And this is historic, I might add, because it is the right side of the brain that develops first and handles the severe impact of early pain. The two hemispheres are different in other respects. The right brain is more global, capable of seeing the overview, whereas the left brain is more detailed and point by point. The right brain is attuned to nuance and subtleties; the left brain is easily deceived, not having a feeling base to call on. Though most of what happens to us during gestation is registered in the right brain, in today's therapy we usually utilize the left brain to get to our feelings. Not an efficient process. We keep going to the wrong address. If we want to understand our primordial ancestors, we cannot only focus on the present; and, in the same way, if we are ever to understand and cure behaviors and symptoms, we cannot neglect history. The left brain knows nothing of feeling; the right side knows just about everything. Therapy needs to go after the right brain, with left-brain therapy handled as the final phase of treatment. That is, left-brain insights must follow, not precede, feelings. As in evolution, feeling must come before thought.

love before birth

When love begins in the womb, the mother is speaking to her baby in "womb-speak," a language that has no words. Nevertheless, it is a very strong language, perhaps the most critical that will occur in our lives. Every "word" a mother speaks has great impact. In her physiology she is saying to the child, "I am calm. I am normal. And I love you." We find the message of love in the mother's energy, passion, and sexuality. When these are lacking, however, basic primal processes may be disrupted.

From a neurologic perspective, a mother's love and calm while carrying not only strengthens the baby's brain but also produces better painkiller receptors, known as opiates, that allow him to manage pain more easily. His ability to feel comfortable also depends on an optimum level of the neurotransmitter serotonin, which animal research indicates may have a good deal to do with how socially gregarious we are (more on this in chapters ten and fourteen). Whereas adverse events in the womb can decimate this neurotransmitter, early love normalizes it. This means a better handling of stress and adversity as the child goes through life. In addition, love boosts the proliferation of endorphins, our internally produced painkillers, which allow us to inhibit intense pain and experience greater joy and contentment. Some evidence even suggests there may be a more extensive network of dendrites (the parts of brain cells that receive information from other cells), which would indicate a better inter-connectivity among nerve pathways and perhaps a more conscious life.

When I use the word "love," I am speaking of more than just physical closeness in the form of kissing, hugging, holding, soothing, listening, and attending to the baby—although these are certainly part of the definition. A baby has needs well before birth, as well as after, and the more these needs are met, the healthier, happier, and more intellectually capable the baby will be. So while it's true that in his first years of life a child may need encouragement and praise, the need for love really begins much sooner.

Besides holding the infant and caressing him, love means looking at the infant with warmth, paying attention to his moods, and caring about his needs. It means sensing what he is feeling; understanding when he needs attention and stimulation and when he doesn't. All of this helps determine how the emotional areas of the brain develop. A mother's physiology while carrying also helps establish the so-called "set-points" for various hormones in the baby. Her system regulates the fetus's hormone output and, to the extent she experiences high levels of anxiety during pregnancy, the child may be at risk for a higher output of the stress hormone cortisol, not just for a few days or weeks, but for a lifetime.

During pregnancy the mother is essentially transferring her patterns and rhythms of mood, in addition to any hormonal imbalance she might have, into the child's feeling centers; namely, the hypothalamus and other limbic structures in the brain. Early love helps determine the maturation and development of these neurologic structures, which in turn has a direct effect on the release of hormone secretions. The main point is that due to high levels of maternal stress early genetic set-points may be reset, modifying how "feeling" we become as adults.

A mother's emotional health during pregnancy also is important for the development of the frontal area of the child's brain where impulses are controlled and integrated.

It is easy to think our personalities and propensities for disease are strictly hereditary. After all, even in the scenario I've just described, these traits are transmitted from mother; however, not in the way we had once imagined. Though the child's emotions may already be fixed when he enters this planet (though he may be lethargic and passive from birth, for example) this personality type may not be wholly genetic. Instead the child's personality may be the product of what has been downloaded at pregnancy, that is, an imprint: either loving or non-loving, down-regulated or hyperactive. This imprint forms the matrix for the child's later physiology and brain development and, of course, his later mental health.

To take an example, a mother on heavy drugs or alcohol may shape a suppressive tendency in the offspring—a newborn who rarely if ever cries or reacts strongly. The child is such a good boy, in fact, that we rarely comprehend something is wrong until months later. He is born passive and lacking in energy, unresponsive and non-reactive. He may even get "love" for being so undemanding and out of the way. His prototype is based on the dominance of the rest-and-repair nervous system, what I call the parasympathetic system. Later in life his drug of choice, most likely a stimulant such as cocaine, will tend to normalize his deficiencies for a brief time, but inevitably it will wear off. Like many addicts, he will try to recover the lost half of himself, the part that was missing at the start. That is addiction; we should not look at this pejoratively any more than we should a child born with kidney problems. It is a lifelong sentence, and there is good reason to believe its physiologic roots are planted in the womb.

Besides abstaining from alcohol, drugs, junk food, and other toxins, a primary way a mother can express love is by fulfilling the child's dietary needs. Recent animal models have found that changes in the protein input of the carrying mother may significantly affect the baby and produce a propensity for later obesity. The baby is learning to adapt to its most important environment; the problem is that the adaptation endures, so the adult continues to expect conditions found in the womb. He sees food at age thirty and immediately gobbles it up. This is known as one-trial learning, and it is one of the reasons womb-life is so important to our long-term health.

A proper diet also means breastfeeding right after birth. There are mothers too busy or too harassed to do that, and so a nanny or caregiver offers the bottle. No matter the rationalization, the child is unloved. Later, when he sees a breast, that very same early stimulation may be present again. He will feel sexually excited (as an adult male), but the real excitement is primal. The excitement is in anticipation of fulfillment—to be touched and caressed, to suck—which later takes a sexual turn. There may be orgasm and relief in adult sex life, but the relief is only temporary; it is only a substitute or symbolic fulfillment of the early unmet need. As with overeating, the gratification does not last. The impulse soon returns because it is driven by a basic need which has found an outlet, albeit a counterfeit one. Alas, many of us go chasing symbolic love for the rest of our lives.

In one experiment, women were encouraged to place their babies at the breast right after birth. The earlier the contact, the more physical the mother was later on with the newborn. In general, we see more loving contact with early bonding. In fact, if there were one word to describe love from birth on, it would be "touch." Intimate contact between mother and child in the first weeks and months of life regulates the opiate receptor system, ensuring optimum levels to make us comfortable. As adults, we are then able to make our own children comfortable, enabling them to handle stress without being overwhelmed. The loved parent exhibits a calmness that is translated to the baby.

Without sufficient touching, however, inhibitory neurohormones fire in overdrive, attempting to shut off the pain caused by deprivation. If a lack of love has been imprinted, as we will see later, inhibitory or repressor neurotransmitters may be called upon to do that for a lifetime. Eventually, serotonin supplies become depleted. And, in the worst cases, the brain will be compromised: there will be fewer neocortical, top-level neurons to deal with arousal, fewer brain cells to suppress feelings or hold back impulses. The result may be chronic anxiety throughout life—a tendency which begins its life during gestation and infancy.

So what do parents do that is so damaging? Obviously, a tense mother who handles her child roughly is not imparting a feeling of calm in him. Similarly, a mother who desperately needs love may use her baby to fulfill her needs, demanding too much from him so that he cannot be himself. The autobiography *Open*, in which tennis star Andre Agassi discusses how his father drove him unmercifully in order to fulfill his own failures, is an excellent cautionary example. What drove Agassi to drugs? Above all, a parent's greed for love. And, indeed, how a mother treats her child after birth is frequently indicative of what went on during womb-life. For instance, a mother who is narcissistic may try to keep her weight down to look pretty and attractive, without adequate thought for the life inside of her.

Indeed, there is little doubt that a mother's physiology while carrying is reflected in the baby's biology. The mother's lowered output of key neurohormones may show up in a baby who is imprinted in the hyperactive mode. On top of that, there is clear evidence that mothers who smoke produce smaller babies, at high risk for asthma, slow lung growth, and lower respiratory conditions. If the mother has been a drug addict, newborn babies may go into withdrawal, showing symptoms such as sweating, shaking, and vomiting. And, understand, trauma to the system is not just chemically induced. Pregnant rats repeatedly exposed to loud noise produced smaller offspring, an experiment that seems to indicate that maternal stress has a direct effect on the newborn. A tense system is an improperly functioning one, and research concerning how tension levels of pregnant women affect the condition of their babies should certainly be a priority for the future.

the die is cast

Scientists claim that the brain is plastic, malleable. But based on my experience, once the critical period when needs must be fulfilled is over, the brain is incapable of a great deal of change. The brain adjusts its shape and function based on very early experience, and rarely makes any radical departure after that. As long as imprinted memory of pain endures, and it does, we cannot expect a different kind of brain. I disagree with most of the current therapeutic efforts to change the brain. Yes, the hippocampus and a few other brain structures go on changing for most of our lives but, in important ways, the brain is inflexible. What is more flexible is the part of the brain that thinks, spouts words and ideas, and holds beliefs—the top layer known as the neocortex (or frontal cortex). What are intransigent are lower brain levels that function as survival mechanisms. In fact, it is in our best interest if these do not undergo great change, for they allow us to react instinctively. If we cannot feel the rightness of something, we are handicapped; if we cannot react immediately, we are likewise handicapped.

In a 2010 study, Justin Feinstein, of the University of Iowa, compared the effect of sad films on those adults who had their hippocampus damaged versus those who did not.[1] Adults with a damaged hippocampus, he reported, could not form new memories. They had little memory capacity and could not express their feelings about the films or even remember them, but physiological markers showed that they continually felt sad. Amazingly, their feelings continued even without the ability to call them up. In other words, we don't need higher-level input to feel sad; we respond instinctively, with or without it. Feelings are inscribed as feelings. And these primitive instincts can be imprinted long before we have the cortical capacity to define them.

Feinstein is not alone. Michael Meaney, a genetic researcher at McGill University in Canada, has done experiments with rats.[2] He compared the offspring of normal mothers, who frequently licked their babies but subjected the offspring to stress during pregnancy, with a second group of pups who were also under stress but experienced no licking. Not surprisingly, those babies who were heavily licked turned out to be the most normal and well adjusted. What is a surprise, however, is how much womb-life counts. For animal mothers, licking is tantamount to hugging and caressing in humans. And, just as we see in the rats, a woman who is unhappy or depressed while carrying can influence that child for a lifetime, even if she later normalizes and feels better.

The notion of a maternal imprint—a sort of physiologic signature passed from the pregnant mother to the child—has sparked interest from journalists and science writers, in recent articles on stem cells. Scientists, it appears, have found a way to avoid using embryonic stem cells for research by using current skin cells, instead. Through a complicated procedure, they've managed to wind back the clock and return those cells to an embryonic state. In general, embryonic refers to a time within twelve weeks of conception. Embryonic cells can be used in stem-cell therapy because they are not, as yet, "dedicated." Known as pluripotential cells, they have not become what they are destined to be: bones, blood, kidneys, etc.; thus uncommitted, they have no special identity and researchers can make them into anything they want. In a way, this is similar to what happens to infants who are short on experience; they can be molded into what their parents need and want.

Once cells take on their imprint, however, they often cannot be changed; their identity (the skin cell, George, for example) remains unshakeable. In recently reported studies, researchers found that some skin cells that were rewound back to their primitive selves could not be used later to rebuild a different organ or tissue—bone, for example. The cells retained the memory of what they were originally. And the danger of all this, if some exaggeration may be allowed, is that you start using imprinted cells for therapy and suddenly you have a patient growing teeth in his throat. More likely, you get what is called a teratoma (not particularly pleasant, either), where a patient will grow tumors instead of the desired organ.

The point is that the imprint is rock solid, engraved even into microscopic cells that do not shed their identity easily. Our human imprint, I propose, is found in every fiber and cell of our being and retains a precise memory of its past. It cannot be pinpointed to any particular location in the system since it is everywhere, from our hormonal balance to our neurology. The imprint says, "This is what happened to me and this is who I am." And because the imprint is everywhere, when we relive it there may be changes throughout the system. That is why we need to relive experiences: to reset the set-points and, in so doing, exercise a profoundly new approach to medicine and psychiatry. We need to "remember" with our entire physiology and being, not just the neocortex.

There is more to this story, for early gestational stress leaves a mark on the genes. That mark is then hard-coded and becomes a part of each of us, an epigenetic memory. The way this happens is through DNA methylation—meaning the gene expression pattern in cells is altered, so that cells can "remember" their history and suppress certain viral or hazardous elements. Early trauma tends to add part of the methyl chemical group to the cell so that it becomes fixed as memory: epigenetic memory that is easily confused with genetics, more generally.

In short, stress or primal pain is encoded into the most basic aspects of our cells; it endures and can mark us not only in terms of lowered resistance to disease but also by producing changes in hippocampal cells that affect later memory. The way methylation evolves helps to define the critical window—the time in which our needs must be fulfilled or we run the risk that pain will be permanently imprinted; it also defines where the patient must go for resolution. In my view, only major imprinted pain that alters the system occurs within the confines of the critical window. Thus, when we see methylation of cells it means that the mark of trauma was stamped in during the critical period before birth and at the very beginning of life (more on this later).

What scientists are finding is that it is largely due to methylation that genetic switches are altered. The methyl chemicals seem to cling to the gene and control whether the switch is turned on or off, and whether it is on when it should be off, such as in serious disease. The good news seems to be that, unlike pure genetics, methylation can be reversed. Thus, epigenetic-caused disease may be normalized at last.

And in truth the distinction between heredity and epigenetic "heredity" must be made, if we are ever to reverse disease. When a mark is made on certain anxiety-regulating cells, for instance, we may be stressed until that mark is revisited and relived (perhaps for life). What's more, the mark can be relived unconsciously, without our specific awareness of it, if connection is made through the proper memory circuits. But the process of methylation also can be temporarily reversed with medications such as Prozac. So what is really going on?

Certain regions of the brain altered by drugs are the same areas that may be affected by reliving gestational events. That is part of the reason it is so easy to confuse genetics with epigenetics: our moods and personalities are shaped early on, so we believe psychological disorders are passed down through the bloodlines. After all, if both the parents have blue eyes, it is not a mystery that their child also has blue eyes. But when it comes to behavior and feelings, it is another matter. Genes can be changed through experiences the fetus undergoes while in the womb. On the basis of those experiences, the offspring may then "decide" whether certain genes are expressed or repressed.

And it is here that some of the mystery of cancer may be uncovered, for it may be that cancerous cells would evolve as normal cells if not for the physiologic force of repression provoked by maternal stress. It may be that as benign cells surge forward along foreordained pathways they are blocked from their destinations. They are then "crushed" or deviated and can no longer be themselves; they lose their identity and become lethal. And as they are changed, we are changed.

What all this means is that by examining our womb-life in detail we can often predict our future: our sexual problems, the possibility of later cancer, psychosis, heart problems, Alzheimer's disease, and a whole host of afflictions. The question is, "How do we do that?" How do we get to those early driving needs that preceded our first steps in a new world? They may seem so "far-out" as to be unbelievable, but many thousands of patients have gone through my therapy, reporting what they went through even when I was unprepared to believe them. At last new research is confirming what they told me.

2

are we already who we are at birth?

When the Nazis occupied Holland in 1944, there was a period known as the Dutch Hunger Winter when mothers in the west Netherlands were deprived of nutrition; this starvation had a pronounced effect on the babies that were born. Most of the children had insulin deviations, none of them were normal birth size, and there was some evidence of mental retardation. Since then scientists have found that when pregnant rats are undernourished, their offspring are less likely to spend time in the daylight. For whatever reason, malnourishment has that kind of effect. It could be that the rat, expecting to be born into a hostile environment, grows up to be less adventurous, smaller, and more anxious—all in the interest of self-preservation. These, of course, are the same features we find in adult survivors of the Holland famine, and that is no accident. The aftermath of the Dutch Hunger Winter is undoubtedly disturbing, a chilling reminder of the Nazi's brutal legacy, but we must not ignore it, for it could hold the key to our proper understanding of pregnancy and childbirth.

As you may have guessed, one of this book's leitmotifs is this: things that happen after birth will not have the incredible impact that they do before birth. The critical window is before birth; irreversible changes are taking place, changes that will determine everything from personality types—phlegmatic versus energetic—to what kind of drugs one will take. Much of this, of course, has to do with the supply of oxygen and nutrients to the fetus. A baby starving in the womb can expect a wholly different physiology than a baby very hungry at the age of two; and it is my belief that the prenatal period may be the more critical.

During pregnancy the fetus lives alongside a sac called the placenta, which is the key deliverer of information from the mother to the child. The placenta is not only about nutrient transfer; it is also an important source of hormones that influence maternal and fetal function. From about the seventh week onward, the placenta will make the hormone chorionic gonadotropin, which enters the fetus and stimulates the developing testis of the male to make testosterone. Late research has found, further, that the placenta helps provide the frontal brain of the baby with serotonin so that the mother's emotional state while carrying is transferred to the fetus directly, influencing the development of her baby.[1]

As I've suggested, it is the environment of the carrying mother that changes the development of the fetus. He is learning about his environment, the only one he knows during his life in the womb. And events during this period are stamped in the child's biology as an imprint that endures for a lifetime. He is learning what to expect from life; his brain neuron apparatus and physiology are changing to meet those expectations. If the mother has too much of the stress hormone cortisol, then there is a physiologic expectation on the part of the fetus that the world is fearful and threatening. To meet the anticipated threat, he may beef up his alerting hormones—an imprinted strata that will affect all later physiologic and psychological development.

Interestingly, experiments with mice have found that the placenta is a key source of serotonin, a neurotransmitter that is crucial to how the brain develops. In the early stages of life, serotonin helps shape neuronal circuits, and also may produce deviations in those circuits. Later, learning disorders, schizophrenia, dementia, and many cerebral functions may be compromised due to this womb experience and the deviation of serotonin output. The placenta, it seems, is in itself a hormone factory that responds to outside influences. It is here that the outside experience of the mother is translated to the fetus.

The fetus or newborn cannot conceptualize fear, but he can certainly feel it and react to it. His early response forms a template that dictates how the child will respond to later stress. Those responses are governed by lower brain structures, which do not as yet think, analyze, or develop images of the scenes of misery. They do, however, react.

As the brain develops there will be, first, a way of understanding discomfort and tracing scenes to their origin, and second, a way to fabricate ideas that conceptualize the agony. All levels of the brain resonate with key counterparts so that a rejection at age ten can resonate down to the prototype and set off a big reaction—a so-called prototypic reaction. This response will seem inordinate at first, but it is not; it reflects the current source of hurt combined or compounded by the original source.

Research now helps clarify how this happens.[2] The point is that the newborn's brain is often chaotic, a bunch of brain cells looking for a place to connect. They seem to be searching out their neurological peers. Depending on experience in the womb and at birth they begin to form solid circuits, or deviated circuits as the case may be. Much of this is a function of interneurons, the controller cells promoting new cell contacts and new connections to other brain cells. Interneurons help prepare the brain for how it functions later on; and this depends a good deal on the experiences of the fetus and newborn.

toxins and the body's "conscious" defense

If the mother absorbs a toxin, that toxin can cross the placenta and harm the fetus. When a mother smokes, for instance, the levels of nicotine and carbon monoxide in the blood rise, as contaminants cross the placenta and enter the fetal bloodstream. The developing fetus is chronically poisoned, yet cannot cry for help. More precisely, it cries for help in the only way it can—through changes in its physiology and biochemistry. Smoking can also affect the calcium that is transported across the placenta and change the make-up of amino acids. It's not that the fetus is aware of its environment, mind you, but that it is responding to this environment. It is "aware," on a different level of consciousness, reacting without the cerebral cortex intervening, and its reactions are deadly accurate. Later, when the neocortex top level is developed there will be the opportunity to detour or re-circuit neural connections, to deny the reality of whatever is going on inside. But at this early stage of development the body's natural reactions cannot be deluded. A rapid pulse is saying something and its message is usually true.

One woman we saw at the Primal Center relived being poisoned. She had been in a bar where smoking was permitted. She felt sick. She came in and complained about the bar and all its smoke, began to feel upset about it, and then became nauseous as she summoned the feeling of being choked for air while undergoing primal therapy. Soon she descended into birth trauma, reliving the conditions of her fetal environment which her carrying mother, a chain smoker, had polluted. Make no mistake, when a child is prenatally exposed to tobacco, he is literally being poisoned. And that child's hypersensitivity to pollution remains engraved in the brain and biologic system for a lifetime. This woman when describing her friends or relatives consistently painted them as "toxic." She moved to a desert community because she was so sensitive to air pollution in the city. She was fixated on toxicity and "overreacted" (although that's not the right word) because she was already carrying around the burden of pollution. The primitive imprint had wound its way to the highest reaches of the nervous system and made her obsessive about "toxic" conditions.

Of course tobacco is just one of many drugs that can harm the fetus. Recent research by Albert Hollenbeck,[3] a specialist in fetal life, reports that any drug given to a carrying mother will alter the neurotransmitter systems of the offspring, especially during the critical period when these neurotransmitter systems are forming in the womb. Hollenbeck theorizes that administration of local anesthetics, such as lidocaine, to aid the birth process during sensitive periods in gestation, may produce enduring changes in the offspring's behavior. According to Hollenbeck, brain chemicals such as serotonin and dopamine can be changed permanently, even with the administering of a local anesthetic, when an animal undergoes birth. This affects the so-called gating system—the brain's mechanism for dealing with pain.

In essence, gating means closing the doors to pain so we are no longer aware of it. When a woman is given anesthetics, neurotransmitters in the child's brain may slip into the synapses between and among nerve cells to block the message of pain from reaching higher levels of awareness. The more painkillers a woman takes during labor the more likely her child will be to abuse drugs or alcohol later in life.

Karin Nyberg of the University of Gothenburg, in Sweden, looked at medication given to the mothers of sixty-nine adult drug users and thirty-three of their siblings who did not take drugs.[4] Twenty-three percent of the drug users were exposed to multiple doses of barbiturates or opiates in the hours just before birth. Only three percent of their siblings were exposed to the same levels of drugs in utero. When the mothers received three or more doses of drugs, their child was five times more likely to abuse drugs later on. Enough animal studies have been done to virtually confirm this finding-exposure to drugs in the womb changes the individual's propensity for later drug use.

There is now even some evidence for a countervailing effect: a mother taking downers during pregnancy will have a child at high risk for addiction to amphetamines ("uppers" or "speed"), while a mother taking stimulants during pregnancy—coffee, cocaine, and caffeinated colas—has an increased risk her child will be addicted to downers: Quaaludes, for example. Why is it that an adult can drink two cups of coffee before bedtime and still sleep easily and well? Most likely, because there is a major deficiency of stimulating hormones—the catecholamines. The opposite is true for the child who can never get to sleep. In short, the original set-points for activation or repression have been altered during womb-life and persist for a lifetime.

One reason toxins are so harmful, as we'll see later on, is because of the threat they pose to the fetus's breathing. During gestation oxygen delivery is determined by uterine blood flow. Two vascular systems have to cooperate to exchange oxygen between the mother and the fetus, and the fetus has to live with only 25 percent of the blood oxygen of the mother. Living on a quarter of the mother's oxygen supply is the fetal equivalent to living on top of Mount Everest without oxygen cylinders; and whenever oxygen delivery to the fetus is compromised, say, through a smoking mother's elevated blood carbon monoxide levels or high anxiety, the fetus must take urgent steps to conserve it. It must diminish the functioning of various systems, including the respiratory system. In some cases, this will lead to reduced fetal growth as an adaptive survival response. Breathing can be affected for a lifetime in the offspring, and all sorts of lung problems may arise. The imprint is the diminished oxygen.

When the fetus gets short of oxygen it shuts down non-essential functions and shifts blood flow to protect supplies to the most vital organs, including the developing brain. The brain reduces non-essential functions when oxygen is low, and most of the energy-consuming activities of the brain stop. If the oxygen shortage continues for a long time there will be a placental failure, and the fetus will stop the most energy-consuming activity of all: growing. That is why size and growth are such strong indices of trouble.

A number of animal studies have shown that when mothers are given tranquilizers while pregnant their offspring will suffer from anxiety or depression. It is important to understand that such studies could have several possible implications. It may be that pregnant mothers who take drugs are giving birth to a different kind of child as a direct result of their painkiller use. However, these studies often compare children of the same mother born at different times, and it may be that the mother's mood or life circumstance on having her first baby is far different from when she had a later baby who was exposed to tranquilizers.

In any case, the impact of prescription drugs on the child is worthy of close attention and one we are likely to learn more about as new studies emerge, attempting to explain the effects of prenatal exposure to antidepressants such as Prozac and Zoloft. According to one such study reported by Susan Gaidos in *Science News*,[5] children exposed to antidepressants while being carried were more likely to be sad and withdrawn, even as early as age three. In the article, Gaidos points out that serotonin acts like a nerve cell lubricant, helping alleviate pain and tempering impulses such as sex and aggression. Some nerve cells "feed" on serotonin to develop properly, Gaidos notes, and when the mother is low on supplies due to her own deep depression, there isn't enough for the baby. That is why the child may crave painkillers and tranquilizers when he grows up.

Moreover, there is enough evidence to show that selective serotonin reuptake inhibitors (SSRIs)—the chemicals that drive our repressive urge—can cross the placenta and affect the brain organization of the fetus. In one study led by Barry Condron, a neuroscientist at the

University of Virginia, fruit flies engineered with high levels of sero-tonin showed swelling around neural branches similar to what is found in Alzheimer's patients or Ecstasy users.[6] It seems that, biologically, the baby learns to ingest, and adapt to, the mood-altering affect of the drugs; he learns in a most profound physiologic way that drugs can soothe.

What is important, here, is that set-points for serotonin can track us throughout life. Once the serotonin system is rendered defective, it will take a lot more pills to begin to balance the levels internally. So the addict is not making a choice; he is, instead, afflicted by his early defi-cit; his physiology drives that addiction. And it is not only tranquilizers that will do this; any painkiller can produce the same effect.

What you have, additionally, with diminished serotonin is a heavy tendency toward impulsive, daredevil behavior. Individuals without sufficient serotonin levels tend to drink more than others, announce whatever is on their minds, and, in some cases, develop sleep and con-centration problems, for their internal impulses are surging forth with-out proper inhibition. The only good thing that comes of this serotonin deficit, in my opinion, is that the chances of later cancer may be re-duced. Somewhat counterintuitively, massive repression can lead to an aberration and chaos of the cells that turn to cancer. Of course we must remember that this is a mixed blessing, at best; weakened repression—faulty or leaky gates—can just as easily produce an overload on the brain system, resulting at times in episodes of cerebral stroke.

Let's keep in mind that the total environment for the fetus is the mother. Her hormones, neurotransmitters, and vital functions, are what the child must adapt to. So when the mother takes tranquilizers during pregnancy the baby must make accommodations, and some-times that is not easy. The newborn may go into withdrawal—shaking, becoming irritable, and crying inconsolably: showing, in a word, the symptoms of deprivation at birth. Later in life these symptoms take on new qualities and may emerge in the disturbed sleep patterns, high blood pressure, and breathing and lung problems we find in so many of our patients.

Serotonin has a great deal to do with brain development, and tranquilizers given to a mother during pregnancy may interfere with that development, causing the brain's neurons to grow abnormally.[7] We may not become aware of this until some egregious symptom appears out of the blue decades later. At times the appearance of this symptom is a total mystery. Twenty years elapse and we as therapists try to bridge the gap, but our insights fail because it is only the person himself who can connect the early trauma with later symptoms. Often recovery requires that a patient be locked into a symptom, such as a migraine, which stems from very early experience. That symptom may eventually lead to a feeling from which we can explain the origins of the patient's afflictions. When the patient relives the original feeling, the symptom disappears, quite suddenly at times, and we know we are on the right track.

It is important to note that the effects of gestational toxins often are magnified by early trauma. As we've seen in studies on birth defects, premature births, and other anomalies associated with intrauterine trauma, aberration often can be explained by a difficult birth in which the fetus was deprived of oxygen. In other cases, we need to look at life in the womb, and many times both factors are at play. A vulnerable fetus who is carried by a smoking mother, for instance, and then undergoes a traumatic birth as a result of exposure to anesthesia will have a serious oxygen deficit. It is this kind of compounding that makes the imprint more serious.

It appears as though the earlier the trauma the worse the consequences, particularly during the first trimester of pregnancy. That makes sense since this is when many organ systems are forming and brain development is taking place. But before we hastily place all the blame on drugs, we must keep in mind the reasons why mothers take drugs. It is often because they are emotionally upset, depressed, or anxious—and it is that mindset and feeling state that drives them to seek calming agents.

Still, drugs taken during pregnancy are a problem. Tranquilizer and antidepressant doses are intended for an adult body, not a five- or six-pound baby. When the mother transfers massive amounts of drugs into the fetal system, the developing child is often overwhelmed; the drug dislocates normal functioning, and, over time, the baby comes to "need" the drug. Because early on the child's normal function has been interfered with, he now adapts to a drug-optimized state, which may well follow him throughout life. His physiology, hormones, and vital signs, have been warped. He doesn't have enough chemicals to properly repress, because these were depleted at two months in the womb and have permanently altered the set-point: what the system comprehends as normal.

imprinting: the signature of pregnancy

As a natural survival mechanism, children react in anticipation of what the future may hold. History in the womb is coded and stored, and then dictates later reaction types. That is why a mother who takes downers and sleeping pills may have an offspring who is addicted to uppers and stimulants years later. Imprinted in the baby is a repressed system, a shut-down world that is depleted of energy, lacking the physical resources to motivate the child without artificial reinforcement.

Please understand, when I speak of imprinting I'm not referring to some transcendental hocus pocus or Huxleian science fiction. I'm speaking of a specific and medically identifiable signature that exists at the deepest levels of a child's biology. The fetus uses information that it receives from the mother to make choices and physiologic predictions that help maximize its advantage after birth. More precisely, the fetus is reacting to the womb environment by readjusting its vital signs, hormones, and neurotransmitters to adapt to a new reality; he is getting ready for life in the outer world.

The problem is that a very anxious mother, or a mother using drugs that mimic an anxious system, will translate her anxiety to the fetus, who must deal with it, often by repressing. The fetus that cannot do that effectively will feel overwhelmed later in life. So much so, in fact, that the most insignificant task will take on life-or-death importance. Moreover, a mother under stress is likely to show a sharp increase in the stress hormone cortisol, hastening the maturation of the fetus and, at times, producing premature birth. Though preterm birth is often perceived as a mystery because, medically speaking, no one can put their finger on the cause, it may be that we aren't looking in the right place.

Indeed, the high level of anxiety in the carrying mother is not always evident to the naked eye, but underneath the layer of the cerebral cortex high levels of cortisol may be quietly shaping fetal development.

One of the ways the imprint happens, which we'll return to later, is that the fetus exhausts serotonin supplies in the service of gating. A little later, in the child's first years of life, he cannot shut down pain so easily. He will need external help in gating drugs like Prozac or Zoloft. This is an anxious, hyperactive baby; a baby who may be later diagnosed with attention deficit disorder. His brain is so preoccupied with internal input that it cannot form a cohesive structure to focus and concentrate; and it is this kind of constant internal pressure, coupled with a harsh, unloving environment early in life, which can result in delusions and serious mental illness. The least that we will see is what I call "booga booga," the belief in far-out ideas and fantasies that have nothing to do with reality.

However, as illogic as it sounds, these later life psychoses stem from the fetus's attempt to improve its chances for survival. The postnatal advantage can be defined in Darwinian terms as the best physiologic trajectory for development in the postnatal period. If the fetus is exposed to a long period of reduced nutrients because of a starvation winter, for instance, it expects to be delivered into a world where nutrients are scarce. Likewise, if there is high glucose level, the fetus will anticipate being born into a carbohydrate-rich environment. And, in the same way, if the fetus's mother has consistently high blood cortisol levels, so might the fetus, anticipating being born into a stressful environment. Of course, diet and a calm environment count, but what really counts is the quiet and calm inside the mother.

These connections may go even deeper than once believed. An interesting study at the Keck School of Medicine,[8] which, hopefully, will pave the way for future research, found that children exposed to a mother who smoked while pregnant had differences in their DNAs. Professor Carrie Breton, the study's lead author, notes that this could be one explanation for how and why in utero experience can affect later health, including heart disease and asthma.

Recently, researchers at the University of Toronto found that children who reported childhood abuse had a 45 percent greater chance of later heart disease.[9] Now we may not think of "child abuse" as something which occurs in the womb, but when the mother is tense or depressed and it adversely affects the fetus it is abuse, though not deliberately done. And abuse during this early period often has a much greater influence on the physical system than that which occurs later. Our own research on this period is currently being carried out in two medical clinics.

And, in fact, there are dozens of studies that show the effect of imprinting on the child. Although they refer to different physiologic symptoms and diseases, all begin with a basis in early environmental trauma. New Zealand scientist Sir Peter Gluckman, the director of the Liggins Institute at the University of Auckland, discusses studies with rats in which the rat fetus was undernourished in utero because the pregnant mother had a reduced caloric intake.[10] These kinds of rats became hypertensive, that is, they had high blood pressure as adults; and they were also shown to have insulin deviations, the latter of which can anticipate such diseases as diabetes. Furthermore, these animals lived shorter lives than the offspring of mothers who had a completely balanced diet at pregnancy; and life-expectancy was further decreased in those rats placed on a high-fat diet after birth, mirroring what happens in humans. Gluckman and his research team also discovered that when you exposed the animals to high doses of stress hormones while they were being carried many abnormalities emerged later in life. In other words, there were pathological changes that endured for a lifetime.

Earlier I spoke of the perils of oxygen deficiency in relation to drugs, but other factors may produce a similar imprint. When the umbilical cord is kinked, not enough oxygen is pumped through to the fetus, who is thus forced to make a set of immediate adaptive changes that are essential for survival. Blood flow is redistributed to the vital organs—the heart and brain—at the expense of blood supply to the gastrointestinal tract. This changes the mother's physiology, as well, and to the extent that these changes occur during a period of transient oxygen shortage, the shift can augur stomach problems in the young infant. Ulcerative colitis or Crohn's disease, for instance, may occur later in life depending on the particular circumstances of the pregnancy. Keep in mind, too, that the fetus automatically slows its growth rate when it senses reduced nutrient supply from the placenta. Generally, this is a good thing, but if the period of the nutritional deprivation is sufficiently prolonged, the fetus adjusts its physiology; it deviates and compensates; it becomes a neurotic system.

Maternal stress may also affect the delivery of nutrients through the umbilical cord, contaminating the blood on which the fetus depends for future respiratory health. Regarding asthma, a fascinating study at Harvard Medical School and affiliate Brigham and Women's Hospital compared the blood of the umbilical cord in women who were traumatized during pregnancy and those who were not.[11] Women who had an upset pregnancy, it was found, had patterns in the blood analysis that were associated with later asthma (cytokines) in the children. So if you're wondering why a child has asthma, the reason may not be due to heredity at all, but rather the mother's tense state while carrying.

Maternal disease while carrying is also critical to a child's future health. If the mother has diabetes, she may have high blood glucose levels; and the fetus, expecting high nutrient availability after birth, will find a gross mismatch with the reality of the postnatal environment. Similarly, if the mother has heart disease, the fetus may adapt to being born into a low-oxygen environment, an adaptation at odds with the conditions found in his first years of life. In short, the state of the mother while pregnant shapes what the fetus will expect and how the young person will feel and behave, even if that physiologic signature is at odds with the environment.

Our own research supports imprinting studies like Breton's and Gluckman's, although in a slightly different context. For the last several years, we have studied natural killer (NK) cells in our patients, lymphocytes (white blood cells) that constitute a very important part of the immune system. We've found that as we remove the patients' pain and anxiety, the NK cells normalize, usually after one year of therapy. There is some indication that NK cells are part of an internal surveillance team that spots newly developing cancer cells and helps to destroy them. Through apoptosis, a process of cell fragmentation, hostile cells are contained and removed before they spread to other areas of the system. That may be why patients with high quantities of NK cells have a strong defense against the herpes virus. Unfortunately, in some kinds of autoimmune diseases, NK cells falter and end up attacking our own indigenous cells, mistaking them for the enemy. I think what happens in neurosis is very similar, on the cognitive level: we effectively attack ourselves. Because we cannot distinguish what is us from what is not us, we alienate our feelings and believe them to be the enemy. And, in a sense, they *do* become the enemy. As those feelings rise toward consciousness, the system goes into alarm mode; our temperature rises as does our blood pressure and our heart rate, all in the anticipation of an attack.

Clearly the immune system, as well as our mental apparatus, is responsive to stress. If the mother is chaotic and anxious, the fetus is going to have an expectation, physiologically speaking, that the postnatal environment will also be threatening and chaotic. The only way that we can reverse this is by reliving events that occurred in the womb, events that occurred before we had the capacity to conceptualize our feelings or attach them to scenes. Stomach upset, lack of energy, a sense of choking and asphyxiation, butterflies in the stomach; all are controlled by the primitive, vegetative nervous system that was already in place during gestation. Reliving great discomfort, summoning pain—that is what we must do to heal.

3

searching for a universal psychotherapy

Usually, what happens with patients undergoing primal therapy is that they relive something in childhood—a rejection—that resonates with an earlier rejection and, finally, triggers a related feeling that occurred in the womb. The feeling aroused during primal therapy, although focused in childhood, carries with it physiologic distress from the fetal period. Rejection by one's mother in the present can thus set off retroactively, without the patient's awareness, a feeling of disturbance from the critical months leading up to birth. In a matter of hours the "Primal," begun with a scene of rejection, evolves into a sensation of fear, which, for the patient, can be a harrowing experience. But I believe there is no other way to alter fixed deviated set-points than to relive the original circumstances during which the set-points were altered.

As we've learned from a number of animal studies, when there is a deficit in the inhibitory neurotransmitter serotonin there will be a later effect on the infant. In humans, too, when there is not enough serotonin delivered to the fetus there can be later physical deformities and deviations in personality. For instance, without enough serotonin we are likely to slip into chronic anxiety: we can't repress well and therefore we can't learn well. In the last ten years, though, we've had a major breakthrough in understanding how to alter the production of this neurochemical therapeutically: using primal therapy, we've managed to normalize patients' serotonin levels after just one year of treatment. This is an extremely encouraging sign that comes on the heels of more than three decades of research. In fact, it is so important that it has the potential, in my view, to profoundly shift the direction of psychotherapy. For it is doubtful we can alter key set-points, such as imprinted levels of the stress hormone cortisol, without recourse to lower-brain primal therapy, treatment that takes us on an emotional voyage that connects the antipodes of the mind.

the Babel of clinical psychology

We in clinical psychology today are in a strange position. We see people, both in and outside of our practices, suffering from an insidious condition that cannot be seen, touched, or pinpointed to any single location. Mental illness, or neurosis as it's often called, is generally understood to be a neurological disorder, but aside from that fact that its origins lie somewhere in the brain, remarkably little is known about its causes. The most skeptical among us question whether the suffering is real or rather a peril of acute self-indulgence and inward thinking. Among schools of psychotherapy that do admit the existence of mental illness, each has very different ideas about neurosis and its genesis. Indeed, no other area of medicine is laden with such widespread disagreement about the nature of a disease, what its symptoms are, and how it is made manifest, to say nothing of how to treat it. In short, the field of psychotherapy today is nothing less than chaotic. So why the lack of cohesion and common understanding?

To begin with, I believe that events that cause mental illness begin very early and remain so barricaded in our unconscious that the notion that early trauma affects how we act at, say, age forty-five, is beyond imagination. Second, we react with incredible diversity to the various manifestations of early trauma, believing that phobias, migraines, compulsions, obsessions, depression, addictions, and so forth, must all have different functions, when in fact there is much more overlap to these afflictions than was once believed. Finally, psychologists themselves have blind spots stemming from their own neuroses—they cannot bear to see their patients' deepest pain—and so they find themselves gladly distracted by symptoms and ideologies that do not directly address pain.

As a result, the field of psychotherapy may be characterized by a remarkable absence of cohesion, and patients' pain is addressed diffusely at best. Some psychotherapists will consistently prescribe anti-anxiety and antidepressant drugs for varying neuroses, in essence trying to kill patients' pain, but not identifying the pain or where it comes from. Others may manage symptoms through various techniques associated with different schools of psychotherapy: they may have the patient dissociate from a symptom in hypnotherapy; analyze it into oblivion in cognitive behavioral therapy; act-out the symptom symbolically in Gestalt therapy; beat it back with mild shock as in conditioning therapy; attribute it to faulty beliefs as in rational-emotive therapy; control it in biofeedback therapy; or re-route it in directive daydreaming and imagery therapy. Yet the approaches we find in present-day psychotherapy are treatments rather than cures, and what's more troubling, the notion of "cure" itself has become an anathema. In the current zeitgeist, for example, alcoholism is considered a disease, presumably because it comes from our birth; not from the trauma of birth but from some kind of genetic source. However, once we see that womb-life plays a key part in later life dependency, we may need to reorient our focus. When we understand that a mother who drinks one or two glasses of wine or takes one or two pills during pregnancy may set up later dependency in her children, we can redirect our preventive and psychotherapeutic approach.

The best hope for lasting help for patients is to address the generating sources of mental illness. What are these sources? It will take a long time to know for certain, but I propose that the conflict between the imprinted pain of early trauma and our effort to repress it is the central contradiction. It is this discord that generates neurotic reactions both internally, in our body chemistry, and externally, in behavior. The resulting psychic dilemma is not easily rectified. Repression involves access to feelings and sensations; it is an evolved function that allows us to survive unmitigated pain early in life. The pain, however, remains engraved in the system, and will perpetually fuel a dislocation of mental and physical functioning to keep itself from being felt.

Therapies that do not address this original, central conflict at the root of neurosis may succeed in reconfiguring a symptom pattern, but they cannot eliminate the fundamental illness. Why do therapies and therapists refrain from delving into our early experiences? In large part, because of our Freudian legacy: the notion that fooling around in the unconscious is dangerous and must be scrupulously avoided. It is true that without a proper scientific theory and therapeutic method, retrieving one's traumatic past can indeed be dangerous; witness the many mock primal therapies that damage patients, every day, by plunging them into rebirthing sequences and other dangerous ploys. It has taken some forty years to figure out this therapy and the theory, and it doesn't surprise me that many therapists avoid it altogether. But it is essential if we want to put an end to neurosis as we have seen it for the last hundred years. The alternative is to continue to move in circles.

electroshock therapy: zapping symptoms, avoiding cures

Believe it or not, one of the most maligned therapies for depression—electroshock therapy—is making a comeback. Once again, there is a discussion in the *Psychiatric Times* and elsewhere about the efficacy of shock treatment.[1] If our diagnosis hinges on some genetic force, some immutable "thing" that needs shocking, then it makes sense. However, what if the cause of our maladies is not immutable but experiential as a growing body of research suggests? What if what happens to produce that depression is knowable, only not in verbal terms? Shock therapy is a last resort. For years it was used when we had no way to access the deep unconscious, including our memory of events that transpired during gestation. But now we do have access, and that makes all the difference.

I remember early on in primal therapy I had observed something that resembled a birth primal but was strangely different. My staff believed it indeed was a reliving of a birth trauma. I knew there was something else to it; after two or three times, I discussed it with the patient. It turned out he had electroshock therapy before coming to us, and he was reliving it. What goes in must come out, and it certainly did: in screaming, shaking, and tremendous pain. It was the patient who figured out the problem. Again, the minute we decide we know what is inside a patient all is lost. We don't and cannot. In this case, we let the patient relive the trauma over time, and he felt greatly relieved and far more relaxed afterward.

Electroshock therapy works by inducing a close approximation of the shock that we find in patients whose parents have died in a car crash, or who have been seduced or raped by a family member—that is to say, a total shutdown due to massive overload. In the same way that a patient must relive the pain of incest slowly over time, he must also relive the shock input. There is no escaping that, for it is what has left a massive residue of pain and tension in the system. Electroshock therapy is truly a perilous exercise—the psychological equivalent of dynamite mining: just blast away, and hope for the best.

We need to be careful about having an agenda as therapists. The old saying, once you have a hammer everything looks like a board, is especially true in the context of mental health. Once we have a method in place, we tend to use it ad infinitum: biofeedback, eye movement desensitization, dream analysis—all have been guilty of the same kind of self-promotion as electroshock therapy, reinforcing their importance at the peril of psychotherapy as a whole. What we need, instead, is science. There are no surprises and our approach never changes. If we are not discussing our history, if we are not *feeling* feelings and reliving our past, we are not getting well. We are historic beings; our brainwaves normalize around events from our childhood and remain fixed, in the same way that our blood pressure stabilizes within a biologic system that has undergone experiences, dating all the way back to womb-life. Why would we want to fiddle with those adaptations? Why not first discover what happened to make our brainwaves fluctuate or our blood pressure deviate from normal?

The reason that the tool bearers (and by this I mean cognitive behavioral therapists and other insight therapists of their ilk) do not generate universal laws is that they focus on appearances and not essences, on fragments not systems. Granted, they do posit general hypotheses, but invariably their theories cannot be tested and verified because they have an insufficient scientific base to support them. It is very difficult to compose a universal psychologic law from idiosyncratic behavior that applies to one person only, or from an id or dark forces that no one can see or verify. Tool bearers' approaches seem to superimpose psychologic laws on humans and then treat them accordingly. We believe, by contrast, that through careful observation of the patient we can uncover the laws of nature, or at least approximate their human implications under limited conditions; after all, natural law derives from humans and biologic truths are of the essence: if we do not explore our own biology, we will be forever at a loss.

As you know by now, my hypothesis is that there are often traumatic events before birth, at birth, and soon after, that were never fully experienced in the first place. Normally, part of the reaction to these inordinate events is stifled, automatically, in the interest of the individual's survival and integrity. Through this blockage, known variously as repression or dissociation, vital functions are dislocated as the system compensates for the intrusion of pain; neural circuits and networks must be rerouted in order to keep the repression going. Serotonin and many other inhibitors also are affected, so that in the serotonergic system, too, there is a dislocation of function, which may result in under- or over-secretion of key repressive hormones or neurotransmitters. In simplest terms, we can expect to find higher than normal stress hormone levels, as the system is ever on the alert against danger. And what is that danger? That the overwhelming pain, never felt and never connected, will rise to consciousness.

But let's take a step back, for a moment, because I want to make clear that the implications of pain are not just psychological. As a case in point, the researcher Mary Ann Ruda and her associates at the National Institute of Dental and Craniofacial Research conducted an animal study showing that pain administered in infancy can permanently rewire the nervous system.[2] They believe, as I do, that the study has importance for human development. Animals injected very early with a substance that made their feet swell had extra nerve endings that sprouted into new areas of the spinal cord (what is known as alpha sprouting). As adults the animals had a greater than normal response to pain. The implication here is that lasting sensitivity can result from early pain.

A proper theory or therapy must have room in it to explore all facets of life, including our time in the womb. There is increasing evidence that real memory is organic; that is, recalling a memory invokes all of the identical neurophysiologic reactions as originally expressed. A study by investigators at the Scripps Research Institute, for instance, found that recalling early events brought forth the same neurons that existed in the learning or imprinting of the event. Investigators reported "reactivated neurons were likely a component of a stable engram or memory trace."[3] The suggestion is that memories live on in virtually exact form, which allows us to reactivate them for the purposes of cure. Keep this idea of a memory trace in mind because later on when I discuss resonance—how current feelings echo and trigger early memories and feelings—it will become clearer.

On top of all this, there is new evidence from researchers at the University of Pennsylvania and Princeton that "as you search for memories your brain progressively comes to resemble the state it was in when you initially experienced the event."[4] In other words the more fully an event is remembered, the deeper and more lasting impression it will leave on the brain. The same is true for reliving: the more fully an event is remembered, the deeper and broader the insight. Understand, I am not referring to the notion of memory found in much of the psychologic literature. I use memory, here, in an all-encompassing physiologic and neurologic sense, not simply as a system of verbal recall. Recall is not curative, organic memory is. If there is not a complete memory in therapy, we have what I call abreaction, which is not a healing process since there is only emotional discharge, not a full memory that includes the historic feeling.

One of the things we need to do in therapy is flush out the pain, although this isn't always easy. The body's natural reaction is to repress pain, and when it rises to the level of awareness the results can be devastating; so jarring, in fact, as to threaten survival. In addition to mental psychosis we have documented cases of massive systemic reactivity (increased heart rate and blood pressure or conversely metabolic shutdown and anoxia) where vital signs skyrocket as patients begin to relive early trauma. One of the amazing things about these reactions is how quickly symptoms can subside. Generally, once patients have relived the event all signs return to, or below, baseline, often with radical changes in patient behavior. (Importantly, in abreaction vital functions do not return to baseline or below. It is one way we know that healing is not happening and that proper treatment is not in evidence.)

Of course one might ask, "What is the magic about reliving that cures anything? How does reliving rewire nerve circuits?" At the most basic level reliving means going back in time, reentering pains that were once too distressing to feel. Although repression sealed them off, deep down they were imprinted and kept doing their damage. However, by lifting the repressive lid in orderly fashion, we can begin to fix the unconscious forces driving behavior and symptoms. We are literally traveling back, both in behavior and physiology, to events that produced the deviations in the first place.

on vital signs in primal therapy

For many years we have measured the vital signs of patients before and after each therapy session and over the long term. Our results often show normalization after one year of treatment. Of course, when we measure vital signs we are measuring vital functions—those functions that keep us alive and allow us to survive. When any of them exceed normal limits we are in trouble. Whether too low a blood pressure, too high a heart rate, or a continual body temperature far above the normal range, when we are dislocated one way or the other the body is telling us that something is wrong; and, if we know how to read the signs, it tells us in what way something is wrong, and sometimes even why. Over the years, if these signs continue to be abnormal, there is a strong chance that disease will occur early in life, followed by life-threatening illness later on; in fact, it is nearly ineluctable.

These vital signs mean vitality. And they reflect our imprints quite accurately. They also reflect what branch of the nervous system is dominant. We know, for example, that many vital functions are either controlled by one of two areas of the nervous system mediated by the hypothalamus. I thought for some time that the parasympathetic system, that of rest, repair, and repose, controlled body temperature. But it may be that the direction of the dislocation depends on two entirely differ-ent nervous systems.

It now appears that high blood pressure is controlled by the sympa-thetic, galvanizing system, while a swing to the low end is controlled by the parasympathetic system. (This may also be true of the systolic and diastolic blood pressure.) Thus, the direction of maladjustment tells us the kind of imprint we are dealing with. We have found that if the vitals descend in sporadic fashion after a session it usually means a lack of con-nection and, hence, abreaction: the discharge of a feeling without proper connection. It means a lack of cohesion in the patient's brain, which can lead to an abreactive style that keeps the person sick and neurotic.

The readings we get tell us unmistakably what kind of trauma the patient underwent and when. If the patient is depressed, there is a greater chance the mother took painkillers or tranquilizers during the time she was carrying. Other times the baby is stuck in the "trough"; that is, the birth process begins but the baby is not able to complete the birth cycle on schedule. Thus the child is born in a passive, energy con-serving mode (so as not to use up too much oxygen) that is reflected in his vital signs, which are characteristically on the low side.

We can reason backwardly and learn from the patient's vital signs what kind of womb-life and birth process existed. Of course there is room for error, but, by and large, among my patients this "law" holds up pretty well. When we see someone with extraordinary vitals, par-ticularly when they are all in concordance: low heart rate, low blood pressure and low body temperature with a passive, phlegmatic person-ality, we can be fairly confident of how life was early on.

Today I heard from an epileptic, whose mother had a breech birth when delivering him. Asphyxiated by the umbilical cord, the man, as a baby, had to conserve oxygen and energy to survive. His modus operandi was to hold back and not use energy. His imprint was para-sympathetic, something that will challenge him for a lifetime and de-termine his interests, his non-interests, whom he marries, and how he will treat his children. In our clinic, for instance, we've discovered that the prototypical parasympathetic individual is a writer who exercises little, chooses an aggressive spouse, and treats his children with indif-ference.

Now why do I claim such things? Why do I insist that our vital signs give us such revealing clues as to our personality and likelihood for disease? Because the very first life-saving effort becomes imprinted. It remains as a guide for future behavior, so that what, in this case, saved this man's life at the start will go on being utilized. Personality is formed out of this matrix, as well as an individual's biologic state. Of course later experience helps shape development, but that first imprint is vital in every sense of the word.

When patients come in for a session and we do measurements, we already have an idea of where we have to go for cure. One of my depressives came in consistently with a very low body temperature of 96 to 96.5 degrees. She was mired in hopelessness—and low body temperature usually means first-line pain is involved. As our sessions went on, almost three hours each time, she started to normalize. It wasn't just the body temperature that normalized but a whole host of biologic responses and personality features. After undergoing therapy she smiled more, showed more energy, and began to feel "up." Not only that, but she could go seek a job, buy proper food, and maintain her house—all tasks she couldn't have done previously. A previous therapy informed her that hers was a "loser trip," a strategy that didn't do much except to put a label on her behavior. However, in primal therapy, as she relived her pre-birth and birth traumas (in this case the imprints of a mother who smoked and took tranquilizers during pregnancy), her body temperature rose gradually until it reached 98 degrees, where it remained at the conclusion of her therapy.

When a patient comes in with the opposite kind of imprint—a very rapid heart rate and brainwave signature—our first job is to bring him into the "primal" zone, where optimum vital signs will occur. If the patient remains at levels above the primal zone, he will not feel and certainly not integrate; and the same law operates when vital signs are too low. We can only feel in the primal zone, and we need to adjust medications to allow that to happen. We cannot and must not cajole a patient into trying to feel.

As I've said, I believe that the depressive personality type, the parasympath, operates on the low end of all vital signs. We can go to one doctor to be treated for a heart rate that is unsteady, another doctor for high blood pressure, yet another for lack of energy, but what ultimately sets the tone is the imprint and, until we recognize this, we will be bifurcated in our efforts and miss the essential. That is why the crucial thing we want to know after each session is, Was there integration? Sometimes, after weeks of feeling therapy, one key feeling emerges, but often there is a dredge effect: the patient experiences one feeling that resonates with a connected deeper feeling (hopelessness in the present leading to helplessness in the womb), and we know that there is more to come. It may be that the patient will need tranquilizers, temporarily, to get over the hump. We need not be afraid of this since it is not an end in our therapy but a means—it is not the therapy, as is the case in so much psychiatry, but something to use for a time. Drugs induce a superficial and artificial state, and they nearly always hold back feelings and aid defenses. That is not the business we are in; quite the opposite, we want feelings to emerge but in ordered, measured ways. Primal therapy, in accordance with our vital signs, follows a consistent path toward our most remote feelings. For those who stick with it the direction of therapy is nearly always right; to understand this fully, let's take a closer look at the workings of the human brain. This is not going to be a highly technical discussion; after all, this is for the non-professional, and I want it to be as understandable as possible.

4

how the brain talks to itself

Brain cells, or neurons, "talk" with each other via a vast network of tiny branch-like connections called dendrites. Dendrites may form a tangled web, but they do not actually touch one another; there are tiny gaps between them, called synapses. When nerve impulses carrying chemical messages travel from one neuron to another, they release chemicals called neurotransmitters, which move across these synapses. The more dendritic neurons there are, the better they will communicate. This can mean increased access to our feelings. However, when the dendrites are sparse, there is weakened communication between the lower centers of the brain and the higher control and integration areas.

Communication within the brain depends heavily on neurotransmitters, the critical biochemicals between nerve cells. The neurotransmitter's job is to bind to a receptor on the dendrite, triggering an electrochemical response, which then causes the release of more neurotransmitters. Once they are used, neurotransmitters are either "recycled"—that is, taken back up by the neuron to be used again—or eliminated. There are many kinds of excitatory and inhibitory neurotransmitters and, as their names suggest, they either facilitate or block the delivery of messages.

As I mentioned, synapses are the gaps between cells that are filled with chemicals that either hold back the message of pain or help it along its journey to consciousness. In these gaps are the neurotransmitters that stop painful messages from traveling any further. With love, the growth of synapses among neurons means that we have a stronger brain, especially in the prefrontal cortex where we connect to, control, and integrate feelings.

Development of these brain apparatus transpires during the critical period when experience will change the brain, often permanently. Malformation or stunted growth of any of these structures—dendrites, neurotransmitters, or synapses—can have devastating effects. It is not any wonder that so many criminals have poor cortical control. Many, I suspect, have had very early gestational traumas when the frontal brain was just getting up to speed.

When we miss a mother's love at the very start of life, there are less synaptic connections between neurons. As I've said, love, for the fetus and baby, means fulfilling needs. When pain begins after months or years of post-birth life it is bad but not horrible; it is not life shaping. However when pain starts its life in the womb—and certain needs for oxygen or nutrients are not fulfilled— all manner of alterations in set-points settle in. If this transpires during the critical period in utero, the brain will change, often permanently.

What early gestational trauma does, in short, is decrease the activity of the neurons in the cortical area. This weakens the prefrontal area so that the adult individual can be easily overwhelmed. When feelings well up, rather than being integrated into the prefrontal cortex, they travel to other parts of the cortex to produce inter alia, a lack of self-control. The brain's integrative repository doesn't seem big enough to store the whole feeling. But because feelings cannot be held back, there is a near-constant malaise later on. Until we had access to deep levels of the brain, those of us in the field of psychotherapy were forced to neglect a subtle but important point: it is very difficult to control oneself when cortical nerve cells have been assaulted and lessened in the womb. Now we understand how critical the organization and connectivity of the prefrontal cortex is to our management of anxiety and pain.

three levels of consciousness

Those familiar with my work know about the three levels of consciousness, a framework for understanding the brain that has guided my therapy for decades. During our formative, very early years there is constant communication between our storehouse of emotional memories and our awareness of them on higher cortical levels. Finally, those memories become, in part, transferred to higher sites for safekeeping, where they remain just out of our reach. This is part of the coding system and, in general, it is a good thing.

In neurotic and depressive states, however, it means the sufferer can ruminate about suffering and pain from early experiences without recalling the experiences themselves. Dissociation, disconnection, and repression see to that. A lot of this takes place via the front, top part of the brain, the prefrontal neocortex, and also via the corpus callosum that blocks emotional memories from traveling from the right to the left brain hemisphere. One way we retrieve those memories is through access to feelings. Neurologically speaking, this means adopting a technique that favors right brain function. What seems to happen as we evolve in personal time, what evolutionary scientists call ontogeny, is that we lock into emotional states that resonate with earlier ones, ultimately connecting us to the earliest brain states.

Here is a brief resume of the interaction of the three levels of consciousness, as I see it: basically what this means is we have three brains in one—the brainstem, the limbic system, and the neocortex. Each constitutes a level of consciousness, and each has its own memory system. We remember smells, sensations, even conversations, on different levels of the brain, yet all are connected.

first-line: the brainstem

The first level, the brainstem, is a primitive or reptilian brain. I sometimes refer to it as the salamander brain because the limbic system and brainstem constitute a good part of the whole brain of the animal. The brainstem was the first to evolve, and the first part of the central nervous system to develop in human evolution. Salamanders, incidentally, have in primitive form pretty much the same limbic system we have. The eminent neuro-anatomist, E.J. Herrick, identified the salamander as a walking, swimming, living brainstem;[1] and it seems we never lost that part of the brain, just added new brain tissue on top of it. When patients are down on that level, there are never any words, nor adult-like screams, nor tears. Mostly what we find is grunts.

The brainstem leads out of the bottom rear of the brain down to the spinal cord. It deals with instincts, basic needs, survival functions, sleep, and basic processes that keep us alive; it also controls body temperature, blood pressure, and heart rate. I call this the "first-line" or survival brain.

The brainstem begins to form around the thirty-third day of gestation. After the second month of life in the womb, we have a brainstem with the ability to code and store trauma. By the seventh month of gestation, most of the brainstem structures are ready to fire and their fiber connections are all in order. Even if the frontal cortex were destroyed at this point through some trauma, primitive brainstem reflexes such as sucking, grasping, withdrawing, etc., would continue to function.

Importantly, however, the fetus can only communicate in the language that its brain has the capacity for at that given time: writhing, grunting, turning, twisting, butting against an obstacle, spitting up, and turning red. Along with these are the vital signs triggered at the time—a fast heart rate and high body temperature, for example. We know when in therapy we get close to first-line imprints because the body temperature can rise several degrees in minutes. Generally, second-line feelings will not push the body and its physiology so hard.

Besides very deep breathing, the brainstem is also involved with taste and hearing. It is possible that on this level the fetus can store the imprint of a mother's depression, anxiety, stress, drug taking, smoking, or drinking. Such experience is not stored as ideas, obviously, since we don't yet have a fully functional neocortex: our thinking, intellectual mind. What is important, however, is that the imprints in this storehouse will later motivate certain aberrations of thinking and may produce nightmares, phobias, and compulsions. These imprints will follow the nerve tracts to higher centers of the brain that will then elaborate and ramify the experience of the original trauma and sway our thinking accordingly. So when there is helplessness imprinted on the first-line level, it later can be triggered by even the slightest hint of hopelessness in the present. It all depends on how sturdy the defense system is. Even without the top-level, frontal cortex, which will express pain through words, animals and humans can still wail, howl, and cry.

second-line: the limbic system

The second level of consciousness is largely dependent on the limbic system of the brain, which is responsible for feelings and their memory. The limbic system is built and evolved from the brainstem. It provides images and artistic output, processes certain aspects of sexuality, and is partly responsible for anger and fear. The limbic system also possesses some key structures which affect brain function, including the hippocampus, which is the guardian of emotional memory; the amygdala, which I believe may provide the visceral components of feeling; and the hypothalamus and thalamus.

The thalamus is the relay station or central switchboard of the brain. It sends feeling messages upward and forward for understanding and connection. It can "decide" a feeling is too powerful to be felt and order that the message not be relayed. Actually, it is the valence of the pain that makes the decision. However the main point is that the thalamus provides gating for our pain, determining what our upper level cortical structures can handle at any given time.

According to some research, it is not until the sixth or seventh month of gestation that the thalamus is fully functioning and can disseminate feelings to incipient cortical neurons. It is here, then, that the second line begins serious operation; the thalamus is the dividing line, as it were, between first and second line; the division between pure physiologic pain (suffocation and terror) and emotional pain (hopelessness, frustration, and fear). It is the former pains that are incorporated into the unconscious and drive us throughout life. It is sometime later that the inchoate neocortical cells mature and begin to understand those early imprints. Often, however, the second level remains alienated from those early memories—which is why psychotherapeutic methods aimed at producing cognitive insight may have little influence on the lower unconscious imprints.

The hypothalamus works with the lower structure, the pituitary, to govern the release of key hormones, not the least of which are the stress hormones. When we have strong emotions it is the hypothalamus that organizes our physiologic response. Our emotional childhood lies on this level and is given force and impetus by the already-in-place first-line structures. Importantly, each imprint on a lower level is duplicated and elaborated on higher levels. They are connected, I propose, by similar oscillations of neurons, but that for now is just an assumption. Future studies will need to account for how a top-level feeling sets off its close companion lower down the neural chain.

Within the hypothalamus lie two different kinds of nervous systems; both work automatically. One is the sympathetic, and the other is the parasympathetic. To reiterate, when there is a strong trauma in utero or just after birth, one of these two systems may come to dominate our lives and dictate whether we will be passive or aggressive in the face of problems. Perhaps even more important is the send-off at birth, which, as we'll see, helps to determine whether we will suffer from high levels of anxiety later on; whether there will be massive repression, as in depressive states, or "leaky gates" that limit our repressive capacity. We will return to this later, but for now understand that leaky gates are responsible for unproductive levels of anxiety: they allow terror to surge upward to consciousness, impairing our ability to concentrate.

Above all, the limbic system is a repository of emotional truth. It lies at roughly the temple area and winds back on the sides of the brain like a ram's horn. This feeling system goes on developing for at least two to three years after birth, although one of its components, the hypothalamus, is fully functional when we are born. That is why we can have physical ailments from birth; colic may be one example of the effects of stress to the hypothalamus from birth trauma or earlier events. Patients who feel on this level may at one point in therapy begin to shake or experience coughing fits. That tells us that deeper level memories are surging forward. We then decide to either tranquilize the patient or allow him to begin a first-line sequence, if together we determine it is appropriate. If the trauma is too much to endure, the patient will come out of the reliving sequence and we will wait until he is ready.

third-line: the neocortex

The third line is the neocortex (or prefrontal cortex), the part of our brain that was the last to evolve and the one responsible for intellectual functioning, generating ideas, and thinking. The left prefrontal area deals with the external world; it helps us repress, plan for the future, and, when possible, integrate feelings. It emerges at about the third year of life.

The right prefrontal area is internally oriented. It deals with our feelings, and is responsible for bringing feelings over to the left prefrontal area for comprehension.

Although the neocortex develops rapidly in the first three years of life, it undergoes another burst of growth just before adolescence. So at the same time our hormones begin raging, there is, conveniently, a greater amount of the prefrontal cortex devoted to controlling the impulses. In short, this is when repression really begins its life. By the end of adolescence, it seems to be almost in full force. But unfortunately for many adolescents this is too late: with too many hormones and too little prefrontal cortex, they've already acted wildly and out of control.

The thalamocortical circuits, which send signals back and forth from the cortex to lower areas of the brain, are established very late in gestation. Only when thalamic and amygdala-cortical circuits are in place is it possible to have a mental appreciation of the pain we are in. Before these circuits are mature, we can experience pain without acknowledging it, meaning, for a brief period, the limbic system in the womb performs the perceptive duties later assumed by the neocortex. Once the top level is in place, our emotional system can return to doing what it does best: handling feelings. Thus, pain can be laid down in a completely unconscious way, without words to clarify or explain it. A patient may have a hard time explaining a gestational trauma, but he can certainly describe a sensation of butterflies in the stomach, pressure on the chest, and a churning sensation in the belly. As psychologists we tend to call this "amorphous anxiety," but really these sensations are part of the overall experience of fear and terror while being carried: each is a remnant of the over-arching experience.[2]

Sometimes at the start of a session the early imprint literally jolts the person who has lain for a few minutes, trying to relax, into a hypervigilant state. Vital signs follow suit. Lower level imprints are stimulating ruminating neurons in the frontal cortex to get busy and help out with repression. In quieting the lower levels, there is a sense of calm in the *thinking* area: a false calm, I might add.

Really, what is happening is that patients, by reliving events at birth and before, are tapping into their evolutionary history. Each new brain level in human history (what evolutionary scientists call phylogeny) is an elaboration of the earlier ones. We do not ignore or forget them; we incorporate them on higher levels of neuronal function. That is why we can lock into a current feeling, experiencing it fully, and then automatically be conducted via resonance to similar earlier states; resonance gives us access to deeply hidden feelings, allowing us to dredge up painful memories of birth and even before. It is not a conscious process, but just the opposite: through it we relinquish left-prefrontal, willful, externally focused brain function in favor of the emotional insight and facility offered by the internally focused right brain. More specifically, the right orbitofrontal cortex, which is located behind the eyes and contains a map of our emotional history, dredges up that history for conscious connection and integration.

As I mentioned, it is the right side of the brain that contains our emotional history, and contains it quite accurately, I might add. Emotional memory is not approximate; it is precise, which is why during a primal reliving the individual's vital signs will accurately reflect those of the original imprint. We will know the force of that imprint by how far from normal it drives the deviation and dislocation. A constant body temp of over 100 degrees, for example, is pathologic; it may shorten one's life. But also, if our therapy is any measure, 98.6 degrees may not be normal. Let me be clear: when, in the high cortical areas, there is resonance with a lower level of brain function (i.e., the limbic system) the force of the imprint on that level tells us about the power, or valence, of the memory. It helps us understand why someone glides right over the feeling.

Recently, for instance, I saw a patient who was getting wound up (her words) because she was moving into a new home and her mortgage lender was making things nearly impossible. She was at a standstill, anxious but unable to move, until finally a neighbor told her what she could do. He had found a "way out" for her, literally. With a new home to move into, her anxiety was almost instantly relieved. Nevertheless, the situation had dredged up an original birth trauma where a tumor had blocked her egress from the uterus and brought her close to death. There was no way out originally and that evoked the prototype: feeling helpless and hopeless.

To recover she had to relive, in reverse order from how they were laid down originally, the third-line, the second-line, and finally the first-line components of the overall feeling. She would not have had such a violent reaction to the mortgage broker, in my view, if not for the birth trauma underlying her experience. In our therapy, we need to have the patient well anchored in the present—meaning we need to connect, first, with the third-line neocortex—before we reach back earlier in our history. We don't want to tamper with evolution, after all.

Of course there is plenty of research to reinforce such anecdotal accounts. Further support is found, for instance, in a 2010 online edition of *Nature*[3] in a report that suggests reversing fear in animals requires that the animals relive the inciting experience. This, incidentally, is also the view of Joseph LeDoux, a neuroscientist at New York University, who reports that each time a memory is evoked all the relevant bits have to be reconstructed or the original feeling winds up missing. For instance, when LeDoux's research team gave rats a medication that prevented the reconstruction of memory, the fear associated with the rats' early experiences was also absent.

As I've said, we can only achieve integration in a therapeutic approach that eschews left-brain intellectualization for a therapeutic atmosphere favoring introspection: darkened rooms, unlimited time, padded floors and walls, and a focus not on a therapist but on oneself.

In brief, we must travel from the last-developed brain tissue to the very first, from the neocortex to the brainstem. Intellectual insight therapy is just the opposite of what is needed. But those who live in their left brain usually cannot recognize feelings much less get patients to relive them in methodical order. I will return to that later. For now, let's look at what clues to our later life lie hidden in the womb.

5

the womb as a black box

When an airplane crashes mysteriously there is an immediate search for the black box containing all the hidden secrets of the flight before the crash. It is an historical record, the silent witness that records aircraft performance patterns, letting investigators know what happened long before the crash to cause it to take place. The womb is also a "black box," containing many hidden secrets that can explain later aberrant behavior. Just as the black box of the airplane has an almost indestructible taped record of previous events, so does the fetal brain; its very early memories are neurobiologic, so fixed not even electroshock therapy can abolish them. Some of the messages in the mechanical black box are in "engineer-speak," providing information that is not in words. And the same is true of the fetus: much of what happens during this stage of development is preverbal, making it difficult to decipher. In order to understand the mechanics, one must have a specialized knowledge of the language of intrauterine life.

The way to learn that language is to descend to the proper level and communicate, inductively, through what I call womb-speak. To eradicate high blood pressure, for example, we need to travel to the brain system that controls blood pressure and attempt to retune it. Likewise, to attack anxiety states characterized by shortness of breath, we must voyage to the deep brain centers that control breathing. Although there are genetic causes to these conditions, often it takes triggering events to make these genetic causes manifest. Without certain triggering events—memories of hypoxia (low oxygen) in the womb, for example—these tendencies may not be realized or may appear in lesser form. This is true of asthma, migraines, and high blood pressure, in addition to a number of other health problems.

What's happening here is that the body, in the interest of survival, is continually reacting to imprinted memory until it is brought to consciousness. The initial information is purely physiologic, and while we may translate some of that information from the original trauma into words, the words themselves are secondary, derivatives of the real experience. Until now, we have not had access to the primitive brain because we did not understand where in our development the black box resided, nor what language it spoke. Our attempts at therapy were the equivalent of trying to understand Cherokee culture while speaking only English, or more absurdly, trying to use human language to reason with a bird. To resolve the equivalent of a human crack-up, we must access our womb-life and relive early traumatic experiences. Then the system can relax because the memories have seen the light of day; they have been connected to our highest evolutionary brain, the frontal cerebral cortex; they've reached their neuronal counterpart and made themselves whole.

the brain that doesn't sleep

Our brain is a constant beehive of activity, even in its resting state. For years we have been measuring the brain's ability to respond when given a new task. Lately, however, work is going on to assess the brain's response to sleep. As it turns out, it doesn't actually rest much. Parts of the feeling-centered limbic brain, such as the hippocampus, are highly active, expending energy, glucose, and oxygen. It appears that when we rest or drop off to sleep, our feelings are mobilized for integration with higher centers. Thus, during sleep, the prefrontal cortex also remains very active; and when we have a good deal of unresolved pain, the brain must remain constantly busy in the service of repression. Some researchers now call this resting state the "default mode," as the brain does not have a specific task. Or, rather, the task is to deal with submerged feelings that interfere with our sleep and suppurate to cause attention deficit disorder, distractibility, and a fuzzy, unfocused mind.

Apart from repressing pain, the default mode seems designed to update memories, turning short-term memories into long-term ones, sorting out what is important and what is not, and eliminating superfluous information so the brain is not overwhelmed. Too much internal input and a person can no longer sort out the trivial from the consequential. On the telephone they will leave the most detailed message, omitting nothing and informing us, also, of nothing. In a car they will drift off into daydream, missing a turn, or worse, risking an accident. For when the brain is overwhelmed, there is no one in charge to give the marching orders; anxiety takes over and we have a state of cognitive Armageddon.

Understand that anxiety is not, strictly speaking, a feeling; it is a sensation, a terribly uncomfortable one, begun in gestation, that is ineffable and cannot be verbalized. I give a thorough explanation of the root causes of anxiety later in chapter fourteen. For now, suffice it to say that any attempt we make at helping patients verbalize or "talk through" their anxiety is, at best, incomplete, as the fetus's neural system had no words to describe the experience in the first place. The minute we attune ourselves to sensations, we must bypass the verbal brain and address the source of our anxiety: the brainstem and limbic system.

Generally speaking, an event is registered at the highest level of brain function possible, but early on the brain is not fully developed; so until roughly the fourth month of gestation trauma is registered at the brainstem level. There is a neural highway on which memories of early events travel: various pathways send information upward and forward, informing higher levels about what is happening lower down; each level makes a contribution in its own language to the overall feeling. This is what I refer to as resonance: information traveling upward and forward in the brain, and later traveling in the reverse direction, so that early events can be simultaneously integrated at all levels of brain function.

Ordinarily, there is a smooth interpenetration of each level. But when there is constant trauma—during gestation, at birth, in infancy and childhood—the barriers between brain levels are too diffuse and information from below surges to the top. That is why, at our clinic, in their very first weeks of therapy, we see pre-psychotics reliving experiences from birth. Their gating system is insufficient (their default mode over-the-top), and these early events rise to the frontal cortex prematurely.

This is an important concept and worth a word of additional explanation. Each very early imprint during gestation leaves a mark, a mark that is registered higher up as we evolve and informs of what happened earlier. It is informed, perhaps, by similar electrical frequencies or by similar chemical compounds. The imprint is then engraved on an emotional and later intellectual level. When something bad happens later on, a rejection or an insult, it can trigger off sister imprints deeper in the nervous system. And the reaction is greater than one would expect because of the analogue or residue of pain already engraved.

Resonance works in two directions: one, it works upward to inform an event that is happening in the present that there is a similar pain—hopelessness, for example—lying deep down; two, it works top-down, so something in the present resonates with or triggers off something low down that rises to join the current reaction. We need to look at the resonance factor when trying to understand behavior and symptoms.

In reliving it is possible that in those with leaky gates, a current event can trigger off all of the earlier similar imprints to produce inordinate symptoms, a migraine, high blood pressure, or terrible anxiety, for instance. A therapist needs to learn about this and make sure that the lower levels are blocked for the moment with tranquilizers so that the patient can focus on the single higher-level feeling. If he feels rage and hopelessness at the DMV he needs to stay there, well anchored in the feeling before descending deeper. If the early feeling emerges all at once there can be no integration of even part of the feeling because the experience is overwhelming.

A simple bit of research is relevant here. The psychologist Daniel Schacter, in an issue of *Science*, reported the results of a memory study in which subjects watched portions of a TV series before having their brainwaves measured.[1] Schacter's research team at Harvard University found that when the subject remembered the event, the single brain cell signature was the same as in the first viewing. He wrote that it seemed like a reliving, which has been my position all along. What do you call it when a memory arouses one's exact history with its precise early physiology? Reliving. With the right triggers, the brain conjures up its history, intact.

All of this explains why rational, insight therapy cannot eradicate anxiety, but can only provide defenses to control it. As we'll see later, the prefrontal cortex can at times work against the limbic system: the more active the top-level thinking brain, the less active the feeling centers. Cognitive therapy, by strengthening a patient's verbal defenses and fencing off lower levels of feeling, may actually prevent him from getting well. We do not need the frontal cortex to feel anxious; lower levels handle that just fine; we need it to report on the sensation of anxiety, to signify it with a name. You might say that anxiety is terror disconnected from its roots. Because severe anxiety or panic attacks often come from traumatic events that occurred before birth, our therapy must target the primitive, non-verbal nervous system, the part of the brain that originally reacted to the intrauterine alarm.

hormones and homosexuality

One of the secrets revealed by the womb's black box concerns finger length. An imbalance in the ratio of one's ring finger to index finger length may indicate an original imbalance in hormones during gestation. In men, the ring finger generally is longer than the index finger. In most women, the two fingers are roughly the same length. When the ring finger is much longer, we may have an index of masculinity. The smaller the ratio, the more feminine the individual is likely to be. Finger ratio is important, in other words, because it may suggest the secretion of sex hormones and, possibly, the very origins of hormone secretion in the womb. When the male hormone androgen is in balance, even at birth, the masculine index is high. Androgen, in addition to other hormones, is transmitted by the mother through the umbilical cord. When she is upset or anxious, that transmission may get garbled. Altered finger-length ratio is just one of many indices of a scrambled message, however it points to a lifelong series of changes occasioned by altered hormone balance. The result may be low libido, feelings of defeat, suicidal tendencies, hypertension, hypothyroidism, and the list goes on.

Gay women tend to resemble heterosexual men in finger ratio. Although this may be explained by genetic factors in our development, there is good reason to believe that environmental influences, particularly in the womb, are extremely important. One study hypothesizes that finger-length ratio may point to later high blood pressure, as well as heart attacks and cancer. This would appear to make sense, since traumas while in the womb alter the hormone balance of the baby, which in turn affects the evolution of the fingers, heart, and other key organs. Presently, we know that at the third month of gestation, the hands are beginning a critical development as key hormones are coming to life. So, too, are the brain, sex organs, and heart. Some evidence suggests that when trauma occurs during gestation, the thyroid output also can be changed. Thus, the actual anatomical development will be affected—the child may be born with wider hips or chunkier legs—because of deficiencies in thyroid secretion.

Additional evidence of the link between gestational trauma and hormone production is found in research with young children. Children with high levels of testosterone, as indicated by the ratio of ring finger to index finger, are more likely to be quicker with their left hands, showing right-side dominance. Right- or left-handedness, in short, may be one more sign of hormone balance in the womb. Other research has used samples of amniotic fluid in which the fetus was bathed to directly measure hormone levels. From this, we find that poor language skills may be associated with fetuses heavily exposed to testosterone.

Too much of the wrong hormone in gestation may, in fact, be the culprit in any number of later aberrations. Heart disease in adult men has been associated with inordinately high levels of progesterone. Breast cancer in adult women has been linked to elevated levels of estrogen. And it is my observation, despite some objection in the scientific community, that early trauma upsets the balance in hormones and continues to destabilize us throughout our lives. A study at Harvard, for example, proposed that breast cancer may get its start in utero, with excessive estrogen in the mother contributing to later catastrophic disease in her offspring.[2] Eventually, we may come to look at our fingers in a whole new light, realizing that they may be the index of what lies in the antipodes of our nervous system—a clue to the mystery inside the black box.

As a final point, it is worth noting that the differences in whorls and ridges of the fingers create yet another marker, indicating the possibility of homosexual orientation. There is now some research pointing to the differentiating ridges on the fingers of homosexual men. Finger ridges are formed roughly in the tenth week of gestation, and those of homosexual men appear to be different from controls. My early hypothesis is that trauma not only changes the hormones that alter finger ridges but may change sexual orientation as well. Granted, this is a preliminary idea, but how else than by testing such theories can we begin to understand the meaning of finger ridges? My belief, still to be tested, is that sex problems are not just sex problems; they involve a host of internal changes that may have begun in the third or fourth month of gestation. Those events, I propose, leave a mark and may eventuate not only in homosexuality but may provide a fertile soil for other serious afflictions later on. In addition to later sex anomalies, there may be a tendency for high blood pressure, impaired or weakened immune system, and even cancer.

If homosexuality were a native state, that is, strictly genetic, then these ridges would not differentiate from those of heterosexual control subjects. As I explain in *The Biology of Love*, homosexual men, in general, undergo more trauma while being carried in the womb than those in the general population. It is possible that the "fertile soil" of maternal hormonal imbalance makes homosexuals vulnerable to serious afflictions later on. This is, of course, a debatable point we can discuss ad infinitum.

depression: the black box perspective

Early hormonal imbalance has psychological consequences, as well. It can be the basis of later depression—feelings of "What's the use? Nothing I can do will make any difference"—because, originally, the newborn was overwhelmed by anesthesia or other drugs. Often we find that if a pregnant mother was constantly on painkillers and tranquilizers, the child develops the same kinds of anesthetized feelings as the drugs produced originally. This can provide the underpinnings of later resignation and hopelessness and, in turn, can lead to such things as high blood pressure and suicidal tendencies, both confirmed by recent research.

I have found, disturbingly, that those who were strangled close to death, at birth, by the umbilical cord, often choose hanging in their suicide attempts. Nature doesn't play dice with biology, to paraphrase Einstein. The memory and reactions to it have an inexorable logic. What enters one's head in times of stress is history, resurrected knowledge of what happened under life-and-death stress early on; of what exists on a lower, earlier evolutionary brain structure. It is this history that emerges in the cortex and creates specific ideas about life, death, and the means to achieve them.

What we generally label as feelings are antedated by deeper, more remote memories that are not feelings, per se: strangulation, choking, pressure in the head and chest—all are pre-feeling states processed by internal brain structures. One follows a progression: feeling crushed originally in the womb, further crushed by overwhelming odds in early childhood, and finally feeling hopeless at the slightest adversity. Depression is basically a sensation of paralysis—a feeling of having no energy, being overwhelmed, and experiencing labored breathing and slow movements. From the black-box perspective, the idea is to convert those sensations to their generating sources; to locate, in the limbic system and brainstem, the fetal language that says, "I can't move." "I am overwhelmed," "I am crushed, suffocated," and so on.

Delving into that language is, of course, never simple. When we look into the black box we find a feeling history, a partial explanation of later development. It may be that depression stems, in part, from an overpowering and dominating father who crushed his son; however, often there is a more remote explanation—a memory of being crushed at birth by the mother's inability to dilate sufficiently or cooperate in the birth process due to gestational drug use. If research moves forward in the way I hope, the black box will soon give us a much richer sense of the contributing factors that lie behind depression.

For years there has been the common belief that emotional pain is different from physical pain, but researchers are finally starting to equate the two. In one study a UCLA team of psychologists[3] used MRIs to monitor the brain activity of a group of college students. A game was rigged so that the subjects would feel rejected and experience emotional pain. Brain scans identified the locus of this kind of pain in the center of the brain, in a structure known as the cingulate, as well as in parts of the right prefrontal cortex. Interestingly, the cingulate also plays a key role in processing physical pain. It appears, at least from the evidence of this study, that the brain doesn't differentiate among various kinds of hurt; pain is pain no matter what the origins.

Emotional illness, then, is something that really does hurt. And similar to the experience of severe physical injury, when the pain becomes too intense, the system shuts down. Emotional hurt becomes embedded in the physical system, and there it remains. Being abandoned, for example, is perceived by children as extreme rejection and experienced as a *physical* agony often too fierce to feel. Some say, "Ah, it's just in your head. You'll get over it!" That's not always true. In psychotherapy we need to be reminded that addressing emotional pain means experiencing all of its *physiological* accoutrements. Shedding a few tears or sobs, however cathartic, won't get the job done; not if we want to undo the damage of emotional deprivation in infancy and childhood.

Why is emotional pain so hurtful? Because we need strong emotional interaction with our parents if we are to survive as a species. As babies, animals with damaged cingulates may escape the safe watch of their parents because, when separated, they are unable to express a call of distress. The cingulate is important because the cry it produces is what lets a mother know her child is in peril.

the brainstem in primal therapy

In primal therapy, patients may regress to relive an experience that happened during their gestation or birth. In such an instance, as the frontal cortex quiets and recedes and lower brain centers assume control, the patient will experience coughing and gagging: this is the first sign they are tapping into brainstem imprints. During this time the late-developing prefrontal cortex is relatively inoperative while the lower levels are highly active. There are less and less thoughts, less articulations of words, as the patient slides down the neural chain, first into early-life feelings and sensations, and then, later, into pre-birth memories.

In some respects, a primal session is very much like dream sleep. During dream-life the prefrontal thinking cortex remains relatively inactive while the feeling centers are churning away. After a session the patient usually has no idea how much time he spent immersed in the feeling. Just as in a dream, the top-level neocortex has been momentarily turned off. Indeed, if a patient has a precise notion of the time spent in the Primal, it may be because he was not wholly reliving the feeling.

During primal therapy, the patient typically has little awareness of the therapy room: he is transported to a lower level of consciousness—inwardly, rather than outwardly, directed as in sleep. A key difference between a dream state and a primal state, however, is that in dreams the feelings are symbolized, whereas in therapy one is plunged into the feelings themselves; as a result, patients typically report fewer symbolic dreams as therapy proceeds.

When we talk about the primal approach, we must remember that a brainstem memory means a brainstem *reaction*. That means that the vital signs that accompanied the original trauma must be in evidence again. Without complete reactions to a memory, the improvement is only partial. This is terribly important so let me clarify and embellish a bit. As I've said, whenever there is an imprint that happened while we were being carried it is done on the most primitive level of our nervous system. That imprint is grinding away all of the time: driving us to keep busy so we do not feel helpless; affecting heart function so that we may have a premature cardiac arrest. To correct the pattern, we need to reawaken the memory through resonance.

The brainstem, as I've said, is particularly important when it comes to intrauterine memory. Developed during gestation, it contains the imprint of our deepest levels of pain and handles life-and-death matters that occurred before we were born. Early in gestation the fetal brainstem will respond to external noises, even the sound of the mother's voice. We see the brainstem at work in ultrasound images of head turning and reflective body movements, as well as in heart rate changes. If there is a serious accident to the mother while she is carrying, it will undoubtedly affect the brainstem of the fetus, and perhaps its heart function, as well. The baby may be born fragile and delicate, plagued by a constant underlying fear, and quick to startle.

Later problems such as high blood pressure or colitis arise when the brainstem is carrying an imprinted memory of a trauma and tries, unsuccessfully, to tell the frontal cortex about its near-death experience. The high blood pressure or colitis we find in adulthood is, thus, a remnant of stored terror. The brainstem is shouting at the neocortex: "Listen to me! I need to tell you about something, you've got to hear this. I've got a connection to make. Let me through." It is screaming by way of biochemicals: high levels of noradrenaline, glutamate, and cortisol that are the language of its biology. And the cortex is responding, "Sorry, you've got information I don't want to know about. I am going to push you back into the basement. Try later!" "Yes, but if you don't let me out my blood pressure is going to rise dramatically." "Sorry, that is how it goes."

Somewhat paradoxically, the neocortex serves as a portal for entry into the suffering component of a memory, a portal that cannot operate by itself. It's the first door we walk through when retracing our history and attempting to understand our pain. When the neocortex is impaired or damaged due to early trauma, it is difficult to block feelings that arise from lower brain levels. When it operates less efficiently, imprinted memory seeps upward to the surface. There may be panic, malaise, depression, and anxiety—all driven by the imprint. Beginning with the neocortex and progressing gradually to the brainstem, we must identify and recalibrate the originating source of the pain.

In this process, the therapist is a kind of guide. He can never help us be familiar with Cairo, however, if he takes us to London instead. We need to go to the right address, the right nervous system where the facts lie. Each nervous system is a repository of certain truths and no others. We cannot understand the birth trauma and its effects on us if we remain on the cortical level: sitting up, discussing and enumerating, ad nauseam. We must push the envelope back. Just when some of us caught on that birth trauma affected us for a lifetime, now we must consider pre-birth events as even more important. We don't "get over it," nor do we grow out of it. We live with it. We do contain that black box I have mentioned; and we should know that it exists and how to access it, for it will give up so many hidden secrets that have governed our lives. We have made an interesting switch from palm reading to predict our future, to finger reading to uncover our past. I prefer the latter; it's a bit more accurate.

PART TWO:
THE SCIENCE OF
EARLY HUMAN
DEVELOPMENT

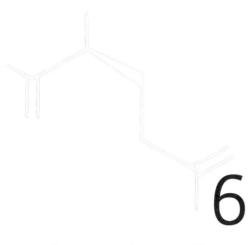

6

how we internalize our external world: telomeres as a predictor of life expectancy

How we develop is due to the transformation of the external into the internal. If external life is harsh and unloving, even in the womb, it is considered, in my schema, a lack of love. It will be internalized, and that environment will shape our brain. Later, if deprivation is compounded, the person may develop a cynical outlook, believing life is terrible because life was terrible in the womb.

I have pointed out that experiences in the womb can stimulate neurons to develop new synapses, and dendrites that enable more diverse connections to other neurons. Access to feelings, therefore, is begun during womb-life. We may think that one sibling is stronger mentally than another due to genetics, but it may well be due to the gestation period: the brain of one child has better and stronger connections than the other, because the mother was calmer during pregnancy. Womb-life is not identical for twins; their position counts. When we internalize our outer-world experiences, our neurophysiology is reformed in the process; it literally becomes part of us. So an anxious pregnant mother, in her response to her outer world, is revving up the metabolism of her fetus. It is a joint environment: for the mother, it is her internal needs that she responds to, while for the fetus, it is the intrauterine environment. It is the effect of the mother's blood system, hormones, and attitudes that the baby internalizes. Body development and formation adapt to this internalization.

If the pregnant mother drinks a cocktail, the baby will be exposed to the toxic effects of alcohol; if she smokes or inhales secondhand smoke, the baby's respiratory system will be affected; if she is depressed for a lengthy period of time, her baby may be imprinted in "down" mode, showing lower vital signs. If she is anxious—with high blood pressure (180/110) and a consistent heart rate above 90 beats per minute—the baby may be fixed in the "up" mode. The main point: a carrying mother is shaping her fetus. All this may endure, as altered setpoints are being imprinted into the baby's nervous system. The outside, in short, dictates the inside.

For some time now, we have been preparing a research project to take a closer look at how primal therapy may influence life expectancy. Our proposed study involves telomeres, a region of repetitive DNA which cap the chromosomes and keep the DNA of the cell stable. Researchers at Brown University have found that when telomeres are longer, we live longer, and vice versa. Moreover, it turns out that telomeres are correlated with the stress hormone cortisol and tend to get shorter as cortisol increases. Through therapy we have reduced cortisol levels in our patients, and it may be that this reduction also slows the shrinking of telomeres; hence, perhaps a longer life. In the Brown study,[1] researchers discovered that the telomeres of those adults who had been abused as children had shortened more rapidly than nonabused adults. As Audrey Tyrka notes in the journal *Biological Psychiatry*, "It gives us a hint that early developmental experiences may have profound effects on biology that can influence cellular mechanisms at a very basic level."[2] Again, the kind of abuse we know and write about— gestational and birth trauma—may be even more profound than much of what is ascribed in the literature. Certainly, the relationship between trauma and telomeres warrants further study, but I am convinced, for now, that very early pain does indeed shorten our lives.

Every day more research is coming out about telomeres. At the point of conception our telomeres are at their longest and most viable, roughly 15,000 base pairs, per cell. Each time a cell divides it shortens the telomeres so that at birth we have about 10,000 per cell. By age eighty, telomeres can shorten to one tenth of the original length. I have discussed this research with Noel Thomas Patton of Telomere Activation Sciences, who believes that there has been no definitive research, until now, about womb-life trauma and telomere length. So all we can do is make an assumption: trauma in the womb may be the precursor for how telomeres evolve and endure. I hypothesize that adverse conditions in the womb may influence how much telomeres shorten across a lifetime and, therefore, how long we live.

Recently, a Finnish group led by Laura Kananen found that shortening occurs often in those who suffer from chronic anxiety disorders.[3] At older ages, up to age eighty-seven, individuals with high anxiety were found to have shorter telomeres than healthy controls. In those who had multiple abuse factors in childhood, there was, again, this shortening. The conclusion: adverse events in childhood adversely affect telomere length, which may predict how long we live. We can forgive our parents for all their transgressions during our childhood, but their apologies won't help us live longer.

A feeling therapy, in short, may do more than help social adjustment; it may help with longevity by reducing cortisol levels and shrinking the size of telomeres. That is the kind of outcome study in psychotherapy that is not usually considered but, perhaps, should be. One of the conclusions drawn by the psychiatrist Elissa Epel, for instance, in her pioneering work on telomeres is that prenatal life has a significant influence on telomere attrition.[4] And researchers at the Hypertension Research Center, a clinical facility at the University of Medicine and Dentistry, in Newark, New Jersey, support her view.[5] Their conclusion: "The variability in telomere length among newborns and synchrony in telomere length within organs of the newborn are consistent with the concept that variations in telomere length among adults are in large part attributed to determinants (genetic and environmental) that start exerting their effect in utero."

I don't think we can say it any clearer than that. It may well be that womb-life is a major determinant of how long we live. This is another way of saying what I hope I've made apparent: that it is urgent that doctors, mothers and mental health professionals do not neglect this critical period.

7

how repression works

Earlier I mentioned that there is a gating system in the brain that inhibits the message of feeling when it becomes too much to bear. This is such an important point of primal theory that it is worth a few more words. I have discussed the amygdala, in earlier works, as the emotional center of the brain; information from the amygdala must arrive at the prefrontal cortex to make us aware of our feelings and help us to understand their emotional significance. When the amygdala's gating mechanism against rising feeling fails, there is a direct impact on the frontal cortex: we start to become aware of our pain, which in turn can lead to anxiety and panic. When the cortex is activated by up-surging feelings the third-line brain gets busy; it races, manufactures ideas and beliefs, and in general does what it can to attenuate the on-rush.

Ordinarily, we need our feelings to guide us and to make crucial life decisions, but the key is balance—and this is where repression can be beneficial. When we are overloaded with feelings there is a shut-down of the thinking apparatus; we become confused, enmeshed in ideas but still hopelessly lost. We need a fluid interchange of feelings and thoughts; that is what a normal brain should do—integrate the two into a smooth-working mechanism. And that is what our brain research found: harmony between the right and left brain and the lower and higher brain affords the best chance for mental health (see *Primal Healing* for a full discussion of this). Constant imprinted stress from gestation and the first years of life can actually shrink the connecting wires among neurons and lead, ultimately, to memory deficit and brain dysfunction.

Essentially, what gating does is interfere in the synapses between nerve cells. Chemicals that stop the transmission of pain are secreted into that gap, thereby keeping the gates closed against the arrival of surplus feelings of panic. There seems to be a time in gestation, however, when pain impinges on the nervous system, yet we are unable to produce gating chemicals (such as serotonin and endorphin) to alleviate it. The result is a residue of ungated pain, which will continue to affect the brain later in life and may lead to chronic anxiety. Some evidence now suggests, for instance, that free-floating, unbound terror may manifest as a variety of phobias—snakes, spiders, open spaces, etc.—delusions which are not due to heredity but events in the womb.

Talk therapy has become quite fashionable of late, but it may have little benefit for patients with high levels of repression: for many, the imprint lies in a vegetative, primitive nervous system that is indifferent to words. This region of the nervous system is adequate to register pain and terror experienced during womb-life, but it cannot translate these feelings into language. That's why the neurotic often goes on having the same experiences without improvement: the limbic brain where the trauma originated is not specifically targeted. Attempts to "talk through" the trauma offer little, if any, real benefit, and the feeling remains an inaccessible memory. You cannot, in short, discuss feelings with a lizard; he will go on doing what he must despite our exhortations.

Early trauma may compromise our ability to repress pain. To relay information to higher brain levels, often via the thalamus, there needs to be a smooth flow of information. What regulates the passage of these signals and keeps them from overloading higher levels of the brain is a neural system of gates, not unlike a series of locks and dams. Normally, we produce chemicals such as serotonin that impede the flow of information when it becomes overwhelming. Early trauma, however, can overtax the gating system, producing "leaky gates." Thereafter, feelings and sensations may intrude into our mental apparatus and cause us to feel miserable and unable to concentrate. If lack of love continues in early childhood through emotional neglect or abuse, the gating system, now under assault from surging feelings, may be further weakened. Chronically anxious or upset, we then can no longer produce the chemicals we need to hold back pain and keep the gates functioning properly.

What that intrusion does, as well, is impel us to seek out chemicals that were originally weakened or depleted in the service of repression. We are looking to be and feel normal. For the depressive, that means taking pills such as Prozac or Zoloft to enhance serotonin. Someone in the passive, lethargic mode, on the other hand, takes cocaine or drinks cup after cup of coffee and suddenly feels better. The ADDer often needs a boost for the prefrontal cortex and is prescribed Adderall or Ritalin—uppers that make the frontal neurons more efficient. None of these chemical enhancements, however, correct the gating problems at the most basic level of the imprint.

What's worse, the converse to leaky gates—an overactive repressive system—may be equally problematic. If the pain is great but our defense system holds, then we may be looking forward to cancer and a shortened life. Admittedly, this is my presumption, not a scientific fact; however, it derives from decades of clinical work. When massive repression is required to inhibit the transmission of life-threatening feelings, tremendous pressure is exerted on the system; pressure which may lead to cellular dislocation and deformity. If we can see the source of the pressure in a Primal (as we now can), we may, one day, be able to uncover how early pain increases the risk for certain forms of cancer.

Freud had his own word for leaky gates: hysteria. The word comes from the Greek word for womb, *hysterion*, and Freud initially applied it in the case of Vienna-born, Jewish feminist Bertha Pappenheim (Anna O), who suffered from hallucinations, paralysis, and suicidal impulses among other things. Freud's interpretation of Pappenheim's case—that hysteria was rooted in repressed sexual desire and could thus be treated with talk therapy—is considered the emergence of the psychoanalytic age. Although Freud's view of hysteria is widely discounted, his identification of the symptoms remains applicable today. Individuals with hysteria talk and move constantly; they are often unreflective and prone to overreact to the smallest of inputs. I believe this is due to leaky gates: input from the limbic system pushes fear and terror upward into cortical regions. When the gates can no longer modulate these reactions, impulses spill "over the top," producing panic, alarm, and the need to solve problems immediately. That is why individuals with hysteria lack restraint and will say whatever is on their mind.

Gating is good, in moderation, because it keeps us sane and functioning; however it becomes dangerous when gates become impervious and access is blocked to ourselves and our feelings. Problems arise, as well, when gates are too porous, and in both cases we can usually make an accurate diagnosis and a prognosis for therapy. Leaky gates lead to a hair-trigger response system, in which our vital signs remain consistently above normal. Dense gates, on the other hand, leave us phlegmatic, bankrupt of feeling. A truly loved child lives somewhere in the middle: continually in the balanced, primal zone.

small feet, small chest: a sign of cancer?

Our own research suggests that stunted body development may be a key marker of repression. Before cells commit to what they will become, they have a script: DNA that plots a course for their development. When the genetic destination is short-circuited, however, that script may not adequately suit its chosen actors. Are small feet and a small chest desirable? Are they good or bad? It's more complex than that. They are neither good nor bad; rather what's important is whether the script for size has arrived at its genetic destination. That is, on the basis of heredity do small feet (or very large feet) fulfill the genetic intention? If not, there can be serious repercussions. When size is in conflict with what we'd expect from heredity, and now we leave the arena of strict science, it may be that repression has interceded to slow down or inhibit growth.

Some of my patients have reported foot growth, chest growth, breast growth, and other kinds of aberrant growth after about a year of therapy. What has happened in such instances, in my view, is the lifting of repression and the liberation of pain. Constant pressure in key sites resisted growth and blocked genetic destination, until the repressive lid was lifted through therapy. And, as I've said, that internal pressure may mean the later possibility of serious illness, possibly cancer.

For now, we can only say that small feet or small breasts appear to be abnormal if, at the end of therapy, they begin to grow. And I believe that only happens when the patient arrives at deeply implanted pain, at and before birth, when numerous hormones are affected and when many set-points are fixed. In this strict sense, I think our therapy may help forestall the development of cancer. Again, this is not a promise, only a possibility we should explore.

Of course there are effects in other areas we cannot measure: for example, the kidneys, heart, and liver. Wherever we've looked, though—in studies of serotonin and natural killer cells, among others—we've found significant changes. We would expect the same with key organ systems. In other words, pain and repression are laid down as a total experience, which means that just about every system is involved in the imprint. But at the same time we would expect that those systems that are inherently weak and vulnerable would be the most seriously affected by repression. So how do we prevent such effects? A good gestation, birth, and infancy. Failing that, by reliving the key pains that were set down early on, so that we may help undo massive repression and reduce potential health risks to our patients.

8

epigenetics:
the inheritance of acquired characteristics

When we discuss repression there is something else we must add to the theoretical mix: epigenetics—how very early events in the womb and at birth can alter the genetic unfolding. Research has shown that one genotype, a single genetic predisposition, can give rise to many phenotypes depending on what happens to those genes during gestation. So what we might imagine is genetic, is actually genetic—plus what happens to us in the womb. I was astonished early in my therapy when long-term patients reported that their wisdom teeth descended. Now I understand it better; the genetic unraveling toward the teeth's destination was deferred due to repression.

In the early nineteenth century, a French scientist named Jean Baptiste Lamarck decided that we acquired characteristics from experiences that our parents underwent. Russian communists applied this to agriculture but, no matter, it was a widely discredited theory . . . until recently. Now this scientific view is being resurrected; for the emerging field of epigenetics largely upholds what Lamarck believed. So what is the evidence for epigenetics? And how does it work? What Lamarck said, quite presciently, was that individuals may acquire characteristics as a result of their environment and pass these characteristics on to the offspring. This could be anything from stress-related mood disorders, to dietary adaptations, to respiratory conditions caused by tobacco exposure.

Children may thus have vastly different life experiences without radical differences in genes, but, rather, in how the genes are expressed, whether they are shut off or turned on. A mother's interaction with her environment is vital, in this way, for it may determine if the potential of her offspring's genes are fully realized. A fetus in the womb is always trying to adapt to its environment; its genes will evolve and be expressed depending on that adaptation. However adaptation may cause problems, if the carrying mother's neurochemical signals are imbalanced. As first reported in a 2007 study by Vivette Glover and her colleagues at Imperial College, London, the transmission of high cortisol levels to the child may lead to lower IQ, as well as anxiety, ADD, and depression.[1] Canadian research is supporting those findings. Following the 2009 Royal Society Summer Science Exhibition in London, Suzanne King, an associate professor of psychiatry at McGill University, concluded: "If there is anything we all agree on it's that the fetus is incredibly vulnerable and fragile, and that even subtle perturbations in the mother's mood can have measurable effects on the fetus that last for years."[2]

Epigenetic changes occur while the fetal brain is developing rapidly and needs proper neuronal input to evolve the way it is supposed to. If input from the mother is not successfully integrated, the child may not be able to form cohesive thoughts, nor to focus and concentrate. This is the kind of person, thereafter, who cannot accept high levels of stimulation because his internal input is so great that anything from the outside—two term papers due immediately, a job interview, a move to a new city, anything most of us would perceive as inordinately stressful—is, quite literally, overwhelming.

To get an idea of how early all of this may begin, consider a recent study at the University of Miami School of Medicine. Researchers there suggest that when mothers are depressed during pregnancy "fetal activity is elevated, growth is delayed, [and] low birth weight common."[3] In fact, newborns of a depressed mother show a profile that mimics the carrying mother's physiologic state, meaning high stress hormone levels, low levels of dopamine and serotonin, and above-normal right frontal brain activity.[4] The research on the subject is fairly consistent: higher resting levels of stress hormones in the carrying mother can have an effect on the later life of the offspring. All of this presages the child's later need for tranquilizers, since the early imprint has lowered hormone levels permanently. With even minor setbacks later on, taking painkillers may become a matter of urgency.

I often talk about our internal pharmacy. When pain enters the body, our brain goes to the pharmacy, as it were, to order what it needs: more serotonin to help with repression, for example. What the commercial pharmacies do is produce the precise molecules that we manufacture inside our brains; and they do it because we cannot manufacture enough ourselves. I am convinced that, were it not for early events, most of us would manufacture the chemicals we need to feel content in the ordinary course of our lives. But in some cases, just as the brain is developing in the womb, traumas beset us, altering the serotonin setpoints; that is, we cannot secrete what we need because pain has caused the brain to use up its reserves in the battle for survival. And this sets up a permanent deficit: a new set-point. The child of an anxious mother is thus chronically anxious because the mother's gating mechanisms were faulty and exposed the fetus to high levels of caustic hormones; thus, the cycle goes on.

There is a debate going on now about the advisability of using tranquilizers to normalize the carrying mother's system. Both sides have valid concerns. If there is no medication given to the mother, then she will likely continue to be anxious or depressed, and pass her chemical signature on to the baby. On the other hand, if we do give tranquilizers to the carrying mother, then these drugs can be transferred to the baby, thereby overloading the fetus's serotonin levels. There is really no great solution, except this: normalizing the system before pregnancy. That can be done, and we have shown in any number of studies that we tend to normalize the brain system after one year of primal therapy. This is preferable, in my view, to messing with our inner neurology.

In July 2010, Frederich van der Veen presented new findings on serotonin to the Forum of European Neuroscience in Amsterdam. In a landmark study, he gave a serotonin enhancer to subjects before they watched sad films, finding that those on medication cried much less.[5] The serotonin infusion effectively blocked the study participant's access to tears and, presumably, the sad feelings themselves. Keep in mind that we are not normally low in serotonin except when in trauma; and those traumas that occur the earliest in our lives are the most powerful, dealing, as they do, with life-and-death matters. Accordingly, crying less doesn't just mean less tears; it also means less access to ourselves and our feelings. The purpose of serotonin enhancers is to numb our feelings and our reactions to those feelings. But taking shots or pills does not eliminate the pain; it disguises it, making us less conscious, which can hurt us in a variety of ways. Taking medication, in short, needs to be seen as a stop-gap method and not a cure.

epigenetics, birth, and stress

As the field of epigenetics grows, we are finding more and more research citing the birth experience as the hidden cause for a variety of common diseases and thinking and memory problems. Researchers at Karolinska Institute, in Stockholm, have found that cesarean births can result, for instance, in increased incidence of allergies, diabetes, and leukemia. The neonatologist Mikael Norman, explaining these findings, points out that "altered birth conditions could cause a genetic imprint in the immune cells that could play a role in later life."[6] The assumption is that the fetus is not prepared for an "unnatural" birth. Unlike a vaginal birth in which stress gradually builds and can thus be adapted to, cesarean birth is a shock to the fetal environment, which can affect how the genes behave.

Several times a year epigenetic research provides us new insight into cancer. There is such a thing as a tumor-suppressor gene, which may cause cancer cells to die by halting additional cell growth. However er something can happen early on to affect our cellular braking mechanism and allow unrestrained growth of cancer cells.[7] What seems to happen when the mother is under stress, that is, is tumor-suppressor cells are momentarily disabled. This is similar to when a mother stops a child from expressing his feelings: pressure builds in the system and disease may occur as a result. Here the only difference is that the suppression is purely physiologic and happens very early on.

There have been other studies of the epigenetic effect of maternal stress. A research team led by Thomas O'Connor of the University of Rochester Medical Center studied 125 pregnant women at roughly

seventeen weeks of gestation,[8] using samples of amniotic fluid to measure stress levels in the mother. When the children reached seventeen
months of age, researchers tested the interactions between the mothers
and their infants to find out, among other things, if the babies were
secure, and if they cried when separated from their mothers. Longitu-
dinal results showed that children of anxious mothers could not concentrate as well as those of mothers who were calm. Interestingly, if
parents were closely connected to their children in the first months and
years of his life, some of that harm could be undone—the implication
being that the negative effects of gestational trauma can be eliminated
in a loving home. I am skeptical of this conclusion, however, because
once a trauma is imprinted it tends to endure. It can be softened by a
loving homelife, but not eliminated. We cannot eliminate our history;
it is the crucible that determines whom we will become.

heredity turned on its head

Let's make sure we understand this notion of epigenetics because in
the coming years it will likely be one of most important areas of scientific research. As I've mentioned, one reason for its preeminence is
that many of the serious diseases we think are genetic are actually epigenetic and, therefore, environmentally caused. The thinking is that
with lower brain therapeutic techniques, such as primal therapy, these
diseases may be able to be successfully treated.

When a harmful event occurs while we are being carried there is
an imprint that remains for a lifetime. It is aided and abetted by a process called methylation, in which part of the chemical methyl group is
added to the mark to help it endure. In other words, the imprint is laid
down, in part, by a change in the cell, as certain chemical reactions
are taking place—hydrogen removal, methyl infusion, and so on. For
our purposes, we need not be so concerned with the process, which
we'll leave to the biochemical scientists. Suffice it to say that methylation does exist, leaving a heritable imprint. So what we always thought
was genetic may well be the result of very early experience diverting the
genetic legacy.

Trauma causes methylation—that is what's important. Perhaps given a good environment there may be a way of demethylating the imprint. But what it looks like, for now, is that adding methyl may be one way to protect the cell against the adverse effects of a trauma. In other words, the imprint is a survival mechanism; it helps guide us in the future so that we avoid danger. And what is even more astounding is that the imprint can be transmitted across multiple generations, so not only is the parent important in all this, but so is the grandparent. A memory has been engraved into the epigenome and so passed from one generation to the next.

Animal experiments have shown that separating a baby sporadically and unpredictably from its mother causes severe stress, and the same applies to a human baby who is not touched right after birth and in the first weeks of life, as we find in babies raised in incubators. The effects of this stress become heritable from the epigenome. This imprint then affects many aspects of our biology, including the memory system. As we'll see later, that may mean that a condition such as Alzheimer's disease may get its start from birth, and not show up for another sixty years.

Research by D.K. Lahiri and B. Maloney, at the Indiana University School of Medicine, for instance, indicates how this all might work—first by the imprint and then, they suggest, by the methylation that carries on the imprint. The mark or tag, not so easily seen, can change or delay the development of a genetic trait. Again, the imprint changes how heredity manifests itself—which is why epigenetics is so confusing and why, until now, we have considered a number of serious diseases to be inherited when, in fact, they may not be inherited at all.[9]

As we saw earlier, Michael Meaney and his research team found that deprived animals, when later raised by a more loving mother, experience a partial recovery as higher-level brain processes override some of the effects of early imprints.[10] The neocortex can provide compensations for the pain, masking the imprint, but cannot eradicate it. Meaney's rats, deprived and damaged early on by a disappearing mother, were later put into an enriched environment where they seemed happier and played well together. But their stress hormone level was still high; they still suffered, as do humans under similar conditions. Masking the pain is not the same as resolving it, and we may die prematurely from that masking. You might call it a devil's bargain: if we mask the pain we may die early, but if we don't we suffer. However there is a third possibility: relive and integrate the pain, and thus be done with it.

There seems to be a window of opportunity before methylation sets in when the imprint can be partially reversed.[11] But it is a narrow, short-lived window. After that the imprint remains for a very long time. What scientists are working on now is how to undo methylation. Investigations into using methionine to reverse the effects of methylation are bearing fruit, and other drugs, including some tranquilizers, are helping to accomplish it. I believe reliving early experience in a Primal may also partially undo methylation and help to normalize the system. This should be a subject for future research.

epigenetics and pain

Although the study of epigenetics can get fairly complex, one of the keys to proper understanding lies in accounting how the brain develops during the fetal period. The thalamocortical circuits are established very late in gestation. Only after they have developed and the amygdala-cortical circuits are in place is it possible for us to have a mental appreciation of the pain we are in. Before then we can experience pain without acknowledging it. Thus, pain is laid down unconsciously, without words to explain or clarify it.

There was a study reported in the British journal *Nature*,[12] in which the investigators noted that when babies are under threat the amygdala sends a signal to the prefrontal cortex, triggering the expression of fear in behavior. The cortex becomes the "decider," as it were, planning for action. As part of the study, the researchers trained mice to associate a tone with an accompanying shock delivered whenever the tone was issued. Each time the mice heard the tone, there was commensurate brain activity in the prefrontal area, signaling a threat. But when the amygdala was surgically removed there was no longer any prefrontal activity; the former could no longer signal fear to the top level. The same is true when we drug that structure or tranquilize it: we thereby diminish the force that mounts in the prefrontal area. And, as we learned earlier, gating problems in the amygdala may be part of the reason so many of us have trouble either falling asleep, staying asleep, or even concentrating. Lower level imprints voyaging upward and forward keep us from traveling to a lower level of brain function by jolting us into a hypervigilant state whenever we lie down to relax. There is simply too much activity in that deeper level to permit sleep.

revisiting family history

When can a fetus begin to feel pain? A better question might be this: when can it signify pain? Research from K.J.S. Anand, a professor of pediatrics and neurobiology at the University of Tennessee, suggests this happens once the neural circuits are in place.[13] When Anand placed a needle into a fetus (in a process known as amniocentesis), the fetus grimaced in pain and its stress hormone levels rose dramatically. Not only did the baby suffer but, from our point of view, that suffering can be coded and registered in the memory system, thereafter awaiting connection. This is what we in feeling therapy are about—connection— restoring the missing links in the circuitry. Some serious diseases have been considered only in the domain of inheritance, muscular dystrophy being one of many. The cures for these afflictions have been slow in coming, in my view, because our emphasis has been on inherited factors rather than in utero experience. If we don't regard gestation as critical, our diagnoses are bound to be flawed.

Early childhood is important, as well, when attempting to identify the origins of later life problems, as evidence of imprinting can be seen in the experiences of very young children. There is a study by a Canadian group from the Douglas Mental Health University that found when child abuse exists there is a change in the gene NR3C1 that affects how the child will deal with the abuse.[14] Measures of the gene were much lower in abuse victims who eventually took their own lives. It appears that childhood abuse had changed the gene's structure, making the gene less active. And these modifications endured throughout the children's lives, affecting the way the stress apparatus, what is called the hypothalamic-pituitary-adrenal axis (HPA), functioned.

Patrick McGowan, one of the study's principal researchers, implies that the changes are more or less permanent; they alter the gene's activity, leading to later illness and suicidal tendencies. When the NR3C1 gene is ineffective it cannot produce the kind of alerting, galvanizing chemicals that help one fight through things. As a result the body behaves as though it were constantly under stress. Moreover, what this research group believes is that mothers can affect the fate of their children even before they are born. Epigenetic changes passed on during gestation may contribute to depression and suicidal thoughts later on. So what looks like genetics, in reality, is a much more complex interaction between biological and environmental factors, an intricate "if-then" sequence which spans generations.

Finally, there is a study by the Israeli researcher Micah Lesham indicating that a mother who was stressed before getting pregnant can affect the life of her offspring.[15] In experiments with rats, Lesham found that those rats that underwent stress before pregnancy had offspring who were hyperactive; the females displayed symptoms of anxiety and were generally more nervous. Over and over we discover, uncomfortable as it may be to our notions of pregnancy and motherhood, that an anxious mother does not provide a good soil for having children.

Every day there is new information and research on this subject. A new study by Alberto Halabe Bucay of the Research Center Halabe and Darwich, in Mexico, now suggests that when parents are happy it can change the egg and sperm germ cells that affect the offspring. As reported in *Science News*,[16] Bucay's study shows that a parent's psychology and emotional state even before conception can affect the child's genes. For now this proposal is mostly polemical, but it is intriguing. It is for all these reasons that epigenetics will soon be a very important area of study, something that did not exist when I was coming up in psychology.

It turns out that heredity has become an "iffy" item. Michael Skinner, a molecular biologist of Washington State University, has been experimenting with the on/off switch of genes and sperm in animals. What new information is showing is that experience is altering the sperm and eggs of the parents and creating micro-changes in "hered-ity," so that it alters the offspring and their offspring. These changes are not about altering the DNA sequence but about changing the switches so that when a switch should be on it is off and vice versa (a process described earlier as methylation). This process determines how hered-ity unfolds; it means that experiences of the parents and grandparents funnel down to the babies who are changed ever so slightly.

What this may mean is that my notion of the imprint has to be wound way back. A more accurate framework holds that the experi-ence of the parent leaves an imprint on the sperm and egg. This imprint endures and affects our physiology for perhaps a lifetime; although it seems like pure heredity, it is actually the effect of experience on the genes and their action. And here later adverse effects on the kidney, liver, or heart begin. One experiment by researchers at the University of New South Wales was done with male rats who were fed a high-fat diet.[17] Their sperm seemed to change—that is, many of their babies had adult-onset disease, even though the mothers were normal. The children had a greater frequency for deviated insulin and glucose re-sistance, hence a propensity for diabetes, even though the fathers had no previous history of the disease. So what looks like pure heredity is actually a molecular memory of the experiential effects on that hered-ity. These research animals had defects with their on/off switches. For humans, this may mean the tendency to be fat derives, in part, from what a father ate before conception. If that father overate as a child, his offspring have a much greater chance of being fat and developing dia-betes. Clearly, we need to change our focus in order to understand who we are. Our idea of what is heredity is rapidly changing.

There are all kinds of intriguing possibilities. In one recent experi-ment, some animals who were raised in an enriched environment and appeared smarter had offspring who seemed to inherit that intelligence (finding their way through mazes more easily) even though they were not raised in an enriched milieu. Let's be clear: when the parent had a chance to develop intellectually his offspring had a better shot at be-ing smart. Somewhere there are indelible and permanent marks on the sperm and egg.

9

oxytocin: the hormone of love

There is a relatively unknown hormone called oxytocin that is critical in making a strong, emotional rapport with others. When the level of oxytocin is low, there is less emotional attachment, less interest in social engagement, less caring and bonding, and less touching. In short, there is less love. The level of oxytocin, like so many other key biochemicals, gets its start early in our lives—again, in womb-life, at birth, and in infancy. It can be found as an imprint, which affects many systems later on. Besides influencing how much affection we will be capable of, the imprint affects sexuality, altering the way key brain structures such as the amygdala and hippocampus translate pain into sexual behavior. When there is little oxytocin a child will have weak or no attachment to parents and feel starved for love. Oxytocin is thus a key survival mechanism, as well, critical to building the relationships so important to human social commerce and survival of the species. As we shall see, our choices of work, partners, and interest have a lot to do with oxytocin levels.

One wonders why a hug from mother is relaxing. Well, it raises levels of oxytocin. But as it turns out, even a phone call from Mom raises those levels. In an article published in *Scientific American*, Leslie Seltzer, a biological anthropologist from the University of Wisconsin, noted that a mother's voice had the same effect, neurologically speaking, as a hug.[1] Seltzer challenged a group of girls aged seven to twelve with spontaneous speaking tasks and math problems in front of a panel of strangers, a scenario which effectively elevated the young girls' levels of cortisol. After being subjected to these tasks, one-third of the girls were comforted by their mothers with hugs, one-third watched an emotionally neutral seventy-five minute video, and the rest spoke with their mothers by telephone. For those who hugged and those who spoke to their mothers, the effect was the same: oxytocin levels rose significantly, as cortisol levels diminished—a remarkable example of how soothing vocal communication and touch have comparable stress-relieving effects. Forget tough love: as this study reveals, one makes psychologic improvements through love, not fear and anxiety. And, as I repeat over and over, early love is the best painkiller extant.

Of course there are other neurotransmitters at work here. When a baby smiles and coos the area of the mother's brain that signals reward, the dopamine system, is activated. Dopamine like oxytocin is an agent of love. Maternal behavior is based partly in the reward areas of the brain and, accordingly, the sight of a happy baby urges the mother to cuddle and love him. Recently, evidence has emerged that oxytocin and dopamine work together to produce a feeling of well-being; in addiction, as I'll return to later, it may be that a lack of good-feeling due to low hormone output is what hooks one permanently to drugs.

For now, suffice it to say that we know that oxytocin inhibits tolerance to drugs such as morphine and also prevents withdrawal symptoms when one is taken off those drugs. Rats given cocaine become compulsive sniffers; oxytocin reduces that behavior. Lab animals provided the choice to self-administer painkillers by pressing a lever do not do so when given oxytocin. These studies suggest, interestingly enough, that with adequate levels of oxytocin, those on drugs do not need higher and higher doses to achieve the same high. It is the rush and feeling of warmth users experience from drugs, not a physical need, that leads to dependency.

Oxytocin, found only in mammals, is perhaps best known for its role in inducing labor. In women, it is typically released after enlargement of the cervix and vagina during labor, and after stimulation of the nipples. Through the latter it promotes birth and breastfeeding, respectively. When levels of the hormone are high, one experiences a sense of relaxation, repair and healing, and loving emotional attachment. Low oxytocin levels, on the other hand, may indicate early neglect and lack of touching. Worse, they may point to dysfunction of the entire system and serve as a prognosticator for later mental and physical health problems. An abundance of oxytocin is the body's way of saying, "I was loved and could develop normally." A lack of this hormone says the opposite: "I was unloved and now my system is in disarray."

mother-child bonding

One of oxytocin's chief roles is as an agent of bonding, the strong emotional attachment that helps us want to be with one another, aid and protect each other, and interact sexually. High levels of oxytocin encourage and strengthen bonding, and the converse is equally true: those of us who are not able to bond with others generally have low levels of oxytocin. Because early trauma and lack of love affect the output of this hormone, the ability to relate to others and have gratifying sexual experiences later in life may be determined before birth and just after. Attachment is not something that can be taught, and it certainly cannot be taught in later life. It is something we feel: something organic and physiologic, something biochemical.

Mother's milk contains high levels of oxytocin, which is one reason why breast milk is so important in nursing the young. Shortly after being ingested, the milk's nutrients are sent directly to the suckling baby's brain for comfort and calm. Research shows that mothers who nurse are calmer, more sociable, and better equipped to handle stress and monotony; they have more regular skin-to-skin contact with their baby, as well. This last point is particularly important, for when a newborn suckles the mother's breast right after birth the gentle massaging by the infant's mouth and hand increases the mother's oxytocin level, which in turn enhances mother-child bonding and produces even greater closeness. So we have an increase in milk production and maternal feelings, a wonderful combination for the baby.

However, if we prevent oxytocin production in baby animals, preference and closeness to the mother do not occur; bonding does not occur. The result, sadly, is that the baby suffers, perhaps for a lifetime. One must understand that attachment is a two-way street: lowered oxytocin in the baby prevents him from feeling close to his parent. He becomes a baby who does not relish being cuddled, who squirms while being held. Even though the mother's oxytocin levels may make their predictable increase upon the birth of the child, he will not respond in kind. That is why biology—especially the biology of our early survival instincts—can speak volumes.

Unfortunately, those who do not bond early on with their parents may be constricted to a lifetime of fragile, tenuous relationships. That may be in large part due to deficits in the child's hormonal wherewithal, which is to say, the child has below-average amounts of key neurochemicals such as oxytocin. But because bonding takes place so early in our lives, it is almost impossible to know, later, where specific problems come from. For a patient in his twenties, it may be painful to try to get close to someone because of the lack of early love; the person lacks the necessary chemicals to ease his social anxiety and help him relate. Contact itself may become painful. It is my belief, furthermore, that if someone has constant trouble getting along with others, a good first step is to seek therapy where he may have his oxytocin levels checked.

Remember, though, that these problems may begin very early and be difficult to correct. Oxytocin researcher Thomas Insel has remarked, "Many of the affectional ties to the mother observed postnatally could be laid down by prenatal experience."[2] Here again we find the same apothegm: life in the womb may determine life outside the womb for decades to come. Of course this research presents a bit of the chicken and the egg. The question we now face is what came first: lowered oxytocin and then the inability to love and to bond, or the lack of early love, which lowered oxytocin set-points. We don't yet know. What can be said is that if one's early relationship with parents is distant and glacial, no matter the cause, it is likely to be a harbinger of his relationships later in life, the consequences of which are empty friendships, poor sexual function, and failed marriages. In fact, if the sampling of our patients at the Janov Center is any index, the association between a child's early relationships and later interpersonal functioning approaches something of biologic law.

trauma, sexuality, and the maternal instinct

Whenever the traumas of birth, pre-birth and early childhood inundate the system, there will be a corresponding overload and breakdown of the neuro-inhibiting, suppressive systems—serotonin, as well as oxytocin. Supplies of neuro-inhibitors are not inexhaustible, and it is the very earliest pains that have the highest valence and require the greatest amount of inhibition. Eventually, as biochemicals are used in the battle against emotional deprivation, the system becomes less sexual. Research shows that oxytocin is responsible for many ejaculations, including the "ejaculation" of mother's milk to the baby and sexual ejaculation in men. A mother who was loved as a child is apt to have more milk to breastfeed her baby; and the male who was loved early on is likely to have more active sperm as an adult.

Though the relationship between oxytocin and human sexual function is not entirely clear, at least two non-controlled studies have found increases in plasma oxytocin at orgasm–in both men and women.[3] The authors of one of these studies speculated that oxytocin's effects on muscle contractibility may facilitate sperm and egg transport. In addition, oxytocin injected into the cerebrospinal fluid of rats caused spontaneous erections, reflecting actions in the hypothalamus and spinal cord.[4] Finally, a recent study of men found that oxytocin levels were elevated throughout sexual arousal, though there was no acute increase at orgasm.[5]

More studies will be needed to corroborate these results, but the research suggests that oxytocin levels may hold important clues to understanding human sexuality. A therapist can ask us, "Were you loved?" and we may insist, "Absolutely," yet we are betrayed by our low oxytocin levels and elevated stress hormone levels, as well as by other hormone levels, which may be quite deviated. Biologic indices speak in important ways. Indeed, we may have been loved after birth but suffered severe traumas in the womb of which we remain completely unaware.

What do we do when we measure biologic indices? We ask the body to give us key information. Diagnostic machines from brain scans to blood samples produce data that help us with our therapy, and they do that commensurate with how the body communicates; that is, nonverbal parts of the system generate nonverbal biologic information. Naturally, we don't expect verbal explanations from these machines. And it seems equally silly to expect them, on the human level, from nonverbal regions of the brain where this information doesn't exist.

In the case of oxytocin depletion, therapeutic approaches must look further than the patient's self-admission or denial of the problem, identifying, as well, where emotional dysfunction manifests irregularities in the brain. When there is trauma early in the brain's development, the maturation of the brain is hampered. A brain that suffers such impairment is a fundamentally different brain. It is crucial when synapses and nerve circuits are being organized that there is a proper balance among brain hormones; and disruptions in this balance may take place before we see the light of day.

New mothers are often confused because they have no milk for the newborn, yet no one can explain why. Many insist on returning to work immediately. They contend, perhaps justifiably, that their career is very important, and that decreasing milk production is a signal to resume work as before. For many mothers, however, it may be that the experience of an early lack of love stifled the production of their maternal hormones, while elevating cortisol levels. As a result, there is a need to stay very active; a mother may claim that she loves to work, but in reality work functions primarily as a way to expend excess cortisol. The mother's priorities, in this case, are not likely the result of her attitudes but rather her neurochemistry and its history. She not only is less maternal as a result of her early experiences, but also she cannot sense the needs of her baby, nor how much he needs her. It is tempting at first to ascribe many of these alterations to genetics, but we must not overlook the start of life during which the brain and body are forming. I have noted elsewhere how womb trauma results in lowered serotonin levels, and I speculate that the same may be true with respect to oxytocin. Of course hormonal set-points can be established in early childhood, as well, and we need to be careful in determining when and how the imprint is laid down. Frequently women who resent being mothers had, in their infancy, parents who refrained from physical contact. This, too, may lower the production of maternal hormones later in life.

vasopressin: the male love hormone

Another hormone, vasopressin, contributes to male nurturance of offspring—it makes for caring fathers. It also has painkilling effects and helps animals venture out and become more exploratory. Animal studies show that if vasopressin is blocked, there is immediately less paternal behavior. When injected directly into the brain of male voles, moreover, vasopressin increased their paternal behavior. The animals became more social, more caring about female partners, and more willing to spend time with them; in short, they become more loving fathers. In addition, vasopressin is a counterbalance to oxytocin, creating more aggression and territoriality in animals.

Our hormones of love, vasopressin and oxytocin, similar in molecular structure, can be traced back millions of years through evolution. Love and attachment have always been important to mammalian organisms and are closely related to sex and reproduction. In sexual arousal, vasopressin is at its peak, while oxytocin levels peak during ejaculation. Vasopressin cells are concentrated in the amygdala, the feeling center of the brain, and it is this region that has much to do with our capacity for love. In my framework love motivates us toward reproduction and sex; and in the varied roles vasopressin plays in our development, it is almost as if nature is telling us not to separate the two.

Vasopressin, released when there is stress to the system, can be combated by oxytocin. This may seem strange since they are so molecularly similar and may use the same receptors. However the difference may lie in the fact that vasopressin facilitates the type of aggression commonly associated with male sexuality. Known to be an essential element in pair bonding in animals, vasopressin plays a role in determining partner preference and, in some male animals, encourages the selection of specific female partners. It is also associated with testosterone, which we find in greater quantities as vasopressin levels increase.

What all this means is that when we "love," there is a chemical component: chiefly, oxytocin and vasopressin. And it is my hypothesis that the more intense the love feeling, the higher the oxytocin level.

(The converse may also be true—the higher the oxytocin level, the more love there is to give.) When the bellies of animals are stroked, not only is more oxytocin secreted into the system, but blood pressure drops, as well. Most important, there is a shift from sympathetic to parasympathetic dominance, as the relaxing, rest and repair system takes over to promote survival and good health. All this is to say that love is calming and normalizing; oxytocin helps lower blood pressure, while pain raises it. Thus, it would seem reasonable that an infusion of love may decrease blood pressure, which is precisely what we see in our patients; after one year of reliving pain, blood pressure drops an average of 24 points in the group. This also accords well with animal studies that show that oxytocin inhibits the secretion of stress hormones known as glucocorticoids. When the system is in a vigilant mode, oxytocin levels drop as the anxiety system takes over.

synthetic drugs and therapy

From a therapeutic standpoint, future research into these love hormones will be particularly important. In the same way that we increase sexual drive in males with testosterone injections, it may be that we can "inject love" into people, or at least inject a hormone that encourages it—give people a shot of love, so to speak. This hormonal injection may help us to bond with partners, to empathize with their feelings and pain, at least for a time. Although we may think that an injection is something special, the same chemical process takes place naturally. We can inject oxytocin into an animal, or we can massage an animal and increase its oxytocin levels that way. Similarly, we can create stress for a pregnant woman, or inject her with steroids: the psychological effect is the same. And just as a kind, loving mother may raise the serotonin levels in her offspring, so can a doctor who injects serotonin into a patient produce a temporary calming effect. Furthermore, a mother routinely "injects" oxytocin into her baby through her milk, which contains high levels of the hormone. All of this is to say that love, or what manifests it, can be injected. When "injected" naturally and at the proper time, mammalian hormones will produce a loving human being.

Oxytocin, translated from the Greek, means "quick birth." Synthetic oxytocin known as Pitocin and Syntocinon is given to mothers who need stimulation for contractions; and I surmise that some mothers who need oxytocin to expedite the birth process may have had a history of pain that lowered hormone levels, making labor and childbirth exceptionally difficult. Statistics indicate, for instance, that mothers who give birth by cesarean have lower levels of oxytocin than those who do not. At the same time, when oxytocin is given to mothers to facilitate the birth process, it enhances the love they feel for their child; they nurse better and are more relaxed with the baby.

An individual may swear she is full of love when clinical evaluations of her hormone levels show low levels of oxytocin. However it is actually good news that "less love" has a physical base, for many times there is something we can do chemically to alter that state; and there is certainly something we can do psychologically. The main point is this: If early on we were not loved, looked at, touched, listened to, nuzzled and adored, then biological changes, subtle though they may be, will follow us throughout our lives. Yet a mother who takes good care of herself, is not depressed or anxious, abstains from drugs and alcohol, and eats properly will usually produce a loving child. At some point in the future, we may even be able to determine what proper love from a parent to a child looks like neurochemically through measurements of various hormones.

Many may find it hard to believe that we can really inject oxytocin and induce love, albeit for a short period of time. But remember, other animals share many hormones with humans, and studies of sheep and rhesus monkeys have found improved maternal behavior following oxytocin injection. If you're still skeptical of the applicability of animal studies to humans, consider the Human Genome Project, sponsored by the U.S. Department of Energy and National Institutes of Health, which has found that humans do not have that many more genes than rats. In other words, what applies to animals has a good chance of applying to humans. We can take virgin female animals, inject them with oxytocin, and within thirty minutes they become maternal. So, yes, we can inject love if we define it carefully. We can help someone temporarily feel something they ordinarily couldn't. At the very least, we can inject the qualities of love, which give rise to greater attachment, touch, and nurturance. The critical point here is that by changing hormone levels, we can alter behavior toward the loving. And, by inference, if we can create a therapy that changes the set-points of those loving hormones, we may offer patients the capacity to feel and express love permanently.

10

womb-life and serotonin output: the origin for later mental illness

I am building the case that life exists in the womb and dramatically affects the rest of our lives. Animal research sheds light on all this: in mice, it is only after several months of gestation that the fetus produces adequate amounts of repressive chemicals such as serotonin. In fact, a mouse fetus does not even start to make its own serotonin until close to the third trimester. It seems like the mother supplies what is needed until the baby can take over. But, unfortunately, when the mother is low on supplies, she cannot compensate for what the developing baby lacks.

Now let's extrapolate this to human mothers. Whereas the beginning of serotonin production in mice is sometime in the third trimester, in humans it seems to begin slightly earlier. Research on the fetus appears to indicate that it can experience pain after thirteen weeks from conception but that it only really experiences pain after twenty to twenty-four weeks of gestation (about five months of life in utero).[1]

What is critical here is this: there is a time during gestation when the fetus cannot produce inhibitory chemicals and must "ask" for help, physiologically, from its mother. When the fetus does begin manufacturing its own neurochemicals it sends some of these to the mother. It says, "I can soothe myself now. Thanks for the help." Above all, serotonin is a soother. Its purpose is to bolster the gating function so that pain does not slip across synapses and inform higher levels of the predicament. It enhances the unconscious; that is its job. It is merciful and does its best to keep us out of pain, which is why it's such a big part of our humanity.

The serotonin system, our defense against pain, is ancient, dating back to the most primitive of animal forms. I once heard that mankind's greatest discovery was the anesthetic. I submit, less cynically, that the greatest contribution to our humanity is the anesthetic that we produce within our bodies: serotonin. Killing pain is essential for humans to move forward and progress. Otherwise, half of us would be stretched out on the floor all day long, wallowing in pain. But at least we would know we were in pain, know that we were in danger and could take evasive actions. Now, few of us are even aware of the pain we carry because the pain is absorbed into ideas and beliefs that mask it so effectively.

There are relatively few serotonin cells, but they project all over the brain. Serotonin is primarily a control agent. By blocking fear, serotonin helps to ease social and emotional barriers between people. Does Prozac create less timidity? Not exactly. Deep down we maintain a timid personality, but our fear is temporarily abated by the drug. Other painkillers serve a similar function, relaxing our relational hang-ups and allowing us to be more open, more touchy-feely, to shed some of our cocktail party anxiety. By lowering our inhibitions, we gain greater access to ourselves and, thus, greater closeness to others.

But for all this to happen we first have to feel. Painkillers do not change anything, except to give us a glimpse of what we might always feel if we weren't constantly ravaged by fear and terror. Drugs do not erase fear. Primal therapy does; and it does so through connection, meaning our feelings must be joined up and locked into place with the front tissue on the left side of the top-level cortex.

We've seen in studies of rats that too much serotonin introduced early in life can produce very passive animals; it stifles their *élan vital*. The same, I believe, happens to humans who have been through deeply traumatizing events such as rape and combat: an increase in serotonin production leads to greater repression. All of this can lead to passivity and form the basis for later depression. And what may temporarily help all this? Something like the drug Ecstasy, which reduces serotonin levels while raising dopamine output—the energy-enhancing transmitter. We are entering dangerous waters, here. Ecstasy use in humans has been reported to cause acute systemic toxicity, as well as long-term neural damage leading to mood, sleep, and memory disorders; research into its potential application in psychotherapy must be approached with extreme caution.[2] Of course there are other alternatives. If we add serotonin through drugs such as Buspar and Effexor, we can ease depression. How is that possible? In essence, we lift the body's burden of having to repress in massive fashion. The system is eased and feels a bit lighter.

Similarly, if we raise dopamine levels we ease depression. One way to look at depression, then, is repression raised to a higher level. So if we are neurotic and want to feel better, we enhance our dopamine output. However since dopamine is largely under the control of the serotonin system, we must dismantle the serotonin system to do this effectively. Through a focus on words and thought patterns, cognitive therapy may temporarily increase the activity of the serotonin system, producing a false sense of mild euphoria. I advocate, instead, an approach that results in a more permanent adjustment to the most basic levels of the system.

To turn to dopamine for a moment, I should point out that those who are low in his neurotransmitter tend to be the timid ones who suffer from "social phobia." And the reason their levels are low, I believe, is because of early trauma that produced inactivity, reticence, alienation, and constriction: the imprinted *modus operandi* for survival. Essentially, the biochemical system takes its direction from the imprint: raising serotonin levels and lowering the dopamine set points. The imprint is fixed, and it is fixed by infusion of noradrenaline, a stimulating transmitter released in life-threatening situations that seals in the imprint and says, "This is an emergency. Remember how you reacted this time and create a template in order to save your life next time."

Psychology needs to converge with biology. If we give patients drugs, we need to know what those drugs are doing to feelings. Instead of stopping with the prescription of tranquilizers, for example, we need to go further and see what happens to pain; in order to do that, we must acknowledge the pain and its history. Why is Ecstasy described as a potentially beneficial adjunct to psychotherapy, according to some in the practice? Because it may well stimulate the feeling dimension, which is missing in cognitive therapy. Our knowledge of how drugs affect the nervous system is murky, at best. When we delve into the nervous system, we see that it points the way for what really must be done—a systematic probe into the deepest layers of the unconscious.

Although the painkilling aspects of serotonin are well known, less is known about its role in affecting appetite, gastric symptoms, and heart function. Nevertheless, we are fairly certain it has an important role in these areas. In addition, new evidence points to its role in shaping brain structures early in fetal life.[3] One reason we see serious mental illness emerge in adolescence is because, during this time, weakening defenses permit some of the fetal pain to rise and affect thought processes—hence, the appearance of delusions and hallucinations.

Interestingly, when secreted early in life, serotonin functions to control and shape anatomic structure. As levels drop over time, we can expect changes in our body structure. Later in life, serotonin's chief function is to control pain, and by then most of us have all the serotonin we need to manage adversity. But serotonin production is slow at first and, as a developing baby, one relies on his mother to pitch in to produce serotonin before he starts making his own. If the mother is chronically depressed, she is apt to have low levels of serotonin since much has been used in the fight against her pain. Because of her limited capacity to fulfill the fetal need, the fetus may be ill equipped to guard against pain and be left with a residue of unblocked, free-floating terror from early in gestation. This makes him much more vulnerable to trauma at birth and in infancy. He is defective in coping mechanisms, and any later trauma can multiply the impact on the relatively undefended system.

The low serotonin output is an imprint that remains pretty much the same throughout life, making it difficult for us to go about the tasks of everyday living. That is why we may so desperately need serotonin-enhancing medication: Prozac, Zoloft, and so forth, later in life. The medication attempts to block pain that is experienced, in some cases, before we set foot on this planet. By normalizing serotonin levels, it may make up for a gestational deficiency, giving us a surge of the missing neurochemicals that we need to feel comfortable.

We know from current research that an imprint during gestation remains pristine throughout our lives, whereas an imprint after birth can produce compensating secretions that blunt the impact of trauma during infancy. As I've said, the very notion of the imprint means pre-birth events may create irreversible dislocations of function in the neurobiologic systems. The only way these can change is if we return to the origin of the dislocation and right the ship.

When a developing fetus without effective repressive mechanisms tries to borrow some of his mother's serotonin to help mitigate pain but finds none available, basic physiologic set points may be altered. Yet a completely naïve physical system has no frame of reference to convey the message that such processes have been deviated: the system adjusts and then considers that deviation as normal. So the baby is born with an inadequate serotonin supply, and that deficiency follows him throughout life. What results is a wound that almost no one can see or even imagine, a child who will grow up chronically anxious and be unable to concentrate; or a child with an attention disorder who cannot sit still because he is highly sensitive to the slightest sign of alarm. The deficiency shows itself in anxiety flare-ups that happen when the system is vulnerable and gating weak; the imprint from gestation rises to the top-level brain and shouts out its message, which is profoundly difficult to decipher and remains a mystery to physicians and psychiatrists because its origins are so arcane. What we may see many decades later are panic and anxiety attacks, and then much later, cases of cerebral stroke.

How on earth can we access experiences with such remote origins, events from a time when there were no ideas to help out? It is possible and, to explain how, I turn to a letter I received from one of my former patients, Jan, a Swedish business executive who was epileptic. His letter provides a fascinating picture of what happens when we treat patients with primal therapy.

11

early trauma and epilepsy

When Jan first came to therapy he was in a group session with thirty other patients. His muscles started to seize. I shouted to him that it was a feeling. "Go there, not to the seizure!" And he did. He turned the possible seizure into a Primal, there and then. With his permission I have transcribed the letter he wrote with minor stylistic edits:

I had my first epileptic experience 1960, when I was seventeen. The first seizures were petit mal, and neither I nor my family and the people in our surroundings understood what was going on with me. The seizures started with a short euphoric moment followed by a helpless feeling of losing control; thereafter confusion, which turned into a burning fit of explosive nature. During the seizure I was in a semiconscious state of mind. The whole seizure lasted only a few seconds and I never fell over. Afterwards I was confused and dizzy, but not for very long.

My first grand mal seizure occurred in the same epoch and happened one morning on a train, when, exhausted after a late night, I was on my way to work. A few days later people who had helped me told me about the incident, and they said they thought that I might have epilepsy.

Shortly after the seizure on the train, I was sent to the university hospital, in Lund, and the doctor in neurology who then and for many years treated me was David Ingvar. He could not satisfy much of my curiosity regarding epilepsy. However he treated me with friendly advice and with strong medicine like Phenytoin/Dilantin and Carbamazepine/Tegretol XR. The medicine did not only repress my epilepsy but knocked out, as well, most of my overactivity (in very much the same way as the treatments did in *One Flew Over the Cuckoo's Nest*). Most of my energy was, luckily enough, intact and I could channel it into studies and my career.

After I was given medication, I became obsessed with the idea that in one way or another I would find a treatment which would free me from epilepsy. This idea was always in the back of my mind, whether planning for career, studies, families, etc. So in the beginning of the seventies when I got *The Primal Scream* in my hands, I was totally convinced that I finally had found my remedy. Now I at least had a hope, and my stubborn planning for a change had started. It was not until 1978 before I got it all together to move to L.A. for a couple of years. In April of 1978, I started with the three weeks' daily sessions, and I had my first primal experiences. Very little happened, though, apart from the fact that I relived the pain of when my sister, born three years later than me, dethroned me and captured my position by my father. I could in a glimpse see her with blonde curly hair in the lap of my father, and I had an insight of why I for years had been obsessed with girls and women with blonde and curly hair. In her early teens and as an adult my sister's hair turned very dark, and I had repressed the memories of her being blonde and curly. I brought home a few blonde girls with curly hair to impress my father and to get his attention.

Back in Sweden, in January 1980, things started to happen. I had what I first thought were grand mal seizures during sleep, but which didn't end in unconsciousness. I stayed conscious during the cramp which started in or around my chest, ran up through my throat, mouth, and face, and finally spread throughout my head. My fingers were pressed against my head, at times rubbing it intensively, and my legs were kicking. The cramp turned into heavy hyperventilation, my body took a fetal position, and I had different experiences such as choking, swallowing my tongue, etc. One part of the process which always was repeated was that I was forced to turn around 180 degrees, and I had a feeling of being sucked backwards with my legs kicking frenetically. The sessions mostly finished off with a procedure in which my mouth was contracted (with the feeling of being extremely small without teeth) and a squeaking sound ascended and developed into a baby's cry which could last for quite a while (several minutes). When the crying ended, so did the primal feelings. I felt a tremendous relief.

My mother was religious, though not fanatically, and during more than twenty years she had at several occasions explained to me that she had not caused my epilepsy and that nobody else in our family was epileptic. So when I returned from L.A., I told her about the therapy and the expectation that I had found a solution to my problems. Suddenly she began to cry (which was an unusual phenomenon), and told me about my painful birth which had lasted for more than two days. It had been extremely painful not only to me but also to my mother, but she said that at that moment that was her desire because the Bible had told her: "You shall give birth with pain." And so she did. But forty years later she could understand the long-lasting effects it had had on her first-born baby.

Being back in Sweden meant that I had to start working again and for the next fifteen years I only had the possibility to allow these feelings to ascend when Dr. Janov arranged week-long retreats in France, Switzerland, and Norway. I especially remember a retreat in France (which by the way was filmed by an English television company and aired in the beginning of the 90s) when I went through a birth primal and, after the squeezing sequence, ended up with bruises all over my forehead. During the eighties my fingers were almost constantly aching. After a couple of years I noted that my small fingers had grown into a more normal size and during a six to seven year period my fingers grew 10-15 mm and the aching decreased to almost nil. Furthermore my old problem with my fingers, turning white, numb, and anemic when it was cold, disappeared.

The fits I had were very similar in their build-up to the revolving suicidal thoughts (attacks), which, before 1980, frequently entered my mind when I couldn't find a solution for a problem or a situation. And in that desperate suicidal state I decided to give it a new and reverse try. The birth process was such an extended procedure of tremendous pressure, anesthesia, lack of oxygen, and strangulation by the umbilical cord. During this process, as you've suggested, the tendency for seizures is laid down. In all areas where I've invested my energy a very similar pattern has developed. Any of my jobs or projects could be used as an example. I work hard at a goal (learning the language of the country, getting to know all employees, hiring, firing, meeting customers, implementing systems and company rules, etc.), and I don't rest. Nor do I feel tired. That is, I'm tired but I don't feel it. After two or three years I'm normally worn down and start to look for a new project. During these in between periods I have a tendency for fits (strong medication keeps them at bay). I find a new project, often in a new country, new company, and in some cases with new life partners. I can often start up at once with full energy to work my way out again.

To relive my birth has been a long continuous process from 1980 up till today. The insight I got through my experiences in January 1980 when I had returned from L.A. was that a grand mal seizure was my birth process. It had happened not the way nature had programmed it. After that important connection my intellect had established fragile contacts down into my second and first lines, (lower levels of consciousness), which I would need thirty years to develop.

In spite of the fact that my intellect knew the connection between seizures and birth, I could not change my behavior. I was still a workaholic with the same patterns, fears, and frozen feelings. Most of my intelligence was more logical than emotional. Between 1980 and 1996, I made small improvements and had insights going to primal retreats but nothing really dramatic happened until the late 1990s, when I threw antiepileptic medication away and went straight into the epilepsy, i.e., the birth process. This has meant more than a ten-year period of reliving different parts of my birth, over and over again. This has changed my tendency for seizures. My seizures were collapses which occurred when my system, due to lack of oxygen and blood circulation, couldn't hold back any more pressure. It was the last thing I could do—then death. And the more I can relive the feelings of pressure, anesthesia, choking, confusion and anger the less need I have for outlets, of which seizures were a part.

My life has changed even if I know the same people, speak the same languages, and have many of the same habits. My intelligence is now guided much more by feelings than by thoughts. I can feel my loneliness and cannot understand where my energy to undertake certain projects came from, even if I can see what motivated it. I can feel the sadness of how a whole life has been spent to fight the effects of a difficult birth ...

This letter, I hope, shows what reliving incredible feelings, including birth, may lead to. A couple of days ago I wrote of a beautiful feeling: how my body grew, expanded into its full size from a feeling of being cramped and suffocated. It was such a full and real feeling that I couldn't stop myself from jumping up from my bed and running to my desk to write you a note to share my joy. Yes I could! I could feel OK and it felt OK to share it with you who knows what a long wait it has been!

Two days later I had an equally unbelievable but more absurd feeling of the most ugly and sickening nature. It scared me on all levels and I turned crazy, mentally sick, felt the feeling of dying, disappearing, being humiliated. In this moment when I'm writing it comes to my mind—and I don't know why, perhaps I'm afraid of exaggerating—that my birth experience could not possibly have been worse if I had been burnt.

The torture went on for a couple of hours and I had a deep feeling that I could not take any more. The mental and physical torment in my fits had the same repetitions and rhythms as my birth primals. They built up with pain, pressure, and numbness, but this time instead of hyperventilating, secreting mucus, being strangled and pulled out with my baby's cries, I had the feeling of being tortured. All feelings were twisted around, screwed and turned against me in such a humiliating way that I turned inward and felt the essence of mental sickness.

I don't know how long the feelings lasted (my estimate two hours) but it was like a conscious grand mal seizure of the same length. Though I didn't have the same urge to go and write to you about this hellish experience (I'm still taken by it) it is certainly more important when it comes to describing the composition of my epilepsy. It was a disgusting experience, but I'm glad I had it.

It's amazing what a help I have had of Dostoevsky's Prince Myshkin and how he described the moment before his fits, how "this second in its boundless happiness might perhaps be worth his whole life, however dullness, darkness of soul, idiocy stood before him as the clear consequence of these highest moments."

Last night more or less the same process of absurd feelings, hallucinations, and birth primals took place again. This time, however, I had my Hungarian gypsy music in the background. The length of the pieces of music merged and the crescendos of each piece ended in a hallucinatory explosion of sound which earlier would have meant a seizure. I agree with Prince Myshkin for these moments one could give one's life.

And I experienced no darkness of soul afterwards. "Sanity stood before me."

—Jan

12

imipramine binding study

Let us turn to a recent study of European primal therapy patients, in which we made an interesting discovery: our patients, uniformly low in imipramine binding at the start of therapy, normalized after six months to one year. What exactly does this mean? First of all, one must understand that imipramine is a serotonin analogue, an important component of our brain that we are only beginning to understand, and which can be a measure of the repressive system in action. Early trauma seems to render this area of the brain faulty, though there is still very little research explaining why. However, as I've said, primal therapy may hold clues. To find out more about the effect our therapy was having on patients neurologically, we conducted blind imipramine binding studies of blood platelets. Blood platelets are believed to have a high degree of biochemical resemblance to nerve cells, including those that serve as neurotransmitter uptake and binding sites. We reasoned that we could measure through the blood, by surrogate, the serotonin production in the brain.

Stephen Rose, the head of the neurobiology department at Open University, in England, led the research. Our informal analysis of a small cohort of twelve European patients found that manic patients were low on binding. That is something we had expected. Their frontal cortex control mechanisms, those involved in serotonin uptake, were faulty. We assumed that early trauma compromised the development of prefrontal brain tissue as a number of previous studies have shown.

What we didn't expect to find was that as a result of primal reliv-ing, the inhibitory neurohormones had become normal again. These results, if replicable in controlled trials on a much larger scale, will have great import for those who take painkillers or tranquilizers to manage their anxiety. Rose's research team suggests that there is a way to revisit the destabilizing factors in our early lives and bring them back to nor-mal, without the use of drugs. Think of the implications: reliving the pain of a lack of fulfillment normalizes the serotonin levels. It appears we have further support for our long-time position: *Attacking the de-stabilizing events restabilizes the system.*

One of the reasons why this study is so important is, as I've said, because imipramine has a role as an antidepressant, blocking the up-take of serotonin so that more of it remains to help with repression. That is why it is so important that levels normalized after one year of primal therapy: in essence, therapy is serving the neurologic function of the drugs, without unnecessary intrusion to the system. To give you an idea of how we came to our conclusions, here is Rose's report, with minor stylistic edits:

1. Subjects were self-referring individuals entering psychotherapy and a control group of self-defined normal subjects not in ther-apy. Upon entry into primal therapy, self-referring individu-als had a level of maximal specific binding of 3H imipramine binding to blood platelets about one-half that of controls.

2. Six months after beginning a course in primal therapy, self-re-ferring individuals' average imipramine binding level had in-creased until it was indistinguishable from control levels, and this increase was maintained for a further six months.

3. Eleven of twelve subjects showed some improvement in score on an arbitrary psychic assessment scale over this period, and there was a positive correlation between this improved assess-ment score and increased serotonin binding.

Although the study was informal and assessed a small number of patients, the fact that patients were able to increase their levels of repression, and, moreover, maintain these levels for a full six months is noteworthy. The perseverance of bolstered vitality in the inhibitory system suggests appropriate lower brain therapy may heal patients in an enduring way. What commonly has been called "epigenetics" I call the "set-points of biologic states"; this includes those set-points of the neurotransmitters that will later make us chronically comfortable or uncomfortable. Describing someone as not feeling good in his skin is, in one sense, a figurative way of saying something is wrong with the set-points, including those established for the imipramine binding system.

Of course all of this leads back to the book's central motif: that what happens in the womb while the organism is getting organized can affect the baby for a lifetime. It is so important that we not neglect this period when we attempt to understand and treat those with emotional problems. The more remote the imprint, the more widespread the later effects, in my opinion. As I note elsewhere, a strong immune system with vigorous antibodies is needed to stay on the lookout for newly developing cancer cells. It is not that a deficient immune system can lead to cancer, it is that a weak maternal immune system does not impart a strong immune capability to the baby: the dislocated physiology of the mother while carrying may thus affect the fetus, setting the stage for later catastrophic disease. Womb-life has largely been neglected in the psychological literature. It is time to reorient ourselves.

13

how addiction gets its start early in our lives

All psychiatric drugs administered during pregnancy cross the placenta and enter the fetal blood system. Once the drug has entered the fetal bloodstream, it has easy access to the brain. Drugs can also pass to the infant through the mother's milk. Unfortunately, due to developmental immaturity, the infant remains less able to metabolize whatever amount of drug has entered its body. Some drugs ingested by a nursing mother, such as lithium, can make the infant become low in energy: phlegmatic and passive. Other drugs can make the infant excitable. What happens during infancy can thus set the stage for addiction two decades later. The same is true of womb-life. The critical period occurs when the key brain synapses are being built, which, in humans, starts from the sixth month of pregnancy and continues after birth to age two or three. The drugs, if ingested by the mother, can create an imprint; that resets the set-point of key hormones and physiologic chemicals so that later the child lacks, for example, serotonin or thyroid.

In a striking example of the importance of the mother's emotional health during pregnancy, a group of people was examined over a thirty-five-year period using documentary evidence. Only those children who lost their fathers while in the womb were at increased risk of mental diseases, alcoholism, addiction, or criminal behavior. Clearly, the emotional state of the mother was affected by her partner's loss, and that possibly had lifelong deleterious effects on the child. The results of this study suggest, as I've noted elsewhere, that the emotional state of the pregnant mother may pose a greater risk to the child than the emotional state of the mother during the years following birth.

There is also a seemingly innocuous study[1] of smell in the fetus that may have import for understanding addiction. The investigators studied 24 newborns of mothers who had consumed anise flavor during pregnancy. In follow-up studies, the researchers discovered the babies born to anise-consuming mothers had a stable and enduring preference for the anise odor, while those born to non-anise consuming mothers showed an aversion to it. Although research is limited, there is some reason to believe similar gestational preferences can be developed for alcohol and psychiatric drugs. One can speculate that if a carrying mother consumes alcohol, tranquilizers, and other painkillers it will later affect her offspring, perhaps leading to a tendency for them to use these drugs in their own lives, particularly if there is inordinate pain to deal with. So, in addition to the gestational damage the drugs may produce in the child's frontal cortex, there is the risk of an intergenerational effect: the child has learned what works in alleviating pain, has an affinity for it, and gravitates toward it.

Transmission by the mother to the fetus is, in this case, chemical, but it is a language, nevertheless. The old reptilian olfactory brain has been elaborated into aspects of our feeling brain. That primitive brain is still a part of us—which is to say, once again, that fetal life is critical in understanding later emotional problems and must not be ignored. Addiction, in my experience, has deep and remote roots. We have to dig deep to find those roots.

the limbic system and drugs

A great number of us take drugs to make ourselves feel comfortable. As I pointed out, many drugs tend to work on the limbic system and brainstem. We take drugs to block pain and in so doing we speak to the brain in its own language of what I'll henceforth call "chemspeak." Indeed, researchers have always been looking for chemicals to ease our pain. Chemspeak is a language carried on in the dark trenches of the lower brain where there has never been a language of words. We can take drugs, develop self-protective beliefs, or join a twelve-step program, but the chemspeak is the same. We crave what we are missing. That is why, in dialectic fashion, stopping drugs can immediately lead to a back-up system of beliefs. Beliefs are not as direct a fix as drugs, but they avoid much of the harm that drugs do to the brain and body. It is not haphazard that the amygdala lights up when one needs a fix. It is, after all, a center for feelings; when they are importuning, we seek out drugs to answer the call.

The field of psychotherapy must learn the language of need and travel to that early brain with the patient, if we are ever to understand and root out addiction to both "approved" and "unapproved" drugs. We must ask the brainstem, "What have you got to say for yourself?" It can only answer with its elevated blood pressure, but that is, indeed, a valid language. Not so oddly, drugs that work on blood pressure also work on the brainstem and vice versa. In our therapy, patients speak this language by exhibiting specific foot positions, breathing patterns, grunts, facial expressions, coughs, gags, and heart rates. My patients taught me to "speak" and understand the language, but it took me decades to master its syntax.

To solve any problem through psychotherapy, we must engage the brain system involved in our history; that means we must eschew cognitive and analytic therapy in favor of an experiential perspective. I have made it clear that key experiences that form our personality happen in the first three years of our lives, long before we develop ideas about them. Psychotherapy is typically focused on the years after that. Since new research makes it clear that emotional and physical pains are processed by the same physiologic mechanisms, we know that emotional pain cannot be confined to the psychological. The difference between a historical therapy such as ours and a cognitive therapy is that the latter deals only with the adult brain; there is a neglect of multiple earlier levels of brain organization and consciousness and, therefore, a neglect of memory that lies below cerebral recall.

dopamine and cocaine

The stimulants cocaine and amphetamine activate the dopamine system. These drugs often imply that their users feel a kind of deadness inside; these people are trying to come alive, to feel the life inside of them. It is worth noting, although I won't dwell on it here, that nicotine and marijuana both activate limbic dopamine function, which allows someone to feel "up." We are addicted to cocaine, or any drug, when we need it to feel normal: that is what addiction is all about, the search to restore balance.

Cocaine helps release serotonin, which also regulates dopamine function. So in a way, it does double duty: killing pain and revving us up, all at once. Whatever pleasurable obsessions one has, dopamine is involved. When it is released into the synapse, it increases our sense of well-being. So if we are not happy in our skin, it makes sense to try to increase our dopamine levels. Compulsive sex is yet another way of boosting these levels; in fact, simple touch increases dopamine, which is why touch is so important, particularly in the first weeks and months of life when the dopamine set-points are being laid down.

Through his addiction a cocaine addict informs us of a lack of early love and, especially, a lack of touch and holding. Love even at seven or eight years of age does not fall into the critical period. Yes, it helps a great deal, but the deviated chemistry is already in place. An obsessive craving for drugs or sex means that there is already in place an inordinate, unfulfilled need for love. And where in the brain is that craving organized? In the feeling center—the amygdala. It is literally crying out for a balm.

I often think that cocaine is almost the perfect drug. It enhances the feeling of pleasure and makes us feel "we can" when really we feel "we can't." So what is wrong with that? It is a drugged state, an unreal state that is superimposed over the imprint. Above all, it cannot last. The downside of cocaine, and there are many, is that it can cause cardiac arrest, extreme irritability, and nasal erosion. It also weakens the immune system, making one susceptible to AIDS, for example, and reduces the connectivity of nerve cells, especially in the orbital-frontal cortex.

There is a significant relationship between the intensity and duration of the rush associated with cocaine and the amount of dopamine present in the brain. Previous animal studies have shown that cocaine prevents dopamine from returning, as it normally would, to the brain cells that release it. In the short term, this allows higher concentrations of dopamine to remain circulating in the brain longer than normal. That is part of what makes someone high when he uses cocaine. However, over time, the result is degeneration: a net loss of dopamine to areas of the brain that need it.

As I've said before, love is not ephemeral; it is biologic. And, chemically speaking, dopamine is one way that love is transmitted. An absence of caring and attention by the mother changes the chemical composition of the baby's brain; and when love is missing early enough, it is a permanent affair. If the mother does not want her baby, or if she is unhappy, the change in her biochemistry will filter into the fetal system. I've mentioned that hugs may increase levels of dopamine; kisses also raise the levels of dopamine; and some researchers now believe that frequent hugging early in our lives produces optimum levels of dopamine.

Cocaine takes the place of mother: If we miss a mother's love, we look to cocaine to fulfill our need for dopamine. Methamphetamine produces a similar effect, dramatically boosting the supply of dopamine at brain synapses, which results in an "up" feeling. It especially helps those who are depressed. Why? Because of the parasympathetic imprint at birth that skews dopamine toward down-regulation. The imprint leaves the person with a feeling of weakness and defeat, a real feeling from the early trauma, not some neurotic aberration. Cocaine makes people feel strong and able. Those who use cocaine often have a masked depression that they are not aware of. Reasoning in reverse, it is the drug use that tells us about the depression, and potentially how to fix it.

alcohol

Hormones, though, are only part of the mystery. With the earlier concept of the black box in mind, we can trace learning problems in childhood back to alcohol intake in the carrying mother. Serotonin is one of the key repressive or inhibitory neuro-juices in the brain. When a pregnant woman drinks alcohol, she may reduce the overall output of serotonin in the offspring. That means that as the child grows up, with less repressive capacity and fewer defenses, he may suffer from chronic anxiety—for which he too will need alcohol to feel relaxed. Neurohormones such as serotonin make their appearance very early in womblife. Thus, gestational trauma can leave us seriously bereft of what we will need, later on, to feel relaxed and calm. And not only can alcohol addiction and chronic anxiety be traced back to fetal life, but the efficiency of the repressive system can be clinically measured.

We know from animal experiments that those deprived of touch and love right after birth tend to consume alcohol later on, whereas nurtured animals refuse it. There is a good study of monkeys that demonstrates this point. Eighty rhesus monkeys were investigated; half were separated from their mother at birth. This group responded to any later stress with 25 percent more stress hormone release. Later both groups were offered drinks with alcohol in them. One fifth drank nothing. Among those who did consume alcohol, those with higher levels of cortisol before the experiment were the heavier drinkers. Those monkeys weren't saying any irrational things to themselves, as the cognitivists might have it. They reacted in terms of their history. We may ascribe alcoholism to genetics, but this study makes clear that those who were abandoned early in life took to alcohol as a result. At the same time, if a mother drinks heavily while carrying she may condition the baby to its painkilling effects. So what may look like heredity (i.e., "a drunk like his father") has more to do with experience than genetics. If a mother is anxious during pregnancy and drinks just one to three cocktails a day to relax she may "teach" her offspring how to kill pain. When he is sixteen and has his first shot of whiskey, it is like a revelation; it is what he was looking for his whole life without even knowing it. So of course he takes to drink: it is the ineluctable logic of his biology.

We are still our primate ancestors, but with a cortex added-on; we've put on a thinking cap permanently. If monkeys can be neurotic without words, so can we. If they can be addicted, so can we. Because these monkeys were deprived of love early on, they later felt the need to comfort their pain, and did so with alcohol. We hurt in the same way with basically the same physiological equipment. It is clear from numerous animal experiments, and there are literally thousands of them dating from the early work of Harry Harlow to the present, that words do not matter and cannot permanently ease the pain.

explaining addiction

Needs start in the womb, and what happens to us in this formative period is often what drives addiction and makes it so compulsive. If a mother drank to ease her pain, then the offspring may sense physiologically that alcohol can soothe pain; thus the beginnings of addiction. Should the pain continue, compounded by parental neglect, we have the groundwork for devastating later addiction. Interestingly, we find that addicts typically prefer drugs that induce the opposite effect of those the mother used. If a mother used cocaine, speed, or coffee, elevating the heart rate of the baby in the womb, then we may have an adult who is addicted to tranquilizers, to calm an overdriven system. Although we don't want to ignore genetics, their effect, in my opinion, is minimal; life in the womb is what is critical. What is the addict doing? Fulfilling the need from that time; that is, trying to normalize the chemistry that was warped early on. The depressive takes more Prozac (a serotonin supplement) to calm him. Yet he would have had enough serotonin throughout his life, if his levels were not dislocated by trauma in the womb or at birth. He is trying to get himself back, recover the parts that were missing from the start. That is why drugs make us feel like "ourselves" again. They make up for a deficit.

The objects of addiction may include any number of things: fast food for American families, wine for the French; you get the idea. But the force and strength of the addiction is not cultural. It is biologic, much the same the world over. The need for drugs, food, alcohol, and so forth, is first of all, and most importantly, a "need." If we make the mistake of treating *the need for* as the problem instead of *the need itself* we will never cure anyone of anything. That is, if we neglect history and address only the apparent problems we are bound to fail. Those few words, "the need itself," and "the need for," must be clearly differentiated. One is the need direct, the origin; the second is a derivative of that need, a calming agent that masks the real need.

The second is also what many cerebral therapies address, believing "the need for" to be the problem. No. In fact, the obsessiveness of "the need for" is determined by the degree of the deprivation of the need. Let's not treat the wrong thing. Let's not focus on pills and tranquilizers and disregard the original pain. So many parents wonder what they did wrong because their child was or is addicted. Maybe they did nothing wrong; the root cause of heavy addiction may go back to long before they had a chance to mistreat the child. Never forget life in the womb. The reason that both addiction and psychosis have been so hard to treat in conventional therapy is that the origins lie back before we set foot on earth. Damage during this period is most often the origin of later addiction and psychosis; we need a therapy that can go deep.

14

the birth trauma

Much of my writing in the last decade has been concerned with life before birth; however the birth experience is equally vital. Briefly, what seems to happen at birth is a "now-print" phenomenon at the end of the birth sequence which records for all time how that process turned out. Was there a massive struggle and then failure, as in emergency cesarean, or was there a near-death experience at the time of birth due to other factors such as the baby having the cord wrapped around his neck, or the vaginal canal being too narrow for delivery? Though I've discussed these possibilities elsewhere, more recently I've come to believe that the birth sequence is already largely predetermined by events during womb-life. For example, if a mother has smoked during her pregnancy and then is administered anesthetics during birth the newborn may experience feelings of suffocation. It is a cumulative effect: having respiration shut down by the anesthetic aggravates the earlier experience of a lack of oxygen due to the mother's smoking, thus duly effecting the imprint.

If the newborn has struggled unsuccessfully to defend himself against the anesthetic, the result may be a struggle-fail syndrome: a lifetime of giving up easily when adversity strikes. Likewise, when the baby is stuck in an awkward position and having trouble escaping the womb there may be an imprint of defeat, of hopelessness and helplessness. This reaction may have gotten its start in the womb, with a drinking mother or a mother who took tranquilizers when there was nothing the fetus could do to avoid the input. On the other hand, if the newborn struggles mightily to be born and is successful, there may be an imprint of success, of optimism and perseverance in the face of obstacles. So at birth we get a compounded reaction: the "now print" is still there; however, it incorporates a previous fetal experience that may lead to vastly different manifestations in the progeny.

Generally, during delivery, the fetus has a tendency either to struggle and succeed by trying, or to give up. The first, I believe, is governed by the sympathetic nervous system of the hypothalamus, while the second (the defeatist) is governed by the parasympathetic system: the one of response and healing. These two modes follow us pretty much for the rest of our lives. Normally, we should have a good balance between the two systems. In neurosis, however, there is a skewing to one system or the other, an inclination that may determine our body temperature and heart rate, our levels of stress hormones and serotonin, and a whole host of other physiologic processes.

Recent research reveals that certain gestation and birth traumas can and do reduce serotonin set-points so that a person may be forever deficient in the production of this hormone. Where lower level physiologic reactions are not properly damped, the individual becomes prone to high anxiety or grows up with an attention deficit because he lacks the wherewithal to repress. All lower level input forces its way into the thinking brain and keeps cohesion at bay. To wit, a study was just completed by Jhodie Duncan and his colleagues on sudden infant death syndrome (SIDS), a mysterious condition in which babies in the crib suddenly die.[1] In their investigation, the researchers examined autopsies and uncovered that babies who died of SIDS had low levels of serotonin. I submit that these levels may have been low because of previous traumas both during womb-life and at birth. If my reasoning is correct, this again points to the danger of ignoring key critical times in our development. We will not know how to cope with and prevent this fatal problem until we understand how early experience affects us. A baby in the crib, in the dark, is alone and terrified. With resonance, earlier frightening situations may be dredged up as biologic memories and overwhelm the baby's system, causing cataclysmic, at times fatal, events.

Although I have touched on it earlier, resonance is a fairly sophisticated idea that warrants additional explanation. In short, resonance is the idea that something in the present, a traumatic event or incident, can trigger or "resonate" with lower level imprints. Here I am positing that low level imprints have a distinct signature in terms of frequency. It may be that different levels of the brain recognize a relationship with one another such that something we endured during womb-life—a mother heavily depressed and taking antidepressants, for instance—is stored as a nonverbal memory. Years and even decades later this memory is sent through the nerve tracks and merges into what we undergo currently. One example of this, as mentioned earlier, is how babies of mothers given anise during their pregnancies favored that flavor thereafter—a limited example, perhaps, but one that illustrates how fetal experience carries into adult life. If we consider this from a treatment perspective, the combined force of the imprint and the present-life situation may mean our current clinical approaches are, at best, shortsighted. The problem thus far is that we have neglected deep brain imprints, focusing on knowable events and believing that a patient's current situation is the one to concentrate on. In reality, it is but a fraction of the problem.

Let me emphasize, here, that my assumption is not fact. However, the late Mircea Steriade, a Romanian neuroscientist from Bucharest who had been researching brain topography until the time of his death, offers compelling evidence. I would quote Steriade extensively but the work and explanation are so complicated that it would be meaningless to the lay reader, and often to me, as a matter of fact. Steriade wrote about reciprocal connections between separate brain sites that appear to oscillate at the same rhythm. Specifically, he traced the thalamus and the neocortex and found "excitability changes consisting of depolarizing responses and decreased inhibitory responses."[2] One can read many of his articles on oscillations for a more precise scientific analysis. For our purposes, the point is that many brain structures are linked by reciprocal connections, and frequency oscillations may be one aspect of this harmonization. What I believe may happen is that through these linkages there is a consolidation of the various brain sites. Through resonance later feelings are automatically joined with earlier, similar feelings. They are, in short, "consolidated."

Now let us take all of this a step further. Many animal studies have shown that early-traumatized animals can have their reactions softened by a good deal of touch and caress. That leads me to the conclusion, regarding the earlier SIDS study, that those babies who died did not have enough touch in the first months of life to give them a solid foundation to handle separation. Without the right amount of reassurance and safety, (to the point of sleeping with parents in the first few months after birth), a child who lacks serotonin may suffer grave consequences. However a child who from a young age is provided with affection may be able to short-circuit some of the harmful resonance held over from gestation. At least one study found that animals who were frequently touched early on developed much more resilience to adverse events than those who were not.[3]

Still, it is important to understand the relative permanence of the impact of trauma on the brain. There are many receptor sites in the top-level cortex that can accept lower level projections of serotonin, dopamine, and other modulators; however, pain early on weakens those receptors so that only some projections reach their goal. Eventually, this causes a breakdown in the gating and repression system. For most of us, early memory from the brainstem is replicated smoothly on the uppermost levels of the brain. When the gating system is porous, however, one has little defense against early trauma; it rises up and the brain is overrun. That means the comprehension of early nonverbal trauma, including a lack of oxygen in the womb, is also stored higher up. That top-level memory can be evoked, for example, in the closed space of an elevator and trigger off the primitive brainstem response. That means anxiety.

Each brain level "remembers" early experience in its own way. The neocortical level cannot remember things physiologically without the aid of lower levels of the brain. In other words there is no total memory on a verbal-intellectual level. All levels must be engaged.

To understand this, we need to return to our evolutionary roots. Here we find that as the brain develops, each new structure or area incorporates and re-represents events imprinted on lower levels. Thus there are spokes, as it were, radiating out from our primitive nervous system and traveling all the way to the neocortex, via limbic structures and the thalamus. These channels inform the higher brain levels of what happened down below, even while we were still living in the womb. When we feel helpless in the present—because, for instance, no one can process our job application until impossible requirements are fulfilled—we may cycle back to the origins of this helplessness in the brain. Thus the feeling carries with it the force of the beginnings of that emanation when its presence may have been a matter of life and death. We seemingly overreact, but in reality we are reacting to our fetal history, our memory inside the womb.

K.J.S. Anand, whom I mentioned earlier, is one of the premier investigators of research into fetal imprinting.[4] He and his associates have produced a compendium of studies on the subject, including a recent article published in *Biology of the Neonate*, in which Anand points out that "imprinting at birth may predispose individuals to certain patterns of behavior that remain masked throughout most of adult life but may be triggered during conditions of extreme stress."[5] Here and elsewhere Anand's descriptions look similar to my own, and there is good reason for that: we are describing the same event; Anand from a research perspective, and I from a clinical, observational post, perhaps no less scientific.

According to Anand, the aspects of fetal history that may leave their impression years later are varied and, in many cases, quite serious. As he observes in the article: "For suicides committed by violent means (firearms, jumping in front of a train, hanging, strangulation, etc.) the significant risk factors were those perinatal (around birth) events that were likely to cause pain in the newborn."[6] Harmful factors cited in the study included forceps delivery and other neonatal complications, which were significantly correlated with adult suicide attempts. Later suicides, especially adolescent suicide attempts, were heavily correlated with lack of care just after birth; and sedatives given to the mother during delivery were noted to increase chances for the later onset of drug addiction.

An obvious question arises, however: knowing how important our life in the womb is to our mental and physical health, what do we do for patients who are well into adulthood and still suffering from pre-birth events? Something's broken but how do we fix it? The key is to return to the origins of our feelings so that we can be liberated from their harmful effects. We do this in primal therapy by triggering first-line memories—basically physiologic reactions, not scenes, nor words. And it is these responses that we may then attribute to womb-life and birth.

One of the constants I see in my practice is evidence of oxygen deprivation at and before birth: what is called hypoxia (depleted oxygen) or anoxia (total lack of oxygen). During a Primal, patients may struggle to breathe and experience a choking sensation, in some cases turning red. The literature is filled with studies indicating that babies frequently are born with limited oxygen. Whether caused by maternal smoking or anesthetics administered during pregnancy, the limited flow of oxygen means the baby has to adapt. This may happen in many ways but one is by the child's reverting to the animal "diving reflex," meaning redistributing oxygen to where it is most needed; namely, the key vital organs: the lungs and heart. As a result, there is a deprivation of oxygen to the extremities, a deficiency which sets up a tendency for the individual to have cold hands and feet, not just for two or three days, but for a lifetime—eighty-plus years. Plus the body needs to slow its metabolism; again, not for a matter of days, but for a lifetime. Perhaps most important, there is a fundamental reshaping of the personality, a parasympathetic adaptation in which the individual remains passive and lethargic throughout life.

I have often said that our life is an analogue of the birth process. That may be an exaggeration, but aspects of it are, indeed, true. Trauma announces and foretells that something very important has happened, something that tells us "behave this way because it involves survival." The problem is that those early imprints govern our behavior, even in non-urgent matters, for the neurologic system has an incredible memory and is always trying to do what it can in the interest of survival. Darwin told us that almost two hundred years ago.

It is my belief that newborns are more fully feeling than they may ever be again; they have a wide open "sensory window," which allows them to react wholly as perhaps never again; they are, in short, born experiencing this new life without an illusory veil of ideas. Does it matter why we have children? Do our motivations for childbearing, conscious or unconscious, affect that minuscule bit of life growing in the womb? I believe so. Research is indicating that mothers unhappy about their pregnancies, for whatever reason, produce newborns who are hyperirritable and restless, who cry excessively, eat poorly, and vomit frequently. It is well and good that these matters are beginning to inform us of something so obvious.

We know, too, that morphine equivalents such as fentanyl and pethidime may pass through the placental barrier, providing a dose several hundred times too powerful for the baby, so that neither the mother nor the baby can react normally to facilitate the birth process. After administration of drugs, the mother has fewer and weaker uterine contractions. Worse, the drugs block important neural messages so that the sequence of contractions from the back to the front of the womb is altered. This means the baby is less apt to be propelled forward in a smooth way. Abraham Lu, a clinical professor of pathology at the University of Southern California School of Medicine, has estimated that between 50 and 70 percent of all stillbirths and miscarriages are caused by anoxic lesions in the brain, many of them drug-related.

It might seem that birth by cesarean section would be a less traumatic method of birth, since the infant doesn't have to hazard the rigors of a long labor or a constricted birth canal but is simply lifted out and into the world. Unfortunately, we have found that the traumas to the newborn delivered by C-section, although distinct from those of a difficult vaginal delivery, are no less traumatic. In cesarean birth, the baby may have been literally "knocking his head against the wall" from the first moments of life. When he is removed prematurely, the result is an abnormal birth. Breech presentation is yet another cause of difficulty. Here, the baby cannot get into proper position for birth. He emerges either fanny-first or legs-first, and both his and his mother's life are endangered.

After going through hours of trauma inside the womb, the newborn is exposed to an assault of sensory input: bright lights and harsh sounds that overwhelm the system. The worst that can happen is for the child to be left alone during this time as every minute counts. Imagine entering a whole new world with no one to turn to for succor. The following case histories illustrate a few of the ways the birth trauma may manifest physical symptoms in primal therapy.

case history

I go through each day exactly the same way as I experienced my birth. In the morning the struggle is yet to come-my birth is beginning and I'm apprehensive about the struggle-and the closer I get to that moment when I will relax and go to sleep, the better and safer I feel.

What I felt in reliving the birth experience feelings was a long and agonizing struggle. Incredible pressure smashing my head and back. My mother couldn't help and I had to count only on myself to get out and live. So I did all the work myself to get out and live, pushing and pushing for several hours until I was completely exhausted. At that point I gave up because there simply was nothing else I could do. And that is the story of my life. I work and work until exhaustion. I never know when to stop. I cannot seem to relax.

case history

When I was in Los Angeles I couldn't wait to get out. I was feeling very overwhelmed by the situation I was in, personally and professionally, and so all I could think about was getting away on a trip. But when I finally got away on the trip, I kept having the same feeling that I had to get out of wherever I was—just as I had felt in Los Angeles.

At first there would be a sense of relief when I arrived somewhere, because I had in fact acted out the feeling and gotten away. But after I had been there for a very short time the feeling would come up again, and all I could think about was getting away. The only relief I got yesterday was in the tourist office buying a ticket to leave, which meant I was moving on. I knew it would be only momentary relief, but that was better than nothing. It has something to do with everyday routine where there is no movement, no change. Routine to me is a dead environment, and it makes me very anxious. I used to like scuba diving as a way of avoiding that feeling of stagnation: I could get into the fluid situation (the water) and move around and alter my consciousness. But no matter what I did, the pressure pushed at me all the time; the minute I stopped moving, it would step out and overwhelm me.

It seems like it doesn't matter what the situation is: whether it's with a boyfriend, a place, a job—I have to get out, leave, do something else. I thought I was "burnt out" on my job, but it was that old feeling coming up again that made me focus on the outside because I didn't know what it was on the inside that was coming up.

Until I came close to those feelings I never had any idea that my constant moving around was any kind of acting out. Now it seems as if I had to go from place, to place, to place, and to avoid feeling anxious because of something inside me. I suppose the same is true for people who are afraid to move around and like to stay in one spot. As long as they stay in one spot, they're never going to know how fearful they are about getting out. They control their fear by staying put; I control mine by moving on!" And of course their leitmotif is often, "Let's forget the past and move on.

I used drinking as another way to get away from the pressure and alter my consciousness. Getting drunk helped blot out my mind; it "switched off" my brain, and allowed me to stay in a fog and a haze without knowing what was really wrong. The great attraction for me of being unconscious was relief from the pressure. The pressure was always a physical sensation to me, and I would have to do something physical to drive it away. Booze was one way; moving on was another.

I spent a lifetime searching for peace and yet got exactly the opposite. I see now that I was always looking for movement because I never had that peace, and I couldn't stand it. The irony is that real peace probably would have killed me. A peaceful environment wouldn't have matched what was inside me, which was a lot of turmoil; instead, I kept doing things that would match the turbulence inside.

case history

I am 32 years old, and began therapy a couple of years ago. I'm broad-shouldered, and have a muscular physique. I did well in high school with compulsory classes, but in the intensive atmosphere of college I spent many helpless hours in front of blank sheets of paper. I have always liked physical work, especially agriculture and construction, but found it hard to take the time to do a well-finished job. I despised successful businessmen who could make a great deal of money by one carefully considered move.

I have always done things the hard way—always paid taxes rather than getting a good accountant to lower or avoid them; always bought old cars that needed a lot of work rather than buying a decent new model that I could afford. I find it hard to ask anyone for help. In my job I often worked myself into situations of being under a lot of pressure, surrounded by ringing telephones, rather than working quietly at designing (which is what I am best at). I would then feel helpless and unable to make decisions, and would plunge into irrelevant work instead of focusing on what really needed to be done. I would even do things the hard way to relax: walking as fast as possible, or worse, mountain climbing!

In a recent session I started having birth feelings, in which I went into involuntary reflex spasm. The spasms lasted only about ten seconds but left me exhausted. What happens now is that I get a feeling about an event in my very early life that is accompanied by a scene, but I am then left with the feeling that there is something more to it. I have pressure in my head, and it feels like very hard work to do anything. It feels as though I have to shake off a great weight or struggle through syrup in order to survive. In sessions, I pound my fists and drop into rhythmic spasms of my trunk and legs similar to, but more powerful than, a sexual orgasm. The spasms push my head against the wall. Like the first time they happened, the spasms last about ten seconds, but leave me completely exhausted and breathless. There is no scene, and I feel as though I have been unconscious.

I have made many connections from these feelings. I do things the hard way and take on a lot of physical work as a way of acting out the feeling of having to struggle physically in order to survive. This has structured my life for as long as I can remember. Under pressure I hyperventilate and my heart rate rises, but I feel helpless and confused because my "natural" response from the early experience is to struggle physically. That's why I find it so hard to sit down and resolve a problem. I can't just sit.

As a result of connecting to these feelings, I have stopped volunteering for jobs which put me under a lot of pressure; I find myself more able to sit quietly and solve problems; I can take the time to produce careful work rather than rushing about ineffectually. I am also more able to ask for help rather than having to do things the hard way—completely on my own.

When the feeling of being helpless and under pressure comes up I go running. Often, running one or two miles works off enough of the energy to put me into the space where I can connect to my feelings. When I make those connections I have more physical stamina and need less sleep . . . I can now function well on only six or seven hours. Because of this I can cope with late night overtime much better than before.

The ways in which the unconscious meaning of the birth trauma impels us are numerous and highly individualized. For one of my former patients, "staying put" meant staying in a safe place: the womb. While undergoing primal therapy she experienced this feeling on the second level (the limbic system), recognizing how it connected to a childhood in which her parents were never satisfied with what she did. Eventually, she slipped into the first level: now getting out of the canal was everything; going back to her birth meant reacquainting herself with the original fear of death-the origin of her adult behavior pattern.

A very different feeling frequently comes as a result of cesarean births. Many of our cesarean patients have the feeling that they must go back to where they started in order to feel complete. They have a general feeling of being unfinished and incomplete-that nothing is "settled" in life. And, indeed, there was something left incomplete, a very important part of growth and development that was abbreviated and remains a source of distress. When the birth sequence is not completed naturally, one is deprived of aspects of the maturation process and may have a persistent fear of the future.

The following case report well describes the unrelenting feeling of doom and defeat characteristic of the parasympathetic personality. In it, we see the patient's transition from "everything is too much for me" to "I can do anything I want to do," made possible by her connection to very early trauma. We also see how the type of birth she experienced previewed the type of life she would experience with her mother: both her birth and her later relationship were riddled with fear. We have found this is often the case. The birth trauma is a kind of condensed version of the life to come, for the neurosis that produces it in those first hours unfortunately continues with predictable, pain-filled consistency.

case history

I woke up the other morning feeling that everything was too much for me; even the thought of going out to make breakfast or do a few errands for the day was too much. I felt utterly overwhelmed, and didn't want to get out of bed. That made me want to cry, so I went to the Primal Center to try to connect to the feeling.

The first thing that I said was, "It's all too much for me, I just can't do it." Then I cried for a while and, as I was crying, I remembered what I had dreamt about during the night. My husband and I were on vacation and we were going to motels that were out in the country. As we entered the rooms, I would get a feeling that there was danger present—nothing specific, just a very subtle feeling that someone or something was going to hurt us. It felt as if someone were lying in wait for us: a sense of impending doom.

As I cried about the dream I remembered how terribly frightened I'd been all my life—how I would check my room every night before going to bed by looking under the bed, in the closet, and under the skirt of the vanity table (which, incidentally, I did until I was 21 years old), as well as having a light on in the room throughout the night. I still lay in bed rigidly, expecting someone to come and get me and hurt me.

This feeling led to scenes with my mother. When my father would go away on business trips, she would make a rope out of neckties, so that we could climb down from the second story in case someone came to murder us. She also would put a stack of old plates on top of the table by the window to be thrown down on the cement below to wake the farm manager in case the murderer cut the phone lines. Then she'd lock the bedroom door and we (Mama, my brother and myself) would all sleep in there together. I was always so terrified: if Mama was so scared, then there must be something so big and frightening out there that could really kill us. Who could protect us? I couldn't wait for my father to come home and bring some sense of security with him.

My mother was such a hysterical person; she was terrified of everything: authority figures, money, the world in general— as if everything "out there" were potentially dangerous and hurtful. Her fear was very infectious.

As I cried about all these things I had been frightened of as a child, I came to a first-line feeling of being born, in which I couldn't breathe, and then to a time just after birth when I was left alone. My mother expressed her fear and panic in childbirth by screaming uncontrollably and banging her head against the bedpost. Her terror was communicated to me, and at birth the feeling of fear was further compounded by being left alone when I so obviously needed to be comforted and held. I didn't know then that anyone would ever come to me; I felt a sense of timelessness and eternal waiting. My father said that as he looked through the hospital window I was screaming the loudest, that he could easily hear me over all the other newborns.

I see now why I have always approached something new with the immediate and all-encompassing reaction of "No, I can't do it—I'm not ready yet!" My first experience of "new things" was totally frightening: my mother not helping me to get born because of her own fear and terror, and then not holding me after I was born.

No matter what the new situation is that I'm up against, no matter how well qualified I am to do it, I always feel that I can't do it. This even carries over to when I am doing something well that I know I can do. I think this is because doing new things puts me face to face with my birth and childhood feelings of aloneness and doom. When this feeling is pushing up, I feel that I can't do anything, despite all the evidence to the contrary . . .

It seems like I have a core feeling of fear and insecurity that is the central experience of myself as a person. My therapist once said that when I'm in that state of asking for reassurance it's as if I am grasping out all around me, but nothing that is said helps. He's so right. I feel as if I were falling into space and no one is there to catch me. My mind compulsively goes over whatever problem I am having, trying to make sense of it, when there is none. Even after I have understood how to correct a mistake, I am still not satisfied, but continue to think obsessively about it. No words of reassurance help; only feeling the very early feeling makes the obsessive worrying stop. That is why I have always said that feeling a first-line feeling is something that I embrace happily: because the mental torture that I suffer while obsessing is the true agony for me.

I feel so relieved when I make a feeling connection, because I know it won't be much longer before I can find peace. All my life I have said, "I just want to rest." My body never rests; I am constantly vigilant, with a startle reaction second to none. Only after a birth feeling do I feel truly relaxed and sane. So, "I want to rest" is a physical statement as well as an emotional one.

After I finished feeling [in primal therapy], I couldn't wait to get on with the day and eagerly went about all my errands. The doom had lifted! In fact, I even refinished a mirror in my bathroom, which an interior decorator had told me was beyond repair. At the time, I had just accepted his opinion. But now I've discovered by questioning several people at a paint store that there is, indeed, a way to repair it. In the past I would have never done that; I would have accepted the decorator's pronouncement as an incontrovertible fact.

The "getting ready" theme takes several forms. One of our patients, born prematurely, would always get a sudden pang when asked to go somewhere or do something. He would feel a slight hesitation, a need to gather himself. After reliving the birth sequence he had the insight that his hesitancy was rooted in a premature birth. The feeling was, "I'm not ready when you're ready," and he had acted out that hesitation all of his life. He could never be spontaneous. Whenever anyone set a date for him he would always be late.

case history

I wanted to control what was happening to me; I desperately wanted to stop until I was ready, but I was not being allowed to. The feeling was over in a few moments, but I was flooded with insights that extended over several days. I realized, in a flash, that my life has been dictated by two major birth feelings:

(1) I'm not ready yet. Everything is going too fast for me-I can't keep up-slow down to my pace; and

(2) I can't stand this pressure.

I had felt the second feeling about pressure in birth Primals before, but it has never been resolved; I still crack up when I'm under too much pressure at work. The connections I felt in reliving the first feeling are still actively affecting my life some three weeks later.

> [Primal therapy] has helped me to understand why I'm always late. I am never ready on time because I wasn't ready to be born. My habit of tardiness was one of the reasons I gave for wanting to do primal therapy, as my job had been threatened repeatedly by my inability to get to work on time. Since I made these connections I have experienced improvements in my life which seem out of proportion to the nature of the Primal (after all, it only lasted a few minutes): I have been on time for work every day but two; I have been able to leave the house without having to tidy it up; and I have been able to have friends in without becoming panic-stricken about not having vacuumed the carpets or washed the dishes. I haven't had to "be ready" first. These may seem like minor changes, but they have made tremendous contributions to my being able to feel relaxed.

Another characteristic of cesarean birth trauma is intolerance for unexpected changes; switching plans of any kind may trigger inordinate anger and anxiety. The conventional therapist might label the problem as "arrested development of the ego," a "fixation of the ego at the infantile stage," or other such elaborate concepts. I think of it, instead, in a biologic sense: a system that has been surprised by trauma in the past and conditioned to be wary of a sudden change in plans.

> My worst Primal involved the switch of being born cesarean after trying so hard to be born the right way. To this day, if someone switches plans on me without my knowing it or being involved I am immediately thrown into a first-line Primal.

Depending on the nature of the birth trauma, it's possible that a long labor in which none of the baby's efforts brought success will lead to indecisiveness. If the struggle yielded nothing, the later reaction may be, "I can't decide anything for myself-I have no decision-making power." This then becomes the prototypic response throughout life. It is the early gestational experience of indecision, not a strictly genetic condition, that produces this result.

Such a person will let his parents, and later his friends or mate, make up his mind for him on both major and minor matters. At a restaurant, he'll wait and see what others order from the menu before ordering the same. The more others take over his daily decision-making, the more reinforced the prototype of being indecisive becomes since the directive influence from birth is paramount.

---

case history

One day I went to the Primal Center and lay down in the large group room to feel. I began to feel my anxiety about leaving this environment in which my feelings were understood and it was safe to be just the way I really am.

It truly amazed me when I connected another of my feelings to my birth. I have always had difficulty making decisions. Whenever I make a decision I feel it is the wrong one. I originally connected this back to my decision at age eight to go to boarding school. My parents had offered me the choice of going "next semester or when you're twelve," and I thought about it for a while and then surprised them by saying that I wanted to go the next semester. The message seemed to be, "Don't make a move on your own."

One of the emotional consequences of a long, strenuous labor may be a general feeling of rage and rebelliousness. Many patients report on the intense frustration of not being able to get out; that physical experience of not being able to do what you want and need to do at birth becomes a physiologic prototype, drawing other similar experiences into its orbit. Later, the command, "No you can't!" may set off an inordinate rage and biologic need to act. I often think that the imprint provides the leitmotif for our life: "No you can't get out" becomes, "No you can't!" across all domains.

For those who have experienced a disrupted or prolonged birth, getting in touch with that prototypic rage can be profoundly liberating. The person finally understands why his first reaction to every frustration, even as a very young child, was anger. His parents might have rationalized, "He always had such a temper"; however the long labor may have had just as crucial a role. If after birth the baby is then left totally alone, the feeling of loneliness may deepen into a more serious terror of abandonment. On the other hand, if that same birth trauma of separation occurs, but the parents are warm, kind, and there for the child later on, then the anxiety likely will be lessened. There will be less of a drive to be with other people constantly, an unfulfilled need we see clearly in the following reports

case history

After my birth (which took eighteen hours), I was left completely alone. That really hurt after all the physical pain I had just been through. All I wanted was comfort and contact. As I grew up, I would constantly organize social things-childhood gangs when I was small, and sports activities as I grew older. I would do anything to avoid being alone.

I always fought against going to bed as a child, and when I grew older I would masturbate or drink to help me get to sleep as quickly as possible.

case history

I was born a month and a half prematurely, with a heart defect, and was put in incubator for two months. I survived against all odds, and primarily against my mother's wishes.

I was even fed without being touched hardly at all. At the [Primal] Center I relived being left alone in the incubator, and the first feeling that completely overtook me was that of waiting. At first I didn't know what I was waiting for, but in my enclosed cubicle, it felt like I was waiting for life itself.

I finally felt that they [my parents] were not coming back. With that cold realization, I decided that I wanted to die; there were no more reasons for me to go on living. It has taken me twenty-eight years to feel that waiting for a pair of hands to touch me and keep me alive. I can't say that I have stopped waiting entirely, but the search for someone to make my life better is over. And subsequently, I am now in the process of taking charge of my life.

On entering a Primal, many patients think that something terrible is going to happen. In reality, something terrible *already* happened; however their nerve cells cannot distinguish past and present. Ironically, these people will go to lectures and weekend seminars in order to "learn" how to handle anxiety, when talking about anxiety is inimical to its origins. Primal therapy provides insight by leading patients to the origins of their feelings in the womb.

All of this is still very much theoretical work. The question remains, for instance: Can a child transiently asphyxiated by an umbilical cord around his neck form a memory of this trauma? The self-reports of patients in primal therapy provide a preliminary indication that such memories are in fact formed. The relationship of asthma or stuttering to such an event is congruent with the adequacy of the neural structures integrating the functions of the trachea, respiration, and the larynx in the newborn. Each body part is woven into integrated function by the action of the nervous system. It would be irrational to say that the trachea "remembers" transient strangulation during birth, but there is neuro-embryological evidence that the functioning unit of the trachea and newborn nervous system is a reactive, adequate system—one potentially capable of "learning" from an exceedingly intense stimulus.

Why is it that we behave the same way in our nightmares decade after decade? Why is it that we go on bearing terrible anxiety, year after year, over the same kind of dream story? Our response does seem to be predetermined. Only now we are finding out that what predicts our fate may not be what we once thought.

PART THREE: EXPLAINING ADULT MENTAL ILLNESS & DISEASE

15

anoxia, reduced oxygen at birth and adult behavior

It stands to reason that perinatal traumas are generally all encompassing; we find damage almost everywhere we look. The problem is that without an all-encompassing theory that suggests where to concentrate our attention we will never link later life health conditions to their causes, never connect a heart attack at age fifty with trauma at six weeks before birth. I arrived at such a theory years ago from patient observation—a valid, albeit insufficient, part of the scientific method. At the time my supporters in the psychiatric community were scarce; however, that is changing, for there is now an accumulating body of evidence suggesting the delivery of oxygen to the fetus may play a larger role in our lives than was once believed.

Several studies have examined fetal anoxia/hypoxia and the results, systematically, seem to link oxygen deprivation to severe emotional illness later in life.[1] There is also more and more information about the later ill effects of trauma at birth and before. As psychiatrists entrusted to heal mentally ill patients, it behooves us to take a closer look at both of these emerging fields of investigation.

Among my patients at the Primal Center, problems with breathing, and panic in the face of suffocation, are rampant. Most of this stems from real suffocation at birth when for many reasons there wasn't enough oxygen supplied to the newborn. As I've suggested, painkillers and anesthetics given to the mother during pregnancy, often in massive doses, effectively shut down the neonate's breathing. Even epidurals can cause a partial shutdown. Overwhelmed by the powerful effect of these drugs on its underdeveloped body, the late-term fetus cannot catch its breath and enters into a panicked state as it approaches death.

This is the same panic that adults suffer from time to time, a state of alarm which seems to arise out of nowhere. Anything that is suffocating—a crammed airplane cabin or a crowded, noisy restaurant—can set it off. However these breathing problems are, in my view, part of a more generalized reaction syndrome to the fetus's lack of oxygen early on. Unfortunately, therapists begin a regime of suppression with pills, not understanding that their patients are really experiencing residual effects of hypoxia.

I disagree with researchers who suggest that panic attacks happen because a "trigger" is set off erroneously. It is not erroneous, it is precise, albeit symbolic: the same reaction whether one is confined to a room with lowered oxygen, trapped for years in a job with no room to expand, or jammed against bodies on a congested subway train. In all cases, what is most likely to trigger panic is the feeling of being trapped. Being in a situation that evokes such confinement and helplessness—finding yourself stuck at the DMV in an interminable line only to discover, hours later, you are missing critical documentation—is a maddening ordeal. That is because it recalls entrapment at birth, the feeling that one cannot get through, that there is no way out.

And, indeed, there is real suffocation (and a good deal of compulsive sighing) that goes along with these episodes. Biologically, what seems to happen are fluctuations in built-in emotional barometers known as pCO_2, or partial pressure of carbon dioxide, and lactate. A pCO_2 reading tells us how much carbon dioxide is in the blood at any given time. When it is high there is also a higher level of lactate, and the result is the physiology of panic. But what finally triggers a panic attack? Remember there are higher levels of the brain that inform our physiologic reactions, and each higher level represents the brainstem's reaction in its own way, adding a different quality to our experience. So while the second-line feeling system adds emotional tone and images, the neocortex formulates these feelings into words. And the process works in reverse. Certain words addressed to a person, a demand or an insult, can run down the neural chain and trigger an original feeling of panic.

What a number of researchers now believe is that the imprint of suffocation changes our physiology, locking us into "panic mode." Later on, it may be that painkillers such as opiates are able to suppress this feeling; yet, ironically, the deregulated painkilling chemicals associated with early suffocation at birth are also partly to blame for the panic we are attempting to root out. Deep breathing diminishes panic for the moment, as does a primal therapy session that includes heavy breathing and crying; however, set-points are difficult to reset, and normalization requires intensive, controlled therapy as I've described at length in earlier books.

There was and is a window of healing, although it is not well understood. Achieving recovery means traveling down the chain of pain to its origins before and at birth. Short of this, we are left to continue to try to push down the panic, a struggle which can go on for a lifetime. One of the most interesting discoveries that has been made in recent years is the finding that disordered breathing can be set off and established as an imprint during the critical window. This may be due to the effect of oxygen deprivation on brainstem structures such as the medulla; we are not yet sure. What can be said is that breathing difficulties are first-line symptoms, which can be effectively treated by descending down the levels of consciousness to the first line. For healing to occur, we must arrive at those establishing set-points—the brain structures that determine whether one will have shallow versus deep breathing, for example.

hypoxia and schizophrenia

One important question that has come up in the literature is, why is hypoxia so often seen in patients with schizophrenia? There are several explanations; however what I have witnessed over and again is that the fetus, in danger of dying from lack of oxygen, does not have the wherewithal to combat the trauma. Lack of sufficient oxygen is a terrible stressor, which leaves the baby with insufficient resources to combat future hardship. The danger remains as a substrate so that any later trauma can set it off-hence, the appearance of breathing problems. The result is that anxiety reactions to seemingly non-toxic situations are out of keeping with the gravity of these occasions. In the worst cases, this manifests as schizophrenia, in which the near death experience in the womb is reawakened with hallucinatory vividness. Treating such conditions is never a matter of changing attitudes; it is a matter of figuring out what shaped those attitudes in the first place. Consider a recent article by J.L. Minkel in *Scientific American*.[2] Minkel cites the work of researchers who postulate that the potential for schizophrenia starts to emerge during our early brain development in the womb. Rates of the disorder increased, according to Minkel, when the mother had influenza, was undernourished during pregnancy, or suffered complications during birth.

I have written elsewhere that offspring of mothers who endured war zones have had trouble later in life. Now we're discovering that there is a much greater chance for schizophrenia when children grow up in adverse environments, and that means when a mother lives in a country at war or a region hit by hurricanes, earthquakes, and other natural disasters.[3] According to Dolores Malaspina, director of the Medical Genetics Division of Clinical Neurobiology at the New York State Psychiatric Institute, the early stresses caused by living in a war zone increase harmful effects on the fetus.[4] By early, Malaspina means during the first three months of pregnancy. In addition, Malispina and her team concluded that the death of a relative radically increased stress levels in the carrying mother. This stress, as I've pointed out, can result in serious mental illness for the offspring. The placenta is not an impervious barrier. It leaves the child vulnerable to exposure to maternal stress hormones. So although schizophrenia may seem to be a genetic condition, it is more likely to result from the closely connected experience of the mother and her fetus.

stress, personality, and the immune system

We are finding that the problem, in both psychologic and physiologic illness, is the conveyance of stress. Because a mother under stress may pass stress hormones on to her baby, there is an increased risk of allergies and asthma in the offspring,[5] not to mention a variety of other conditions related to the proper functioning of the immune system. At the Primal Center, we've found this to be true in a preliminary study of ill patients, and it's also been shown in a recent study by researchers at Harvard. The gist is that the mother's stress level can directly affect her immune system as well as her baby's. There may be a genetic factor at work here, but certainly epigenetics plays a major role.

The amount of new research in this area is staggering. Stress in expectant mothers is now implicated in later diabetes, immune disease, hypertension, dementia, and a number of other pathologies. In sheep studies, the researchers Jonathan Seckl and Michael Meaney have found that when a pregnant ewe is given steroids (the stress hormone glucocorticoid), the offspring tend be born at low birth weight, suffer from high blood pressure, and show increased risk for posttraumatic stress disorder (PTSD).[6] Not only do babies born of these mothers show hypertension tendencies just after birth, but researchers studying sheep also note a strong link between the stress hormone intake of a mother ewe and her baby's long-term hypertension. It appears the later in pregnancy this occurs, the more permanent the adult high blood pressure. Described in some articles as "developmental programming," this fetal adaptation has to do with the sensory window when a stimulus is most apt to create alterations in functioning, and the reason it's so important is that during certain periods of gestation an anxious mother is delivering stress hormones to her baby. The fetus is being injected from within, exposed to the same chemicals as when given a shot of steroids.

When I speak of stress, I am referring to serious cataclysmic events that may permanently transform cardio-metabolic, neuroendocrine, and behavior function. While this can occur in very young children, it may also occur in the fetus when a mother is endangered or malnourished. For instance, infants of women who developed PTSD after being inside the World Trade Center or close to ground zero on September 11, 2001, had reduced salivary cortisol levels when their mother's exposure occurred in the third trimester. In addition, offspring of women who were pregnant during the Dutch Hunger Winter of 1944 and 1945 showed increased rates of cardiovascular disease and schizophrenia; and elderly Holocaust survivors and combat veterans with PTSD, both of whom have a statistically higher prevalence of early childhood adversity, have been found to have lower cortisol levels in their urine.

From an evolutionary perspective, stress-exposed children may be adapted to a life of peril—their rapid metabolism, early age of puberty, elevated blood pressure, and heightened response to stress increase chances of survival and procreation when food is scarce and predators are rampant.[7] Over the long term, however, survival rates diminish. For instance, one study of Holocaust survivors living in concentration camps or ghettos during the years of Nazi occupation found that extreme malnutrition and stress correlated with alterations in pathways of glucocorticoid metabolism. In fact, Holocaust survivors were found to be several centimeters shorter than a control group of comparable Jewish adults. Whether these results are best explained by the mother's stress or the stress of the survivor is not clear. What is apparent, however, is that Holocaust survivors who were younger at the time of exposure showed more pronounced changes in metabolism—a similar effect to what we find in individuals with PTSD, and those with evidence of environmental adaptation.

However, while these changes may compensate for detrimental early life experiences in survivors—lowering the risk for stress-related disorders later in life—they may have the opposite effect for those raised in safe, stable environments. The reality is that in most developed societies we do not find conditions even remotely resembling the Holocaust. Thus the adult environment is at odds with the biologic expectation, and the baby is born with a tendency for anxiety and possibly later disease. One way we know this to be true is that mothers who are anxious show elevated cortisol levels in the amniotic fluid surrounding the fetus. This, again, is really epigenetics: how the genes are affected by intrauterine life.

What is most important is that stress in the mother compromises the repressive system in the fetus, so that later it will be difficult to mitigate surging feelings. Low-level imprints from womb-life burst through the repressive barrier, overloading the system, and—in the absence of a cohesive cortex—result in difficulty focusing and concentrating, and problems learning. The prefrontal cortex becomes overwhelmed as it is pressed into service to counteract and hold down painful feelings. In a state of early terror, chronically alert and mobilized, we cannot think clearly. Here is attention deficit disorder (ADD) waiting to happen as forceful information from very early on intrudes the thinking apparatus. The neurons seem to be adrift, the top-level cortex bombarded with internal input, as signals move from the lower to the upper brain and the right to the left brain. In effect, we have a causal chain: too much information creates overload, overload creates shutdown, and shutdown produces symptoms. Over time the effects can range from impulsive tendencies, to migraines, to high blood pressure, all due to the attempt to hold back imprinted input. It is no mystery, then, when a child cannot concentrate or sit still—rising stress produces measurable changes in parameters such as brain amplitude.

What can be done about this? Treating it, first and foremost, then making sure it will not come back. How do we do those things? By reliving early womb-life events. Luckily, each new harmful experience that remains un-integrated is later re-represented in a higher level of the nervous system, where it is coded as the outsider or enemy. These imprints are indeed a threat to the organism because of their load of pain. And, as I stated, it may be that specific brain frequencies tie these events together. Figuratively, what is going on is much like the stone thrown into the pond: a ripple effect in the way the neurons connect to each other in mirrored progression; the difference here is that the ripples travel at warp speed, forging connections almost instantaneously.

When there are certain kinds of triggers, the brain conjures up its related history, intact, kindling like-minded feelings and their physiology together. That is why our behavior is so compulsive and unwavering; our history motivates us all of the time. In primal therapy, when we explore these ramified events and begin to relive them, we are also reliving deeper, earlier related aspects of our pain. That is how we relive purely physiologic brainstem responses without ever acknowledging them.

I will discuss this later on, but we need to be clear about this: lower level imprints send references higher up in the nervous system. These higher-level memories are wired together with their origins down below. They form a neural circuit, a pathway. When a trauma exists later on, it may resonate with earlier imprints and set off the whole memory intact. It is here that there may be inordinate responses to the most banal of events. We are winding down again to the originating sources, the base of the feeling. It is how we get to preverbal events automatically.

When the primal imprint sends its message higher up feelings are added to the impulse, and then later ideas and comprehension are included. Together these form a complete feeling. All are necessary, eventually, in reliving. That is how something in the present, a rejection, can set off such catastrophic feelings. It is an organic process and needs to happen in a precise order, with the original feelings preserved. Discussing feelings is one thing, but feeling them is quite another.

Why is neurotic behavior so incessant and predictable? Because needs do not change. For example, I am now treating a woman who married a man who reportedly has never loved her. She was desperate to be married, and so she offered her hand to the first person who seemed to want her. If she had been more critical up front, she may have realized that he saw her mainly as a sex object; however, all her life she was treated as an unwanted child by her parents, neglected to the point that being wanted became paramount. Sexual promiscuity was her "act-out" until she could finally relive her father's lack of affection. She did this though primal therapy. Until then she claimed she was an "easy lay"; all a man had to do, she said, was show a mild interest in her and she would return the favor with sex. Although she thought she would get love in the bargain, generally all the man wanted was to take something from her: to exploit her for sex and then abandon her, leaving her once again feeling unwanted.

Eventually, with an fMRI, we may be able to measure where anxiety is organized in the brain, and what each brain region's contribution is to the overall state. Already, in four separate brainwave studies, we've found a shift of power from the right to left brain and from the back of the brain to the front.[8]

A key point in all of this is that physiologic reactions are the basis upon which feelings are constructed: thus, what distorts physiologic responses will distort psychological reactions, as well. If the system is highly activated due to early trauma, chances are we will find, later on, a hyperactive individual who will search out projects to keep himself active and busy. If dopamine and other alerting chemicals are in short supply, we may have someone, instead, who is passive and phlegmatic, who concocts reasons for not doing anything, for not following through. It is not a one-to-one relationship, but physiology does direct our psychology. When someone doesn't have all of the mobilizing chemicals he needs to take action, it stands to reason that as an adult, in order to keep matters comfortable and ego-syntonic, he will rationalize why he lacks drive and persistence.

And that's not all: in addition to altering metabolic function and reshaping our personality, traumatic experiences in the first years of life may weaken the disease-fighting ability of the immune system. A report from researchers at the University of Wisconsin [9] demonstrated how children who had had an abusive early life or had spent time in an orphanage showed a compromised ability to defend against disease. Even after the children were removed from the adverse environment, damage was still apparent. The scientists point out that though the immune cells are ready at birth, how they develop and become a dependable cohesive system depends on experience.

As part of the study, the investigators used the control of latent viruses as a measure of immune competence. People with an intact immune system can usually keep these viruses under control. Those who are neglected, unloved and uncared for, cannot; thus, such afflictions as the herpes virus, which often lie latent, are more likely to be activated in those who have poor immune control. In this case, traumatized patients had higher levels of certain antibodies, indicating their immune systems were compromised and, hence, more likely to manifest overt symptoms of herpes. Those later living in a stable environment still showed a higher risk for contracting overt symptoms. In short, early life adversity has enduring effects. Later love, in general, does not affect the background state of damage that sets up a propensity for disease. So some of us react to stress with the appearance of immune diseases of various kinds, including, perhaps, HIV; others are able to prevent the onset of deleterious symptoms with a strong immune system. If there is no evidence of a compromised immune system, there will be less risk for serious disease.

oxygen, metabolism, and cold feet

How oxygen deprivation contributes to such divergent effects as immune system disruptions and abnormalities in personality is far from clear. My theory is that the fetus, in the interest of survival, reduces its metabolic level and possibly its growth rate to meet the demands of oxygen deprivation. Smaller bodies utilize less oxygen; this follows from the evolutionary logic of the human system. Whatever helps survival is what survives,[10] and accordingly the metabolism slows as a self-protecting device; what is important, therefore, is that the survival strategy seems to duplicate itself later in life under stressful conditions—not necessarily diminished oxygen but any kind of stress.

The person blocked from egress may experience hypoxia in the womb and be fixated in a parasympathetic "freeze" reaction until the originating event is addressed and relived. That is, there may be a tendency for passivity and a lack of aggressive or forceful action when such action is necessary for success or well-being. The reason this tendency is so hard to shake is because passivity and lack of aggression were life-saving instincts in the original event. Those reactions become stamped in, engraved as prototypes thereafter. Any later pressure will produce the same behavioral tendency because, prior to birth, there was no evolved neocortex to reason things out and anticipate that things might be different in the future. Later in life, physiology takes over and reacts as it did originally. Makes sense. When we are thirty we say to ourselves, "I wonder why I keep on doing that?" It is not such a mystery. The woman I mentioned earlier always wondered why she was so weak. After she relived her father's mistreatment, she realized the origin of her need to be wanted.

Keep in mind she did not have to relive the need with a more positive outcome (which would entail redoing history), but with the same outcome, experienced by the mature brain for what it was and is. This whole notion of a slowed metabolic response is relevant, here, for insufficient growth may be evidence of an organism's inability to fulfill its genetic destiny. In earlier books, I've written about the growth of limbs as a result of primal therapy, and, as I mentioned earlier in this book, we've seen chest, feet, and hand growth in our patients after one year (usually more) of therapy. We've seen wisdom teeth descend in forty-year-olds. In short, epigenetic factors, essentially inherited changes in gene expression that do not affect the DNA, can block certain aspects of growth and short-circuit genetic tendencies. When that happens, the person, in my experience, is vulnerable to serious catastrophic disease. There is an internecine war going on in the metabolic system between the forces of expression and those of repression. Very often the same person who has cold extremities is the one who has a lag in one sort of growth or another; in women, this often appears in breast growth. Naturally, there are heritable factors involved, but the crucial role of trauma has been largely ignored.

Reconfiguring our oxygen reduction response is one key way to prevent oxygen damage to the brain and heart. The system does this for us, before birth, by sending more oxygen to the heart and lungs than to the feet. Now we understood, perhaps, why someone has cold extremities: in cases of deprivation, this is the body's natural protection for vital areas. Unfortunately, if complications do arise many years later they are difficult to detect. If there is a trauma that affects the heart, it may not show up for fifty years, not until the first heart attack. One way to limit the risk is to provide sufficient oxygen at birth. Failing that, the fetus will reduce its oxygen demands. But that can mean inadequate cerebral oxygen supplies, lower cerebral metabolism rate, and later learning problems. Thus, when we say, "He's got cold feet," we are articulating a physiologic truth about the roots of apprehension. The person with cold feet may be reacting, therefore, to an intrauterine environment of fear and terror produced by an early oxygen deficiency.

the critical window:
like grandmother, like mother, like son

In the scientific community, the question has always been, "How early is early?" and this is where epigenetics is relevant to our discussion. A group at Washington State University led by Matthew Amway found that gestational experience in animals that sways the genetic unfolding can show effects for three generations. They found that exposing pregnant adult rats with defective sperm could engender many diseases, including cancer, in adult animals. Females avoided mating with other rats that were also exposed during gestation. And this went on, not only for the life of the adult, but for the life of their offspring, as well. It seems that the system knows how to behave given certain biologic deficiencies, and it does so according to what is best for heredity; what gives us the best shot of succeeding in life. So when we cannot explain some trait in adults by heredity we may have to reach back several generations to find the answer we're looking for. This gives us a new perspective on so-called psychological problems in adults. When we do an intake interview of prospective patients, it has to be thorough enough to include the prenatal life of the patient, as well as their parents and grandparents.

Without clinical evaluation we can only guess as to what traumas may have occurred in the life of a pregnant mother, and what adaptations continue to show their effects in her children and grandchildren. Of course it isn't just that a mother underwent trauma, but that the trauma has altered her basic physiology and produced lifetime changes in her and her offspring. Did the pregnancy occur in wartime? Were the parents fighting all the time? Was the child's grandmother depressed? Was she a heavy smoker or drinker during her pregnancy? These are all questions we should be asking.

For a moment, let's suppose someone exhibits all kinds of health problems from birth: allergies, a history of emergency clinic visits for infections, asthma, breathing problems, and in general, a very deficient immune system. Here is where we need to push back the envelope and direct our attention to those early months in the womb. When we do, we often find out that the mother was quite anxious, depressed, or both. A quite frequent result of parents who battle and who are not getting along at all are severe allergies in the offspring. This is often punctuated by frequent emergency room visits and bouts of allergies that handicap the person and her social life. Don't forget that the immune system, in some respects, is our first inchoate nervous system, sussing out dangers and menaces and organizing defenses against them. This includes secreting some of the same pain-killing neurotransmitters we know about today. However what starts out to defend us may end up hurting us, for if the immune system is compromised there is a good chance natural killer cells will be, as well. That does not mean all hope is lost. Encouragingly, something we discovered in our research at St. Bartholomew's Hospital in London is that with the right treatment we can correct these maladjustments. After several different measurements before therapy and after one year, we found our patients had normalized natural killer cell levels; we had particularly good results with depressives.

Timing is indeed everything. While Rebecca Huot and her colleagues have shown that a pregnant mother's depression negatively impacts the baby,[11] this was not the case for a mother depressed only at the time she gave birth. The investigators found that stress hormone levels reacting to a minor stress stimulus (arm restraint), predicted negative responses in infants. There was a particularly negative effect if the woman was depressed during the first two trimesters. In short, the effects on in utero life endure, predicated on the timing of physiologic development. And these effects are predictive, given certain kinds of adverse events that affect the fetus. At least in the context of depression, it seems the earlier the trauma, the more devastating. Here again we see how events during womb-life are as important as post-birth experience, if not more so. This has been a saying of mine for decades: The more devastating and earlier the trauma, the more devastating the symptom. And as I've said, we often find the symptom is deeply located because its origins are also registered deeply in the most primitive part of the nervous system—the brainstem and a portion of the limbic system. Thus, symptoms often tell us how early and hurtful the traumatic imprint is: we've found this to be true, for instance, with colitis. Treating these symptoms in adults, however, may be ultimately less productive than preventing their transmission to future generations. To do that, we need to know what to look for. In the case of colitis, for example, we have treated several women and found that their diseases were closely related to first-line imprints. As they relived more and more of these imprints, their affliction lessened.

early warning signs for later psychopathology and disease

red flag #1: low birth weight

Low birth weight is associated with slow fetal growth and the lack of development of various physical systems. If the newborn is abnormal in any respect, even birth weight, it is an indication something abnormal may have happened during gestation. Babies of depressed mothers are frequently underweight; they lack muscle, a characteristic that follows them into adulthood. Furthermore, certain height and weight problems at two years of age are a well-accepted indicator of childhood emotional problems. Equally troubling, the results of the Helsinki Birth Cohort Study show that "the risk for coronary heart disease and type 2-diabetes or impaired glucose tolerance is . . . increased in 60- to 70-year-olds who were small at birth, thin or short in infancy, but put on weight rapidly between 2 and 11 years of age. A similar growth trajectory has been shown to predispose to type-2 diabetes or impaired glucose tolerance." Other evidence has shown that people who suffer stroke tend to be thin or short at two years of age, and some research suggests adverse early events can lead to later hypertension, an important risk factor for both coronary heart disease and stroke.

One unifying theory to explain these risks suggests that the growth of the fetus, which relies heavily on adequate oxygen supplies, slows as a self-protective measure. Because of the fetus's relatively large brain to body ratio, the brain uses a good deal of oxygen, and thus has a physiologic demand for replenishment. If the supply becomes limited for any reason, body growth will slow so the brain can be left intact: hence, lower fetal weight. Another explanation may have to do with drugs taken voluntarily or administered during pregnancy. For instance, birth weight reduction is most severe when steroids are administered in the late stages of pregnancy. No matter what the cause, when a child is born out of the curve of normalcy, either too heavy or too thin, it may be an indication of abnormality during gestation.

red flag #2: high cortisol in pregnancy

Cortisol is a stress hormone that sets in motion the alarm signals to combat too much and too strong an environmental input. When it is released for a long time, however, it accelerates the possibility of dementia and a whole host of other diseases. Primal imprints do exactly that: produce a high level of cortisol for a lifetime; the danger is encoded and the body continually reacts to it. Cortisol has its benefits, of course, one of them being that it is heavily implicated in signaling the birth process to begin. It is when birth begins too soon, however, before the fetus is fully developed, that we have an indication that maternal stress may be putting the child at risk for later pathology. Again, stress levels descend into the fetal system and change the baby's development in ways we are still learning about. One of the earliest and most serious risks is the increased likelihood of a lost or premature baby. And as we've seen, increased fetal cortisol levels may result in elevated blood pressure, anxiety, hyperglycemia, and later cardiac crises.

This is not a radical view. In numerous studies of prenatal life, there is an indication that high stress hormone levels in the pregnant woman can result in later hypertension and cardiac problems in the offspring. What is tricky is recognizing the early signs of heart problems for what they are. As the neuropsychologist Paula Thomson explains, "prenatal stress responses are dependent on the mother's stress level. But how babies show it is through a limited physiologic vocabulary."[12] Thomson theorizes that the fetal stress response is already skewed and, given later stress, the earlier stress response does not change. It can be blocked, diverted, or covered, but the imprint remains pristine. How do we recognize the imprint of stress? According to Thomson, by observing a newborn who shows an elevated heart rate; greater activity levels; mistimed, diffuse movement; grimacing; and a general lack of coordination. These early signals, viewed from a gestalt perspective, predict later heart disease. It's no accident that patients at the Primal Center are uniformly high in cortisol at the start of treatment. Nor is it a mere stroke of luck that they demonstrate pronounced physical activity when undergoing primal therapy. All of these reactions, acting as a sort of ensemble, are how we remember our trauma physiologically.

One of Thomson's worthy goals is to help clinicians understand the hazardous effects of prenatal stress. In a recent article, she points out the importance of acknowledging and mediating the possibility of an intergenerational effect. "One of the most dramatic changes occurs in the first moment of conception. The primitive cell carries the blueprint for an individual who has never existed before and will never exist again . . . It is hoped that increased knowledge of prenatal stress will inform psychotherapeutic treatment protocols, especially when treating severely traumatized and dissociative patients who may themselves have suffered early prenate stress. Further, when these patients become pregnant, appropriate treatment for the mother may benefit the offspring. When clinicians provide therapeutic intervention to a pregnant woman the prenate may also be affected."[13]

It is this indelible blueprint from one's mother, not symbolic and Oedipal but hormonal and biologic, that Freud should have addressed when he was developing his theory of psychoanalysis. Here lies the deep unconscious: a dark place with no exit and no words, a place where biologic responses dominate. Not that Freud is at fault, of course. Lacking our present knowledge of fetal life how could he have known?[14]

In any case, what researchers are now reiterating is that womb-life can inalterably affect the lifetime of the offspring. And it is not only behavior that is altered but our physiology and anatomy, as well. Does this mean a change in primal theory? Absolutely: it pushes the envelope much earlier for when imprints will start and for when they will have their widespread enduring effects. It also means that how the birth trauma is effectuated and reacted to depends on earlier life circumstances: namely, womb-life.

red flag #3: birth trauma and pregnancy drugs

In an article published in the *British Medical Journal* ("Obstetric Care and Proneness of Offspring to Suicide as Adults"),[15] researchers Marc Bygdeman and Bertil Jacobson found that individuals who committed suicide violently were more often exposed to complications during birth. They suggest that "through a process of imprinting, certain individuals might subconsciously create a traumatic situation during the act of suicide that is similar to that experienced

during birth."[16] Curiously, children of mothers who were administered drugs did not commit suicide at all. The implication seems
to be that opiates given during pregnancy reduce the impact of the
trauma and are, hence, less likely to produce suicide-prone individuals. However there is also the implication that the child exposed to
opiates was more likely to be addicted to drugs in adult life. Why?
Because the birth complications are yet to be resolved. When it is
provoked in the present the feeling of hopelessness, though not
overwhelming in itself, resonates with the earlier imprint of birth
trauma to create a magnified effect. Thus, we find attempted suicide
or drug use to try to put an end to the agony. It is not that the person wants to die; he simply no longer wants to live with the agony.
A big difference. Opioids such as fentanyl and pethidine (Demerol)
given to the mother to ease her pain at childbirth also ease the suffering of the baby. Thus, later on, one turns to drugs to combat pain;
a replication of the earlier event. It worked when it was a matter of
life-and-death. Why shouldn't it work again?

One reason that current psychotherapy has not been profoundly
effective is the factors that produce current behavior begin far earlier
than we might have imagined. To ignore this research is dangerous, for
without an understanding of the origin of psychological pathology the
patient stands little chance of resolving suicidal feelings and addiction,
to say nothing of chronic depression.

primal therapy:
toward a cure for endogenous depression

We cannot undo what heretofore has been called endogenous depression with our current focus. We need to address the origins of our feelings. Endogenous depression means originating from inside, usually
without explanation or apparent cause. We know now that there is
definitely a cause and it is often from a parasympathetic imprint during gestation or at birth (see *Primal Healing* for my full discussion). If
we do not go deep enough in our query, however, we will never know
exactly what that imprint looks like.

Suppose we learn that in many cases of acute anxiety there is not enough residual serotonin in the person's system. So we add chemicals that boost serotonin—Prozac, Paxil, and similar antidepressants—and the person feels better, somehow "normalized." We now need to roll back the clock to see why that serotonin level was so low. In some cases, we may find grave traumas in the sixth month of gestation when serotonin production in the fetus was being organized. When the patient relives those kinds of traumas there is again a normalization. It is no mystery as to why; it is a matter of addressing the generating causes.

To reiterate: my thesis is that there are predictable, long-term effects of prenatal, neonatal, and infant experience. Understand this is not some version of "the shoemaker sees only shoes," but a need to emphasize a woefully neglected aspect of the human condition. Now, in my sixth decade of practice, it is gratifying to see statistical science catching up with some of my early observations; but, remember, biologic truths should not defer to statistics only be supported by them. Had we not conducted research into cortisol levels or imipramine binding we would not know exactly how therapy could change a human being, nor understand which aspects of psychotherapy are valid. Thirty-five years ago I thought that forced heavy breathing was essential to our therapy. Now, as a result of refining of our techniques, we know that deep breathing is not necessary; it can be quite dangerous, in fact. The same is true of forcing patients to relive their birth when the neurologic system is not ready. We know how dangerous the whole rebirthing movement is. Here is a therapeutic mode embraced by charlatans and some reputable psychiatrists precisely because it can be so dramatic.

But there are fly-by-night experts and then there is science. My patients, collectively, have been reliving birth traumas for a very long time. These events are minutely measured using an electronic rectal thermistor and a blood pressure cuff, both of which are fixed during the session. Through these tools we observe significant elevations and drops in body temperature, variations a physician would not ordinarily find except in cases of extreme illness. Originally, I never believed what I saw—to the point of threatening to discharge patients who continuously fell into reliving birth. Researchers at the UCLA neurology department told me what I was observing was impossible. But when heavily depressed patients enter a session with a body temperature two degrees below normal and leave with normal readings something significant is happening. When we see this month after month and year after year we are building an objective case. The problem, then, is to find out why this is so; and then further to determine how to treat depression in the general population.

For too long, we have equated memory with what we can recall cerebrally. My contention is that there is also an important physiologic memory that existed before we had thoughts or words. Low serotonin is part of this primitive physiologic language, whose outline gives us clues as to the origin of depression. As I noted earlier, I postulate that depressives are, by and large, parasympaths, meaning their psychology is dominated by a system of rest, relaxation, and repair in the brain that usually produces under-secretions. The key marker for this personality type is body temperature—almost universally low in these patients— and it speaks of a birth or pre-birth trauma that skewed the system into passivity, despair, and an inability to react. It is a system that is down-regulated in every sense of the term. There may be an under-secretion of thyroid, for example, and it has been found that offering depressives a bit of thyroid medication helps the condition. I say "helps" because, although the peripheral effects of the imprint can be alleviated by adding this or that, medication alone is not a cure.

It is tempting to overlook the importance of imprints when treating depression. Often the simplest and most apparent solution is to administer prescription drugs in the hope the patient will become more functional. However this only mitigates symptoms. I am equally skeptical of cognitivist approaches that stress the power of positive thinking: "Looking on the bright side," is a religious idea transported into the realm of psychotherapy. As much as a parasympathic individual may want to look on the bright side, his internal system is "looking" on the dark side. And he has no choice because the driving, dominant imprint is a response to impending death due, perhaps, to a lack of oxygen at birth.

Not only do we need a theory to root out imprinted memory, we need an office structure that accommodates it—a silent, soundproof room with soft lights and a comfortable mattress. No distractions. No opportunity to leave the clinic to visit friends. The person with depression is not in a position to socialize because there is no energy left. In fact, merely seeing others happy sometimes makes someone more depressed. Exercise? It drains the energy of the pain for a short time, however it is not a cure. The crucial flaw of all "how-to" fixes is that one has to do them repeatedly because they are temporary expedients. The prescriptive books on mental illness are endless because, for the most part, they do not address causes. While it is important to treat symptoms and help make the person more comfortable, this should never be an end in itself.

When we label certain problems as patently genetic, we avoid the more difficult job of investigating the influence of traumatic early memories. If imprints are not in the therapist's lexicon, if nine months of fetal life is ignored, then there is no choice: rules and mechanical techniques gain favor and the notion of depression becomes ephemeral and vague. Nevertheless, in most conventional therapies, the patient is "done to." He is the recipient of a variety of manipulations—and why not? When we ignore feelings it is logical to want to be "done to." This is what happened to many of us growing up—being done to, ordered around. But to compound the error, to be done to again, is a grievous mistake.

Primal therapy differs from other forms of treatment in that the patient is himself a therapist of sorts. Equipped with the insight of his history, he learns how to access himself and how to feel. The therapist does not heal him; the therapist is only the catalyst allowing the healing forces to take place. The patient has the power to heal himself. What we do is remove barriers to feeling, and after that nature takes its course. Although there is a specific procedure for the therapist to remove defenses without harming the patient, the process is fairly nonrestrictive. We've found that patients can self-monitor their progress quite well: they only need proscriptive rules about how to behave in impersonal settings, in which feelings are left out of the equation. Unfortunately, the essence of the "how-to" approach is always to temporarily tame the beast. The problem is the "beast" is us: our neurology and biochemistry. There is no known way to conquer depression unless one finds a way to distill who we are at the deepest biologic level. Depression is not some monster, some part of us that we must rip out. It is bound up in how our biology functions, how brain nerve cells interact, and how key hormones behave. We do not attempt to tell anyone how and what to feel.

Practitioners at one eastern hospital, however, believing that certain deep depressions do not respond to heavy medication, have begun to use brain surgery—deep brain stimulation, to be exact—to try to cure depression. To say the least, it is a drastic attempt at a solution. It involves drilling four holes in the brain, inserting four screws, planting electrodes near the midline brain in a part of the cingulate region known as Brodmann area 25 (BA25), and sending a steady stream of electric pulses through the region. The clinicians believe that key areas accounting for depression reside at the top of the brainstem and nested in limbic structures. The idea is to stimulate this area with electricity to ease the pain. My belief, however, is that we can reach this area without drugs or surgery; and certainly natural feeling methods are to be chosen over serious brain surgery. Admittedly, the surgery performed had a high success rate: some 80 percent of patients felt their depression was lifted.[17] But until we have found ways to probe the depths of the brain without surgery or drugs we cannot say there is a cure for depression.

Most treatments thus far have addressed the top part of the brain—the neocortex. This strategy ignores a lifetime of memories lodged in the deep right brain. Because we have found a way to access deep brain centers, I believe invasive surgery can be avoided. Evidence for this view exists in the fact that we've successfully treated many deep, often suicidal, depressions. They are called "deep" because they often emanate from remote areas in the brain formed early in our evolutionary history. Until we access these depths we can never speak of cure; or to put it differently, only when we access these depths can we speak of cure.

Interestingly, if we were to overlay a transparency of the characteristics of depression on those of the birth trauma, we would find they match perfectly: nearly everything a person felt during the birth trauma also describes his or her current depression.

1. Inability to talk
2. Lack of energy
3. Inability to move; feeling of enclosure, of being stuck in a dark abyss

4. Inability to find anything to live for; flat interior landscape; monotonous, inner deadness
5. Repetitive mood; feeling that nothing is going to change
6. Feeling that something wants out
7. Inability to feel pleasure; feeling of constant suffering
8. Difficulty concentrating
9. Extreme fatigue
10. Paralysis and immobilization; feeling helpless to change a situation, make a decision, or make something stop
11. Numbness and ponderous labored movements
12. Recurrence of a wish to die
13. Sense of isolation
14. Visualization of falling into a black hole
15. Persistent feeling of not getting anywhere
16. Overall heaviness or deadness
17. Difficulty breathing or even lifting an arm
18. Lack of interested in anything; no sexual interest
19. Despair, resignation, desire to give up
20. Self-defeating impulses: i.e., "What's the use of living?" "I don't want to go on like this"

So in describing the symptoms of their depression, patients are also relating the sensations of birth trauma and gestational life. Nearly all are in the category of the parasympath, the "down-regulated" group, as mentioned earlier. The sensations and feelings described above accompany the trauma of birth in what I call "the trough." This phase, characterized by the baby experiencing a feeling of helplessness and hopelessness, is brought on by complications that arise as the baby leaves the womb and moves through the birth canal. Whether the baby is turned around the wrong way, entangled by the umbilical cord, has respiratory distress from too much anesthesia given to the mother, or otherwise encounters some obstruction in the birth canal, the trauma leaves its imprint. Later in life, the individual is left with a sensation of not being able to move freely forward, a feeling of gloom and doom. That feeling is what is commonly known as depression.

The most common problem a baby will encounter during birth is the suppression of its nervous system due to anesthesia or other medication given to the mother. Under the influence of these drugs, the baby cannot summon the energy necessary to leave the womb and take its first breath. It takes work to be born, and yet many neonates are incapacitated at this critical juncture. Given a baby's fragile state and the fact that its brain will not be fully developed for years to come, these physiologic impressions take on enormous significance. Laid down biochemically in the child's nervous system, they will ultimately shape his personality and behavior.

After treating several hundred depressives successfully, I can come to no other conclusion than this: endogenous depression is not genetic. What has been known as endogenous depression is simply a state of imprinted helplessness related to gestational life. It seems genetic because we neglect the nine key months of pregnancy. Yet this form of depression does not respond well to any currently known treatment. When we cast it as genetic, or as a mental condition of mysterious origin, we cannot fashion a therapy for it other than to prescribe medication to control it. This is truly a vicious cycle that forestalls any hope for long-term recovery.

16

on the nature of anxiety

Nearly all of us know someone who is anxious. What is less obvious is whether that person is aware of her own anxiety, whether, that is, she's suffering. We recognize anxiety in friends and members of our families who have a hard time getting things done. These people are never without projects: remodeling the kitchen, redoing this or that. One reason for this near-constant activity is that for someone with high anxiety to sit still is to be confronted by helplessness, not in the present, but originally, in the first years of life. Flights of activity take on an exaggerated quality for individuals with high anxiety because behind them lies the threat of death. Acting-out is an unconscious attempt to distance oneself from this fear.

When we are anxious and know it, the chances are we suffer from what I call leaky gates, an inability to regulate pain in the lower brain. For many of us terror is bubbling up constantly. Some repress it successfully; the pay back, however, is sporadic depression, or in the worst cases, migraines, and uncontrollable epileptic attacks. As I've suggested, something in the present resonates with a related feeling in the past and causes a massive release of accumulated, undelineated pain. Most people are unaware of their anxiety. Having successfully rearranged their lives to mask it, they have no idea they are under such an enormous amount of stress. In therapy we open the gates a bit and out comes a roaring, volcanic pain, repressed for years.

From an evolutionary perspective, anxiety is one of our oldest and most remote feelings. It is a survival mechanism that alerts us and galvanizes our body into action to avoid death. The symptoms are controlled by the brainstem and by ancient parts of the limbic system that regulate primitive survival functions. That is why we often see anxiety emerge in physical symptoms: shortness of breath, the need to urinate, pressure on the chest, digestion problems, an inability to sit still, cramps, palpitations, and so on. These are signals that prepare the body to confront or elude danger. The problem is that some people are unable to shut down this vigilant state. I want to reiterate this point: anxiety is not just a pesky feeling that needs to be eliminated; it needs to be understood as a warning signal, a sort of internal fire alarm originally intended to save our lives. For someone with chronic anxiety, however, this feeling is constant and unbearable. Above all, there is an inescapable sense of doom and gloom—a feeling that death is approaching.

As I've discussed, the deepest level of brain function, rooted in the brainstem, is what I call the "first-line." The inability to concentrate comes from massive pain input surging upwards from this region. When input is not properly gated, it disrupts the normal functioning of the neocortex. Poor gating, as I've said, can derive from any number of emotional and physiologic disruptions that occur during pregnancy: a carrying mother who is terribly anxious; a mother who takes drugs; a mother who does not eat enough or properly; a mother who is miserable due to the strain and hardship of a difficult life.

A recent study found that babies in the womb feel their mother's anxiety as early as four months in gestation. The findings, published in the journal *Clinical Endocrinology*[1] show that the baby's anxiety level rises and falls in accordance with the mother's anxiety. (This work is being done at Tommy's, a baby charity in London devoted to investigating the causes of miscarriage, premature birth, and stillbirth). Anxiety was measured in the mother's blood as well as in the amniotic fluid. The point I want to make is that the fetus is constantly adapting to its environment. When the mother's system signals danger so does the unborn child. The difference is that the baby's adaptation is being imprinted and will guide perhaps a lifetime of reactions. It doesn't end when the mother's anxiety ends. The child is learning to be *qui vive*, always a little too alert and vigilant; hence, overreacting to the slightest fear later on. We are finding, more and more, that fear can indeed burn memories into our brain.

Let's return for a moment to the work of K.J.S. Anand. As you'll recall, Anand found that when a needle was inserted into the mother's abdomen in amniocentesis—a medical procedure used for in utero diagnosis of chromosomal abnormalities—the fetus attempted to escape it, grimacing and turning his head, while secretions of in-born, anti-pain chemicals skyrocketed. The fetus was not anxious; he was terrified. When the child grows up and is distanced from the memory the experience may manifest as an anxiety disorder, but it is still the same terror originally imprinted in the salamander brain.

Now take, for example, the feeling of anxiety suffered by one of my patients who went to the Department of Motor Vehicles to renew her license. As soon as she arrived, the obstacles began: long lines, burden-some paperwork, required proof of this or that. The day was interminable. Gradually her worries accumulated, until she reached the brink of panic. Fortunately she was scheduled for therapy later that day. She came in to our clinic frantic and alarmed, still exhibiting signs of the morning's distress. She described a feeling of helplessness; she could not leave herself in the care of someone else, nor trust others with her feelings. For her, death was menacing, and anxiety the byproduct of that same gestational fear. During a Primal, she relived that same help-lessness at birth when complications had meant a struggle to exit the womb. This patient was far enough along in her therapy to have deep access: through resonance she could connect with those early experiences on a physiologic level. However that is not always the case; in fact, waiting to connect to early trauma bothers many of my patients because in the womb this same waiting could have spelled doom. I know as I write this that it seems "new agey," a flight of fantasy, or "booga booga," as I phrase it, but trust me it is not.

In another classic case, one of my pre-psychotics was in a restaurant bar waiting for his table. He kept being put off by the concierge, and eventually he got so angry he started to break the dishes hung on the wall. Characteristic of the pre-psychotic, his pain was right up to the surface, unrecognizable as anything but anger in the here and now. He was desperate and didn't know why. The only way to discharge this pain, in his mind, was by violently acting out.

Granted, neither of these reactions are completely irrational. Who, after all, doesn't get anxious when they have to fill out long forms or wait an incredibly long time to eat? The responses were proper initially but continued on, rising to calamitous levels, because the sensations and feelings associated with womb-life events had become imprinted. We don't harbor malignant feelings as a sort of caprice; we don't manufacture them out of some whim. They should be there. It is our job to find out why.

uncovering the salamander brain

Anxiety means that the lower brain is at work, the brain we have in common with the salamander; and indeed, the salamander brain has remained largely unchanged through millions of years. It reacts immediately, often without reflection, and prepares us for an onslaught of incoming events, both external and internal.

Internal events—the ones we should be focused on—are feelings that seem alien to us and which we attempt to repress at all times. Sensations such as being crushed or suffocated are engraved onto the salamander brain and can be as menacing to the system as a virus. When confronted with such terror, the immune system is compromised, basic repressive chemicals are diminished, and we may well run a fever. In fact, when a patient of ours gets close to those feelings it is not uncommon for his body temperature to elevate by several degrees. Even more strangely, body temperature can drop several degrees, in minutes, during a session, due to a dominance of the parasympathetic nervous system (more on this in a moment).

When we cannot repress effectively we become anxious because brainstem reactions approach consciousness. For most of us, these reactions are largely tamed or mollified by the dominion of the prefrontal cortex. That saves us from being overloaded with stress. But once we descend to lower levels, as we do in primal therapy, we see that early reptilian brain largely intact, as it once was.

I'm quite aware that all of this may sound strange. A salamander rummaging around in our heads? Arthur, please. Yet for the better half of the nineteenth century, before Charles Darwin returned from the Galapagos Islands to publish *On the Origin of Species*, the idea that ancient flippers had evolved into our hands, arms, and legs was blasphemy (and still is to some). And, indeed, today there is growing consensus that we carry around vestiges of our ancient, animal past in many of our organs. Rats, for instance, have brains and kidneys too; and it turns out that their genes are not that different from ours and nearly as plentiful.

We are learning more each day. It now appears that rapists, killers, psychopaths, and others whom I categorize as "acting-out impulsives" usually have a great deal of first-line trauma and pain. Due to gestational trauma their neocortex was never properly developed; that damage appears, as well, as a residue of barely contained, atavistic impulses in the brainstem. So are they human? They are basically primitive animals deficient in neural tissue for control: lizards with an add-on.

Other types of psychopathology may result from impairment to the second-line feeling brain; this typically occurs after the first few months of life and determines how one relates to others and whether he can socialize comfortably and express empathy. Those deficient in compassion, mechanical in their responses to pain and suffering, may be limbically impaired. I often think of this second-line dysfunction as a "missing feeling band."

In primal therapy, the goal is to have our human brain meet up first with the second-line (chimp brain) and then the first-line (lizard brain), so that they can know each other intimately and communicate. When they do we are normal; we are whole. Though wholeness can be explained in many ways, essentially it means getting ourselves back, no longer being driven by imprints in the lower brain that control our lives. One might even say we are not fully conscious until all three levels interact fluidly, for if one-third of our brain is impaired we are stunted, incomplete.

Anxiety is so remote in origin, so seemingly inaccessible as to be considered a "given," something that is inherent in us, something we can only hope to barricade ourselves against. But before we can hope to eradicate it we need to be sure we understand what "it" is.

Originated during gestation and birth and organized in the neuraxis, anxiety is not like a current fear: there is always the element of terror about it. In reliving, those with imprinted terror will again feel terror when confronted with the simple but painful reality that everyone will die. The combined experience of being near-death at birth and recognizing the inevitability of death in maturity produces an exaggerated reaction, often one of chronic anxiety. Ultimately, this connection leads to healing.

Of course there may be a justifiable fear in the present that produces the same hyperarousal as I've described earlier in this chapter, the impending death or severe illness of a relative, for example. Some call this anxiety, but I prefer to reserve the term anxiety for something that resonates with very early trauma; it is easier to understand in this latter sense, for it automatically directs us to our origins.

In the face of trauma, the fetus reacts viscerally. If we've had this kind of trauma, we will have a predisposition to go on responding viscerally for the rest of our life. We then develop stomach problems, palpitations, colitis, ulcers, cramping, breathing problems, and so on, without knowing why. That is why clinicians often don't know the origin of the problem when a patient presents colitis, for example. To find the source, we must look to the brainstem, for it creates the need to keep busy and have plans; it is in a constant state of agitation, and when our patients suffer from anxiety attacks it is almost always a sign of a brainstem reaction.

Because midline structures and organs were the first areas of the nervous system to evolve, they are where we most often see ailments that have an early start in our lives. Digestive and breathing problems are therefore often of first-line origins. Later sexual compulsions and bedwetting are of first-line origin, as are colitis and ulcers, migraines, and high blood pressure. So when we try to treat sex problems with a constrained focus on the sex organs we may be making a mistake; the focus is far too narrow. It is not the penis or vagina that is the problem; it is the brain, specifically the lower brain; the sex organs just follow orders. Anxiety is often attached to something in the present to justify its existence, but that something is often just a rationale. The real problem began much earlier.

The brainstem imprints the deepest levels of pain because it handles life-and-death matters before we see the light of day. Later in life, when the lower level imprint tries to inform the frontal cortex about a near-death experience in the womb, blood pressure goes up as does the heart rate; this is a warning about stored terror: a memory that pushes the system into higher output. Because so many patients normalize after therapy, I am led to believe that most of us are born normal. The only reason we get sick later is because of adverse experiences in gestational life and at birth.

reliving anxiety: away from pills

A memory imprinted in the brainstem may disrupt the functioning of many survival functions. That is why a chronically rapid heart rate and high blood pressure, for instance, can presage cardiac problems decades after the imprint settles in. However when a patient relives early terror and then relaxes his obsession he has solved an important mystery. We see this in patients who cease to compulsively lock their doors. The change happens without any prolonged discussion but by reliving the original imprint. Typically, a compulsive patient reports feeling profoundly unsafe; his obsessions are trying to control the terror. The left frontal cortex is saying, "I'd better check the locks. It makes me feel more comfortable." The feeling of being unsafe, in other words, is seeping over in small increments from the right brain, where it is immediately staved off by obsessions manufactured in the left brain. "I'll be safe if the house is locked" is the unconscious formula. "I'll be safe if no one can penetrate me." If we were to prevent the obsession, however, we would see panic and helplessness again, which is exactly what happens in the early stages of our therapy. Once the pain mounts with force, obsessions trail off into psychosis and bizarre delusions. What that means is two-fold: one, delusion are a last-ditch stand against the onslaught of deep pain; two, their failure gives way to more bizarre ideas: "the mafia is out to get me." The pain simply stretches the ideational brain to trespass into psychosis; that means the deep first-line brain usurps the third-line almost completely.

A reliving of the pre-birth and birth imprint will evoke the same reactions as at the time of trauma. This is why therapy must be done in a safe, controlled atmosphere. When undergoing primal therapy, a patient will often cough and bring up sputum in large amounts; and actually, we've found that doing that (coughing and choking in exaggerated fashion) will help a person feel better. We recommend it to our patients at the beginning of treatment when there is not yet access to deep-level imprints. This approach, of course, may seem unorthodox, yet it allows for the discharge of energy associated with anxiety. None of these reactions require a cortex or higher-level brain function in order to take place. What we have is a visceral and subcortical response: reactions such as coughing and suffocating tell us that anxiety emanates from a very primitive brain organization when there was only an inchoate cerebral structure.

Until a patient undergoes a reliving, fragments of the physiologic memory such as a fast heart rate or high blood pressure are likely to persist; often patients complain of a heightened state of confusion. What's happening is the individual is constantly being stirred by deep-level imprints that connect to the frontal cortex and keep the mental wheels turning. In order to control these renegade signals, we need to resurrect the imprint and straighten out what is happening in the lower brain.

When we relive a pre-birth memory (of which a fast heart rate or high blood pressure was a part), that fragment of the memory will be integrated across all three levels of the brain, and the patient should consequently see relief from the intrusive symptoms. If aspects of the original reaction are missing, however, the reliving is not complete and therefore not curative. So by using medication to lower blood pressure and keep the high-level reaction at bay, we foreclose the possibility of complete and enduring healing. That is one danger of taking tranquilizers: we feel better but, in general, we live a shorter life.

Any deep symptoms, such as a constant low-grade fever or chronically elevated body temperature, point the way to the brainstem and some parts of the limbic brain. That is, they suggest a pre-birth experience and point to the route the patient ultimately will have to travel in order to recover. Unfortunately, problems such as heart attacks or strokes may not emerge for decades, making the origins of such terminal conditions difficult to detect. Realistically, the real way out needs to be the way in: feeling the anxiety untrammeled, for what it is and was—pure terror: panic in the face of the threat of death at birth.

Most forms of neurosis can be traced back to anxiety. We need terror to alert us to danger, which, as I've said, is an in-built reaction we have in common with many primitive animals. Or at least a reaction we *had* in common with primitive animals. Presently, we live in a nation consumed with prescription medication, drugs which forestall any chance at real health by suppressing the warning signs of chronic conditions. This approach makes us feels better but leaves us undefended against serious afflictions, much in the same way angina may suppress the precursors to a heart attack but fail to remove the threat.

Still, I know how necessary getting out of pain can be; it is not a moral position but one of survival. Patients will be openly anxious if they cannot carry out their ritual obsessions. In fact, the sex addict and the chain smoker are not all that different. Both attempt to regulate anxiety through an all-consuming habit. And although the content of the ritual may have little to do with its pre-birth and early life origins, it is nevertheless an adaptation to first-line reactions.

Anxiety appears in nearly all of our patients at one point in a session as they approach the first-line. As mentioned, the reason it is called anxiety and not terror, although it is the same feeling, is that the sufferer does not know where the anxiety comes from, nor what it really is. We therefore treat them as separate entities. Disconnected from present experience, anxiety—at least in terms of severity—seems to hang in space with no specific antecedent. Once the patient relives the trauma at birth, gasping for oxygen where it is scarcely available, the anxiety becomes the terror and fight for life that it is and was. It now has a home—and an owner.

animal terror: MRIs, nightmares, sex, and other clues to our past

Terror is what we see in lower animals when frightened by predators. Their reactions are pure panic—the need to escape being eaten. We see this, as well, in some individuals who undergo MRIs. The minute they are enclosed in a steel and cement sheath panic surges forth. This reaction is approximating what happened originally: it takes the confines of such a machine to reawaken the primitive feeling. The patient may believe it is the machine that is producing anxiety, but it is really the primal panic from the confined, enclosed space; the womb in which he tried to exit to preserve his life. What the MRI does is stimulate a resonating memory, not a memory in the way we usually think of it, but one which sets off a bodily reaction. If we do experience this kind of anxiety when having an MRI exam, we can be fairly sure that we endured a difficult birth or pre-birth. It is, in short, a sort of differential diagnostic tool to separate out those with healthy births from those who experienced traumatic births. We can teach technicians who perform MRIs to tap the leg or foot of a panicked individual at irregular intervals, so that he cannot organize a full-fledged anxiety reaction. Or we may offer an eye mask so that the person stays unaware of the surroundings. When such distractions fail, however, there may well be an anxiety attack.

We are dealing, figuratively, with a non-verbal animal rummaging around in the lower reaches of our nervous system. That is part of the reason why asking for calm or simply saying "take it easy" to someone with first-line damage is not going to help. Slowing this person down is next to impossible. Driven by a very early deprivation of need, he wants to get better now; and, in fact, he needs to be allowed to go to those remote places that drive him, for he likely feels an intense physical agitation. He hasn't the patience to read a lengthy book that tells him what anxiety is; he can't even read the doctor's brochure importuning calm. Indeed, the problem exists far below the verbal level and requires a method like primal therapy, which targets the deep brain. If we cannot reach these lower levels at first, we may administer painkillers to suppress the force of deep-level imprints until the patient can *feel* his feelings. Ultimately, though, the painkillers are a means to an end.

Too often the therapist or physician sees his job as eliminating the symptom, the origin of which is considered an unfathomable mystery. Of course the symptom often is uncomfortable and life endangering; however when the therapist makes the tacit assumption that the symptom is there for no good reason, he is making a serious mistake.

Therapy must begin with a proper understanding of resonance. The concept is important, particularly when it comes to anxiety, because resonance links language centers in the cortex to areas deeper in the brain that induce panic. In sex, for instance, a nude female body can resonate in a man with an early experience with his mother, not in the symbolic Freudian sense, but in the neurological context of early trauma.

I had one patient, for instance, who had a very seductive mother who French-kissed him. The woman was White. Later, her son could only have girlfriends who were Black or Asiatic; too "White" a girlfriend would resonate with the early seduction that scared him. In fact, any association with White women recalled the early childhood experience with his mother and was to be avoided.

In another case, I treated a lesbian woman who was sexually molested by her White stepfather. Afterwards she could only have relationships with Black men, and eventually with no men, since the male presence resonated with the sexual terror induced by her stepfather. When she switched to sex with a woman, everything seemed much safer to her; there was no chronic, low-level apprehension. And why not? Because there was no resonance with the early trauma. Apprehension is located in the limbic system; and it is only transformed into anxiety once resonance takes hold. However, in the absence of a precipitating event at the start of life, the anxiety reaction is far less severe and generally in fitting with the present-day triggering event.

When there is a life-and-death struggle at birth, however—due to lack of oxygen, exposure to drugs, or other adverse intrauterine conditions—the existing reactive system cannot fully respond. The load of pain and terror is unmanageable; to feel it completely would be to run the risk of cardiac arrest or loss of consciousness. Instead, the system reacts within its biologic limits, putting the excess terror away for safekeeping until the system is strong enough to feel and resolve it. Nevertheless, we continually respond to this stored terror with chronically high stress hormone levels, a response which continues to gnaw away at the cardiovascular system, so that we may fall seriously ill at age fifty-five, even though we seem to be living a normal, relaxed life.

Somewhat paradoxically, in order for certain patients to feel the fear and its context, we need to tranquilize them so that terror does not override their other feelings. To do that we offer first–line blockers, the same anti-psychotic medication used in conventional medicine and psychotherapy. Once tranquilized, the patient will no longer be overwhelmed because we have reduced the overall pain load; he can focus on a single feeling without the emotional overload that leads to the generation of bizarre ideas and beliefs. Make no mistake, anxiety is a catalyst for psychotic ideation: feed in too much pain and the system searches for an outlet; reduce the level of pain and the system calms down and no longer needs to concoct delusional ideas to rationalize what is going on inside. In a way, those strange ideas are like an over-flow valve to channel pain away from consciousness; left untreated, however, they can be dangerous.

What is diabolic about anxiety is that many suffer from a chronic, barely perceptible level, acted-out constantly. The person is rarely aware of it, yet it drives him to be constantly on the go: he cannot read a book without that agitated feeling; he cannot fall asleep; he cannot listen to a long lecture or to his children's stories. It is not that such parents are callous or unloving. Rather they suffer and cannot help themselves, and so they rationalize that they must keep busy to feed their children. We know otherwise: the real reason they are desperately trying to keep busy is to discharge excess energy; if they cannot, they suffer.

On this point, lengthy phone calls are particularly telling. Many times the original anxiety begins just after birth when there is no one to hold and caress the baby—no real contact. As a result, the feeling behind the anxiety is that of complete isolation and alienation. Phone calls become a way to reconnect the person constantly. If one stays on the phone for a long time, he avoids that abandoned feeling he suffered just after birth or in the first months of infancy. Moreover, he cannot judge that he may be on the phone too long, because he is acting out old feelings that drive him to talk; he has found an outlet to stave off the feeling of abandonment and exercises it with impunity, unable to detect any impatience on the part of his listener, even when she says, not so subtly, "My dinner is starting to burn; I have to let you go."

At the same time a person with low-level anxiety is prone to ramble: he can rarely listen, for that demands too much patience. When given a list of groceries to buy at the supermarket, for instance, there is a good chance some of it will be neglected or mixed up: "I know she said to buy low-fat but low-fat what?" It is not that these individuals have poor memories, but that they don't process the directions in the first place.

As I mentioned, sleep may be problematic, as well. For when the limbic system mobilizes against early pain, the third-line neocortex diminishes its hold. Pressed into service to control our lower level feelings, the neocortex essentially becomes an escape hatch, allowing for the alleviation of pain. The problem is that we need to let go of that top-level control in order to sleep, and when the neocortex is constantly busy we cannot. Enter a ruminating mind: a very busy mind that cannot shut itself down long enough to give the body the rest it needs.

Interestingly, it is in deep sleep that we move closer to the primitive brain and approach primal feelings. As we rest, they agitate and move upward, making the thinking brain work very hard. As we begin to suffer from the uprising of first-line terror, the brain rushes in to regulate that terror with a nightmare. Most of us think of a nightmare as terrifying—and it can be scary—but that is because it is an attempt to encapsulate a traumatic feeling so that it never becomes conscious. A nightmare is not a willful act. It is a built-in survival mechanism that ensures that our consciousness will not be impaired by overwhelming input from very early in our lives. The story in the nightmare does not count for much, but the feeling in it counts a great deal. That feeling can give us a way in; indeed, it is the royal road to the unconscious. Imprinted first-line pain drives the top level to ruminate interminably; it has the greatest valence, and it is where mental illness is born.

There are at least two main avenues to provoke anxiety and repression: one, the meaning of a certain look or negative reaction by the parent, which means, "I am not loved nor will I ever be"; and two, the physiologic recognition that something is happening that is an immediate threat to one's life. In either case, there is a disruption in the organism's evolution.

When the resonance of an early traumatic experience descends from the top-level cortex to low levels of the neuraxis, terror appears. It is not something new, nor something to endeavor to reach. It is an old friend—more accurately, an old enemy. In fact, willfully trying to reach a lower level feeling is an oxymoron; the more we use top-level will, the less we can descend to where we have to go. The more we let go of the present, on the other hand, the more access we will have. The person in terror suffers anxiety because the body is preparing for extreme reactions in order to survive. Rest assured, you will never be slow to react when there is a lion approaching. The lower brain was in place when dangerous animals roamed the landscape, and its modus operandi is staying alive.

If we want to successfully treat any of the so-called psychosomatic symptoms (migraines, high blood pressure, etc.) we must find the generating sources. Interestingly, when someone suffers a full-fledged anxiety attack—feeling he is going to die—the feeling is correct; it is the subject which may not be. How is giving a public speech or filling out federal tax forms cause for mortal panic? Because, in short, the area of the brain responsible for survival is triggered through resonance, thus setting off a massive reaction. Anxiety attacks may also happen as a response to early criticism or mistreatment from hypercritical parents when one misstep meant abuse and denigration. There is the thought, "I am not loved if I make a mistake," or, "catastrophe happens if I screw this up." And indeed, the chances are good that someone who suffers from chronic anxiety was censured in childhood whenever he made a mistake.

Discomfort with being wrong is present in so many of us, however for someone with chronic anxiety being wrong is a question, literally, of life and death. It is not a reasoned response but a physiologic one. Defending against the possibility of a mistake begins with that very early sensation when being wrong could have been fatal. Defenses sealed in the feeling, which later can make the person seem like a know-it-all, someone who can never be wrong, even when they clearly are. It has become an art form to displace blame onto others.

evolution of the left brain

One reason for the evolution of the left frontal cortex was to produce a brain system that could distance itself from other areas of the nervous system where painful feelings lie—a way of not being overwhelmed by what lay below, so we could comfortably handle the day-to-day vexations of life.

The prefrontal area is unique as a brain system in that it can uncouple itself from massive, damaging input. It is the human part of us, the part that can dissociate from feeling and reason through problems. But it doesn't just bolster our defenses and keep us out of inordinate pain. The left frontal cortex evolved with the use of tools, and it is this area that oversees the precise manipulation of our thumb and forefingers as, for instance, when hammering a nail. If we are looking for a good surgeon we are wise to find one that is left-brain dominant. If we instead want a therapist who can feel and sense things we may want a right-brain dominant individual; but, of course, someone with a balanced brain is always the *ne plus ultra*.

The anxious patient shows us his early generating source as unmistakably as a peacock shows his colors. The key feeling lies deep, a sort of avatar ushering in the catastrophic reaction. We know this because we see the individual's neural defense system at work in studying the brains of our patients. As feelings surge forth there will be higher vital signs and mounting amplitude of the brainwaves, the latter indicating how many neurons are recruited to defend against rising feelings. At a certain point the defenses are lowered, the connection is made, and the brain can relax. We know this is happening because the brain scan will show a precipitous drop in amplitude. Contrary to the popular misconception, we do not use only ten percent of our brains; in fact, we overuse our nerve cells when defending against feeling. Operating above ten percent is like trying to drive a car eighty miles an hour in second gear; we may go fast for a little while, but it will quickly destroy the internal mechanics.

From a therapeutic perspective, there is not much difference between the anxious patient and the patient who comes to us with other complaints but develops anxiety during therapy. In both cases a primitive feeling is being exerted. The difference is that for a patient whose main problem is not anxiety, primal therapy, not day-to-day stress, may be the trigger. Nevertheless, once early traumatic feelings are activated we may see a full-blown anxiety attack, including, in some cases, the announcement of impending death. Both types of patients are propitious for therapy, so long as the anxiety is not terribly overwhelming, and the individual can be brought into the primal zone. Those who have a strong repressive barrier to the cortex will have only transient anxiety as deep feelings approach. When that danger is over so is the anxiety. For the chronically anxious patient, part of the feeling will continue to seep through to higher levels throughout the session. That is the part we need to tranquilize for a moment.

Conventional therapy is often unhelpful for patients with anxiety because it attempts to suppress, not express, feelings. That is quite a different goal. If feelings are erupting it is always better to let them out in some methodical way than to continuously hold them back. Unfortunately, that hasn't been done with seriousness since Freud's admonition that the unconscious is a dangerous place. What we have instead is the psychiatric equivalent to religious doctrine: evil spirits which need to be controlled. To the psychologist they are simply negative feelings; but, whatever we choose to call them, it amounts to the same thing— mysterious, inexplicable forces which need to be silenced. Without a wholesale shift in the direction of our therapy, we will not cure patients; we will continue down the ill-conceived path of alleviating symptoms.

On my desk is a scientific paper concerning how early life affects adulthood.[2] Chris Murgatroyd and Dietmar Spengler, molecular biologists at the Max Planck Institute in Germany, have shown rather conclusively that life events can induce long-lasting changes in our brain, physiology, and behavior. Early life stress can cause over-secretion of the stress hormone cortisol, which in turn weakens our ability to remember things clearly and cope with stress. (For the more scientifically minded, the article includes a detailed explanation of the long-duration effects of methylation.) In their study of mice, Murgatroyd and Spengler found that periodic infant-mother separation just after birth was a major cause of anxiety. And it is my view, as I've noted, that when it comes to humans the earlier the separation occurs, the more likely the anxiety will result in a shortened life span. The published results from the study end with a rather bleak assessment: "Adverse events in early life can leave persistent marks on specific genes that may prime susceptibility to neuroendocrine and behavioral dysfunction."[3] Yet further evidence that early events have a profound effect on later life.

But if the causes are so deep rooted how does one know whether he is anxious? Heart irregularities may be one sign: a chronic symptom of palpitations, for example, is testimony to the possibility of an imprint lying deep in the central nervous system. It is a fragment of the early memory when a rapid heartbeat was called for—one aspect, that is, of an anxiety state. So often we find a patient going to one specialist for heart problems, another for an anxiety disorder, and another for migraines when these are all part of a single imprint, which, if relived, might normalize all reactions. There is a reason why high blood pressure is related to these other conditions. Too often the reason is so arcane as to be disbelieved, but it is there: either genetically or, more likely, as the result of an imprint while the fetus was developing in the womb.

Many times a specialist will offer medication to lower a patient's blood pressure without asking where the deviation came from. He has a task to complete: help the patient avoid suffering. Can we blame him? It requires a certain level of abstraction to tie palpitations in the present to an event that occurred during our womb-life. Luckily, we don't have to make that intellectual leap; the patient will do it for us. When we give the patient the possibility of deep immersion into himself, we learn from first-hand experience; and the patient, too, learns from the experience: not just parroting the beliefs of the therapist—i.e., that there is an id or shadow forces that drive us—rather that there are concrete events in our lives that account for our afflictions: for our anxiety, high blood pressure, migraines, and neurotic behavior. Once a patient has access he may relive oxygen deprivation or other sources of trauma during his time in the womb, and his symptoms—a transient palpitation attack or the pain of angina, for instance—can now be connected to the original threat.

treating the "right" brain

Unfortunately, a good deal of intrauterine trauma is registered in the right brain. It is a vain task to use the later developing, externally focused left frontal brain to gain access to it. They are two universes apart, and, as I explained earlier, they speak two different languages.

At the start of therapy, the patient rarely retrieves memories of life-and-death valence. The laws of evolution often will not permit it; that is, repression does the job for which it was intended. It allows only manageable fear at first. Fortunately, we have found a way to access the depths of the unconscious in an orderly, methodical fashion so that the patient is not overwhelmed by pain. Man is a microcosm of the universe; therefore what man is, gives us clues to the universe. Or, if that sounds too metaphysical, here's a more measured version: We learn about the evolution of the brain by observing patients in our therapy.

As I suggested, much of the research into intrauterine trauma has focused on animals. A study of three-day-old baby rabbits deprived of oxygen, for instance, found radically lower precursors (building blocks) to 5-hydroxytryptamine (5-HT) serotonin receptors. Across their life span, the rabbits never recovered from this deficit. If we later found these rabbits and offered them Prozac, a serotonin enhancer, I am sure they would jump at the chance. And in fact there are many animal studies just like this one that show how oxygen deprivation at birth lowers the set-points of serotonin. The research is virtually inexhaustible, almost always with the same conclusion: early trauma, including pre-birth trauma, alters serotonin and other neurotransmitter levels in the brain.

When we extrapolate these results to humans we find that trauma to the carrying mother may lead to any number of conditions, not the least of which is anxiety in the child. If a husband is unfaithful to his wife during her pregnancy, we may find increased stress in the mother, interfering with the orderly production of serotonin cells in the fetus. Later on when the baby, now an adult, suffers panic and anxiety attacks that appear out of the blue, we understand the origins. We see the early signs in newborns whose bodies are continually restless, and the long-term effects in children who grow up hyperactive and not terribly affectionate.

Are we actually born with not enough serotonin in our systems? Yes, but it is not strictly genetic; we are born with missing serotonin but it is *not* missing at the time of conception. The gene for serotonin production is encoded but not expressed because of experiences in pregnancy. Think of it this way: We take drugs (Prozac, Zoloft, etc.) that boost serotonin levels to help repress anxiety and pain. Does that mean that anxiety is due to low levels of serotonin? Not really. Serotonin is a natural product, something we produce internally, and it can be pathologically low. We are born with low serotonin levels due to epigenetics: because of a mother's anxiety and low serotonin levels she cannot help the fetus out by donating any surplus supplies. So the fetus is born with little defense against pain.

Earlier I mentioned compounding, and it is worth another word here. A child who lives with a cold, distant parent never feels the kind of safety necessary to really relax. The world becomes a dangerous place for him. When the pain is consolidated by a sterile home environment there can be the development of delusions later in life: "They are after me and want to hurt me." We professionals are never going to convince this person that there is no danger. There is, but the doctor cannot see it; only the patient can feel it and know what it is. What is particularly troubling is that the person is often convinced that the danger is coming from outside. I've had schizophrenic patients who nailed and taped their doors to "keep the aliens out." The dynamics of chronic anxiety are almost the same: A neurotic phobia is just a lesser version of "the aliens are coming to get us," lesser only because the pains driving it are not as severe.

One of my patients was involved in an auto accident during gestation. Her mother, eight months pregnant, was pinned against the steering wheel and had the fright of her life as the car turned over twice. As a child, the young girl seemed anxious, distracted—and she remained so throughout her life. She suffered a continuous low-level anxiety, which made her unable to deal with the simplest tasks. I submit that part of the reason for this was that her mother remained anxious throughout her pregnancy, "downloading" a substrate of the stress into the baby. When the father subsequently berated her in a strong, commanding voice, she tended to overreact and be especially fearful. This type of overreacting, in my view, is simply reacting to different epochs of early life, different kinds of trauma and neglect compounded over time.

A big part of the problem is that when parents take our "no" away we dare not disobey because we are fearful from the start. A healthy baby who sees distasteful food shakes his head and says to his parents, "I don't want to eat this." The child who spends his life in an anxiety-filled womb doesn't dare say "no"; the consequence (i.e., triggering the birth and gestational traumas) is overwhelming. As a grown adult, we find that the individual cannot refuse an invitation, nor discipline a child. He cannot say "no," in the same way that he could not, as a child, say no to his father.

For most of us, controlling anxiety is not too much of a problem. When we have normal levels of serotonin we can forestall anxiety or panic attacks through repression. However some of us utilize more serotonin than we manufacture. One of the curses of trauma during womb-life is that it not only can cause us to use huge supplies of serotonin, but it also can compromise the repressive system so that we cannot replenish our supply. The set-point is, thus, forever very low.

Consciousness as I see it—the full integration of all three brain levels—is the end to anxiety. Disconnected feelings are what drive us constantly to keep busy. Their energy is manifest as ulcers and irritable bowels, phobias and attention problems. These unrooted feelings are a ubiquitous, free-floating danger that shapes a personality of defensiveness and the avoidance of pain: a self stuck in history forever.

To put it another way, anxiety is a function of the Janovian Gap: the distance between rational awareness and one's feelings, between third-line cortical awareness and low-level events on the first or second line. Having to constantly repress will cripple us mentally and physically. Consciousness, however, will narrow the gap, and that can mean a longer, healthier life. Once we have felt the depths of our terror, there is the ability to experience joy to its fullest; that is what is liberating. The conscious person, now in touch with the life inside, has a reverence for life in general. And that is our goal; not pain, of course, but joy and contentment. What more can any therapy do? Sadly, the portal to that joy exists in the reliving of painful childhood feelings.

Psychotherapy has been in the business of awareness for too long. Since the days of Freud, we have apotheosized insight therapy, and we continue to celebrate it in depictions of cool-headed, erudite psychiatrists like Dr. Melfi on *The Sopranos*, intellectuals adept at giving patients a sophisticated vocabulary for their feelings. We are so used to appealing to the almighty frontal cortex—the structure that has made us the advanced human beings that we are—that we have forgotten our precious ancestors, their instincts and feelings. Unfortunately, when we emphasize how our neocortex is so different from other animal forms, we disregard our mutually shared feeling apparatus. We need a therapy of consciousness, not awareness.

I have come to believe that a general theory, made of many hypotheses is essential for guiding patients to their original pain. It should contain some philosophy, some neurology, some psychology, and, above all, a strong sense of humanity. Suppose we were like the very early explorers (and current professionals) who did not know there was a down under? Their explorations were random, without maps, a hit-or-miss proposition. We need to know that there is a proper destination, and we need to know how to get there—to be cartographers of all the elements of mind, not just the thinking mind. If physicians and therapists don't know about "down under," they will not solve panic and anxiety attacks, suicidal tendencies, high blood pressure, and sex problems, to say nothing of heart attacks and other catastrophic diseases.

Lower levels talk to us constantly; the problem is we haven't learned to listen. We struggle to do so because that language is ancient, developed long before the verbal faculties that most of us have today. However emerging studies of pregnancy and the first years of life provide us with a roadmap, a direction for the future. Each month in our womb-life and infancy (ontogeny) seem to represent eons of development of the human species (phylogeny). In this sense, in our therapeutic sessions, ontogeny recapitulates phylogeny. What we can do now is go back to our beginnings, and through reliving we can find what happened during our birth. Further, we can discover how that event affected our lives. If, indeed, there was a significant trauma early on, we can discover how and when our neurosis began. Otherwise, there is the slow accretion of pain year after year, until one day we wake up and discover that we are miserable. We fight assiduously against the liberation of the unconscious when that alone spells emotional freedom. We need to get "emotional."

In a recent study at Georgia State University, scientists researched infants (now adults) who spent a good deal of time in neonatal intensive care units where there were many surgical procedures, most involving pain. They noted that later in the infant's lives there was decreased pain sensitivity; or to put it more precisely, there was a permanent increase in the opioid inhibitors that we manufacture ourselves. In brief, more global repression.

Now why would pain signals continue long after surgery? I submit that it is because the danger is now imprinted and becomes a permanent menace. A rapid beating heart is part of the memory. So is a lifetime of anxiety. The focus of most medicine and psychotherapy today is the treatment of fragments of a human being, pieces of an original memory that have lost their connection to the whole. So we have coughing spells, frequent colds, anxiety and phobias, seizures and migraines, all pieces of an original imprint. We then treat the various offshoots of a central imprint rather than the imprint itself; and, because it is all of a piece, we have several different doctors treating the same problem. Treatment becomes interminable. What we get is a fragment of progress—a change in aspects of an early experience, but not a true cure. What we should aim to avoid in therapy, above all, is a false or deceptive sense of health in our patients. We will encourage that false sense unless we assist patients in accessing their inner life and their feelings.

Anxiety is not a normal feeling. There are those who claim it is necessary to drive us and get things done, and that is true if we are neurotic. But we are not born anxious; we become that way due to early experiences that produce gating problems in the brain. We have the power to make an atavistic leap into our past. We can peer down into millions of years of evolution by traveling back in our personal development. We can see that when feelings are too strong, ideas and beliefs jump into the fray and lead to debilitating delusions. On that note, let's turn our attention to psychopathology.

17

on psychopathology

There are certain individuals who look human but never establish any kind of loving relationship with anyone. They are diabolically manipulative. Relating only to what they can get, they exude a false charm that sometimes allows them to get away with heinous offenses. When one tries to extend kindness to them they feel nothing; they only want more. Why are they like this? Because usually there were no love objects to relate to right after birth; in fact, some research suggests that the origins of psychopathology may begin in the womb, even before we have a so-called emotional life.[1] Proponents of this theory believe that during the period of fetal development when key structures are damaged or when they remain neurologically immature, feelings may not evolve the way they are supposed to. The makings of a psychopath, therefore, may have origins long before birth. We often think of psychopathology as "genetic"—something inherited and unchangeable—because it occurs so early. And in some sense that is true: once the damage has occurred, I do not think it can be changed.

If on the off chance a psychopath comes to our therapy—almost never voluntarily but sometimes at the behest of the court—they tend to incorporate the therapy into their psychopathology. These are the ones who, without a day's training, sometimes decide to become therapists. They scream and yell during a session, yet they do not feel, for it is beyond them. In the best interest of our clinic, we finally had to stop taking them years ago as they were causing too much disruption to our other patients. One of the personality characteristics that makes psychopaths seem so vile to the rest of us is that they cannot feel; they do not seem to have the capacity for it. They have learned how to act charming, so as to manipulate others by obtaining their trust first. But it is short-lived and then the truth comes out: they care about no one.

Shortly after I finished writing the above, a research study at King's College, in London, came out with a thoughtful explanation of the origins of the psychopath. He remains as I have described him (and psychopaths are mostly males), but the origin of the personality disorder needs to be located more principally in the weeks leading up to birth. In the study,[2] the investigators used an imaging scan (MRI) on psychopaths and concluded that there were differences in their brains from those in the general population. Two of the culprits were the prefrontal area of the cortex and aspects of the amygdala. There was an impairment between the connections in those two areas. In a normal brain, when there are emotionally stimulating events, the amygdala responds. But in psychopaths there is a breakdown in this response.

It appears—from this study, at least—that in psychopaths the neural circuitry that connects feelings to higher level brain processes is deficient. Another way to put it is that feelings are not part of their conceptual, day-to-day cortical functioning. So while the person can be charming on the exterior, there are no sincere feelings underlying this façade; it is all a dumb show. Perhaps if trauma had not occurred before birth to damage the connection between nerve cells responsible for feelings and those in charge of comprehension, then the lack of touch and affection these individuals experienced after birth would not have such disastrous effects. However, when there is a pre-birth impairment of the connections between feelings and thoughts, the lack of physical contact right after birth is catastrophic. The result can be someone who has not only no control over his impulses but also no means to experience feelings. There may be learning but not emotionally integrated learning.

One of the major implications of the King's College study was that psychopathology could be a brain disease. I think it is more likely explained by epigenetic trauma—a mother who drinks, is highly anxious, is in a marriage that is falling apart, and so on. In any case, the damage or immaturity of development occurs in many key structures of the limbic system: the amygdala, insula, anterior cingulated, as well as in the paralimbic system that surrounds them. These structures among others are necessary for the feeling and expression of emotions. Those with damage to the insula, in particular, can develop psychopathic tendencies because the insula and related structures govern our sense of morality. Other areas of the brain control anxiety, but the psychopath, by definition, has little anxiety and is therefore able to approach people that most of us would seriously hesitate getting close to. The brain structures involved with impulse control may also be adversely affected by complications during pregnancy, such that we have someone who feels no pain, someone who is impulsive and therefore can attempt things that none of us would dare.

Since the insula is involved in pain perception, and is affected by trauma during womb-life, the psychopath cannot feel the damage he is doing. So what about morality? Psychopaths seem to be immoral, but, according to recent evidence, they are more accurately described as "unfeeling." They cannot feel or empathize with others, so anything goes. They cheat and swindle their closest friends, a la Bernard Madoff. They don't feel bad about their immoral behavior because they are biologically incapable of feeling the pain they are causing. That is why when they are caught they can never confess to their crimes; it is always someone else's fault, or "they deserved it."

Those with dysfunctional limbic systems, many of whom suffer from repression and are out of touch with their feelings, often need books to guide them in child rearing. They are frequently drawn to "how-to" books which provide rules (e.g., pick up the child when he cries) that loving parents, in most cases, adopt naturally. This peculiarity of the psychopathic mind may be one of the reasons why professionals have accepted with alacrity Bowlby's Theory of Attachment. It lays out recommended practices for raising children, techniques that someone with feelings would most likely recognize instinctively—even, interestingly enough, that some animals recognize instinctively. Does a chimp need rules to regularly lick their baby? No. Morality, in some sense, seems an invented guide for those who cannot feel. Yet until we accept a theory that puts needs and love first, we will continue to rely on books and advice with specific instructions—"how-to" manuals that do not examine the more fundamental causes of dysfunctional parenting.

The important lesson, though, is that psychopathology, much like other aberrations in development, bears the signature of what went wrong earlier in our lives. Memories are made indelible in our biology because they form guides to our future. That is, they become part of our "apperceptive mass"; always ready to serve our interest for survival.

Or, as one of my students wrote:

> Psychopaths shed light on a crucial subset of decision-making that's referred to as morality. Morality can be a squishy, vague concept, and yet, at its simplest level, it's nothing but a series of choices about how we treat other people. When you act in a moral manner—when you recoil from violence, treat others fairly, and help strangers in need—you are making decisions that take people besides yourself into account. You are thinking about the feelings of others, sympathizing with their states of mind. This is what psychopaths can't do . . . They are missing the primal, emotional cues that the rest of us use as guides when making moral decisions. The psychopath's brain is bored by expressions of terror. The main problem seems to be a broken amygdala, a brain area responsible for propagating aversive emotions such as fear and anxiety. As a result, psychopaths never feel bad when they make other people feel bad . . . Hurting someone else is just another way of getting what he wants, a perfectly reasonable way to satisfy desires.

The absence of emotion makes the most basic moral concepts incomprehensible. G. K. Chesterton was right: "The madman is not the man who has lost his reason. The madman is the man who has lost everything except his reason."[3]

18

on attention deficit disorder

Recently there was a one-hour special on PBS about attention deficit disorder (ADD), featuring four major specialists in the subject. What the special was about and the diagnoses it touched on is, in my opinion, characteristic of what's currently wrong with the fields of psychotherapy, psychology, and psychiatry.

Not once in the hour did I hear what the origins of ADD might be, nor why it occurs. Instead most of the hour was spent spelling out how to cope with the condition. This is the same approach typically applied to other psychological disorders and health complications. It is tantamount to saying that the illnesses remain, they are irrevocable, but how we deal with them changes. After you are diagnosed with an allergic reaction, for instance, you still have the allergies, you just avoid this and that to cope with them. Or you still have a chaotic mind, painful headaches, or whatever the case may be, and you try to avoid the problem by changing how you behave or taking drugs. The problem is that approach doesn't work—not if we are looking for more than just the alleviation of symptoms. The PBS special on ADD is characteristic of a deeper and more troubling cultural problem: our obsession with coping with, rather than curing, our mental illnesses.

One of the first points made in the episode is that diagnosis is essential. Evidently, there are ten things that make you an ADDer. You need to be impulsive. You need to be unable to focus and concentrate. You need to be underachieving, hyperactive, unable to sit still (I am improvising a bit here), unable to listen, and very impatient. In addition, you are likely to have low self-esteem, learning problems, a need to talk constantly, no long-term goals, a quick temper, and a bad memory. If you counted more than ten, that's because some of these descriptors are taken from the Brown Attention-Deficit Disorder Scale. Between the PBS special and the Brown Scale I think we pretty well cover it. But you have to be suffering from these symptoms for six months or more (according to most metrics) to be clinically diagnosed as having ADD.

The experts claim that diagnosis is critical. Once you are aware you have ADD, you are halfway to recovery because you know what to do. Now you can make future plans, adapt your environment to suit you, find a calm partner and a job that matches your personality, and avoid losing your patience. Above all, you can seek therapy: the surest way of realizing contentment and achieving your goals. Once you have a little bit of success, you can build on it, gradually improving your self-esteem until you are no longer an underachiever.

So let me see, you tell the doctor that you are impulsive and impatient, that you can neither concentrate nor sit still, and she says that you have ADD. Okay, there is the diagnosis, now what? She has told you what you just told her in simpler terms. Have we made progress? Is that what diagnosis is? Saying things in esoteric language? Of course after the diagnosis doctors have many suggestions: don't do too many chores at once, stay in a calm environment, jog to work off tension, don't talk. Don't work amid chaos. If you've ever listened to Radiohead's *OK Computer,*[1] these suggestions are strikingly similar to the refrain of the computer's voice in "Fitter, Happier," a sardonic commentary on programmatic advice for healthy living.

> Fitter, happier, more productive,
> comfortable,
> not drinking too much,
> regular exercise at the gym
> (3 days a week),
> getting on better with your associate employee
>   contemporaries,
> at ease,
> eating well

(no more microwave dinners and saturated fats),
a patient better driver,
a safer car
(baby smiling in back seat),
sleeping well
(no bad dreams),
no paranoia. . .
. . .calm,
fitter,
healthier and more productive

The problem is that automated responses to psychological disorders do
not lead us any closer to recovery. I say to the doctor that I cannot stand
crowded restaurants, and he tells me to avoid them. He adds "do not
take so many risks in your life," yet points out that it is the risk takers
who invent and innovate, and who tend to be more creative. Now I am
confused.

Not once in the entire special did I hear the word, why? As in, why
do we develop ADD? Where does it come from, and what can we do
about it? Unfortunately, for too many psychologists and physicians, understanding where ADD comes from has become secondary to mitigat-
ing its telltale signs. What has happened in the field of psychotherapy
is that cognitive behavioral approaches have taken hold. A psychiatric
diagnostic manual known as *DSM-IV* indicates all these problematic
behaviors with a clinical description, and it is simply assumed that to
treat the disorder we need to change the behavior: hence, cognitive-
behavioral therapy.

I say that a better approach for understanding and treating ADD is
to trace its origins back to womb-life. There is a good deal of evidence
that a mother's hyperactivity—frequently the result of drugs such as
cocaine and methamphetamine taken during pregnancy—can leave
an imprint that affects the offspring for a lifetime. Just that early exposure is enough to set up a child to be revved up and jumpy for life.
Of course this may stem from more than just drugs. One Israeli study,
for instance, found that children of holocaust survivors frequently gave
birth to anxious children. At first researchers thought it was because

the parents told horrible stories to the children, but later they discovered that the anxiety came down through the genetic chain; that is, it had descended from the mother's physiology through epigenetics.[2]

Of course, understanding ADD is not simple as knowing whether or not a mother used stimulants during pregnancy. Human reports as well as animal studies have recorded accelerated motor activity, as well as learning and memory deficits in the offspring of mothers exposed to nicotine during pregnancy. One study investigated actual physiological changes of the cerebral cortex of rats after prenatal nicotine exposure. Several groups of experimental rats were exposed to levels of nicotine that, at times, reached those experienced by heavy smokers. Observable effects included significantly reduced thickness of the cortical cortex, smaller neurons in the cerebral cortex, and reduced brain weight. Also noted was an overall decrease in "dendritic branching," an important part of brain conductivity thought to play a role in memory formation. The study also showed that the more cigarettes a mother smoked during pregnancy, the greater the likelihood her child would demonstrate severe behavior problems at older ages.

Prenatal drug exposure and epigenetic factors also may be compounded due to the trauma of birth or infancy, where, for instance, the child may be left for days without warmth and cuddling. Later, if the child is raised in a home with parents who instill feelings of rejection and abandonment, the effect may be magnified. All this, as discussed earlier, sets up imprints low in the neuraxis, codes which are then transmitted to higher centers in the brain. When the neocortex is fed conflicted signals, what we get is a situation not unlike listening to ten people talking at us at once. For those with attention problems, however—and this is important—the information is constantly bombarding them from the inside, not the outside. In children with ADD, the system is trying to pay attention to the additional input—which is normal, not an aberration. The disease, if it exists at all, is the result of electrical input that floods the cortex, much like what happens during shock therapy.

The child with ADD cannot manage complex instructions because he is being prodded all the time by signals in the lower brain. Any new information becomes overwhelming: "Just go to the right two blocks, and then one block to the left, and then go straight to the roundabout, and then . . ." We have already lost him because his internal input is crowding out the information. And, of course, he cannot sit still because there is information that needs connection and resolution. That cannot happen if he has no access to his early imprinted memories.

Naturally, this creates problems in school. The child cannot get down to things quickly and start a project or an article because there is so much going on in his brain. Others get impatient when he does not turn in his work on time, but the reason the child is constantly distracted is because he has little cerebral control. Information is constantly climbing upward and forward in the brain, in attempt to establish a connection so that the system can improve functioning.

These gating problems often get their start late in pregnancy when trauma prevents the evolution of prefrontal cortical cells, and cells that carry information from the right to the left hemisphere via the corpus callosum. Children are left without the cerebral equipment to control impulses thereafter. We know, further, that the prefrontal area often attempts to control right subcortical feelings, shutting them down for a time. When control is weak it is harder to put off an impulse, to reflect and ponder rather than to act. But those impulses are imprints originating deep down in the brainstem centers, and as with the salamander, snake, or shark, they are there for an evolutionary reason: to strike, attack, or flee at the instant when it is necessary to do so for survival. They come out of those primitive brains and are essential, as well, for our survival—for example, needing to swerve to avoid a car accident. In such circumstances, we do not want to be too reflective. We need to act immediately to survive.

Now think of the snake; it too must act immediately for its survival. This fight or flight response is not an aberration unless our primitive snake brain overtakes the rest of our cerebrum and permanently runs the show. In a way, in children with ADD that is exactly what is happening. What are these children fleeing from? Danger. Menace. Feelings that are overwhelming. Pain that is much too much to bear. Suffering that threatens their mental stability. This deep-level pain has to be contained.

The ADDer is often an underachiever because he can never stay focused on anything long enough to learn it properly. Later in life, he may become a salesman: someone with the gift of gab who talks continually to relieve anxiety. If others snub him, he may well suffer from low self esteem, as the PBS special suggested. Often he develops the feeling that he cannot succeed because success requires the kind of sustained effort that his scattered mind cannot handle. Eventually, he may find a job that suits him and will allow for distractibility, but do not ask him to be calm and to follow directions. His brain will revolt. With so much input surging upward from lower levels, even a simple idea becomes overwhelming; it is all too much, literally.

I have treated enough of those who have ADD to know what a successful therapy entails, and it is not advice, even though that might help a little.

One of my senior therapists is a classic ADDer. He never went to college because he was sure he could not concentrate well enough to succeed in his classes. Thankfully, he can now, and he is on his way to earning a doctorate. As his case history illustrates, he arrived there through primal therapy.

case history

I was diagnosed with hyperactivity in 1957, at the age of seven. It manifested the following symptoms:

- Trouble concentrating
- Limited cohesion of thought
- Inattention
- Difficulty focusing
- Difficulty doing daily tasks
- Prone to distraction
- Experiencing boredom quite easily
- Disorganization
- Cluttered and messy room and, later on, a cluttered and messy desk
- Trouble initiating and finishing jobs and tasks, as well as underestimating the time able to complete a task

- Shoplifting as a kid
- Substance abuse as an adolescent
- Impulsivity
- Trouble maintaining temper and being patient
- Interrupting others while they are talking
- Tactless expression of ideas (blurting out thoughts without thinking them through, first)
- Acting with disregard of future consequences
- Functioning in a socially unacceptable manner.
- Struggle with managing feelings, specifically anger and frustration
- Mood swings
- Constant struggle to hide symptoms and work harder
- A sense of underachievement
- Inability to achieve same levels of success as my peers

The feelings associated with this disorder, at bottom, have been feelings of failure. I have grown up expecting failure, feeling I can't do anything right . . .

Therapy has been difficult for me. The feelings have not been easy to feel. It has taken a long time, and lots of work, which is also the nature of my imprint, meaning that therapy has been an analog of my birth.

On one such occasion during therapy, at certain points in the session, I would find myself with the impulse to push my head against the padded therapy room wall, usually after a feeling of frustration (from not being able to "get to" the feeling and get out of the mess I was in) or after a childhood feeling of nobody wanting me. It felt familiar, although I had no conscious memory of its familiarity. It was a sensation in my body, that's all I knew. As I was pushing my head into the wall, my breath gave out, and my throat had completely locked up. The muscles in my throat had completely seized, and I couldn't get air, no matter how I tried. I could not voluntarily relax them, nor change their position. There was no constriction of my body movements, there was plenty of air in the room, but I couldn't move or get any air. There was nothing that I could do, or that could be done, no one to save me. It seemed like a long time, minutes at least, though it was probably about ten to fifteen seconds. It felt endless. After the experience, I realized I had been in the grips of a terrible early memory. It was pure terror—the feeling, connection, and insight all rolled into one. And it's everything. I mean to say, it's my life, where my body never experiences calmness. It's what drives me in everything I do. And it's there because it's always been there, compounded by parents who didn't want me. I once asked my father if I was a planned birth. He replied, "Well, let's just say you came at a bad time." My mother would force me into a corner to sit still and not move. She wanted to be with her friend to talk about her problems, paint her fingernails, or do whatever she wanted to do, except pay attention to—or have anything to do with—me. I wasn't allowed to go out and play, or be held or touched, or to do things that would help discharge any energy I had inside. So the pressure would just keep building and building, without any escape valve for release. There are many childhood feelings involved, such as not being wanted, nor listened to, understood, nor cared about, but the feelings of failure seem to underscore all of it. Both in childhood and earlier. It's what I struggle against.

I've spoken to other primal therapy patients who have had first-line Primals. One said that in her Primals her mouth stretches wide, and that she can do nothing to stop it, that it's completely involuntary, but I found only one other that said he encountered the same experience I had relived. I don't wish it on anyone. I don't go to that feeling voluntarily. It is extremely difficult to feel. But life has been difficult, and nothing else has touched the roots of my ADHD. My feelings of failure are quite strong, and after therapy some of the fear and terror abates. For brief periods of time I can experience what it is to walk down the street and feel what life is like without the "normal" accompanying pressure and fear. For me it is a luxury of feeling, this absence of terror. Although I'm quite aware that for other people this is a normal mode of existence, for me it is an extraordinary achievement.

case history

Throughout my life, in every major endeavor, I have given my all in the struggle for success. Each time I would work long hours filled with enthusiasm, damn the sleepless nights, damn the overwork, damn every obstacle, whether it was my restaurant, my advertising agency, or whatever along the way. With each I would progress to what I perceived as the pinnacle of success . . . then, like magic, it would all collapse and turn to shit. I would be left broken, awash in pain, feeling helpless and worthless, and thinking of suicide. Oft-times it would take years for me to recover enough to begin anew, to go on to the next big project—the next big stone to roll up that hill.

Finally, in my late fifties, at the end of my last great failure, I became extremely ill and convinced my life was over; I was welcoming the opportunity for death. But in 2005 some weird fortune landed me in primal therapy.

I had no trouble getting to my feelings. I was what they call a mélange. All my feelings, at all three levels, were coming up at once. On the surface it was an ugly business with all that pain, but at the end of each session, I would be more relaxed and feel better than at any time that I can remember.

Early on in my therapy I began descending into birth feelings. Now I was quite skeptical of the whole notion of birth Primals. I could not wrap my mind around the idea of having a clear memory without pictures in my head. Nonetheless, here I was: I was in the middle of a devastating toddler feeling. At that time in my life I suffered severe eczema. My parents would put socks on my hands and tie them to the bars in my crib, so I could not scratch myself until bloody, then leave me there alone to cry myself to sleep. The itch, the helpless feeling of being so restrained, and the abandonment by my mother was hideous.

But then the feeling took a new turn. It slowly became all physical. I started to cough. The itch and restraint became the pain of being crushed. I felt smothered. Then as though there was some camshaft-like machine inside me, my body went into a writhing, waving dolphin motion. My head pushed against the padded wall in the therapy room. Time lost meaning. It was just forever. The feeling of suffocation was like sharp needles from deep inside my chest jabbing out through every pore of my whole body. This next part is a little difficult for me to explain because during the feeling there were no words. The words came after, when I was integrating the feelings and connections with the help of my therapist. I pushed and strained and pushed and strained, as the feelings became more intense. I felt like I was doing something wrong. There is something the matter with me, I thought. It's too much. I'm dying. The terror and panic accelerated until I got to a point when I thought I was going to make it through, and was finally going to be free . . . but no . . . too late . . . I was spent. I gave up to die. My whole body gave up the ghost and collapsed. Then my body went into wave after wave of the most radical trembling I could ever imagine.

This sequence repeated itself (I didn't seem to be in the driver's seat) again and again until my body just quit. It had felt all it could stand for now. The feeling slowly dissipated and left me drained but relaxed. It was as good as feeling gets. No fear; no panic, terror, nor tension. Life felt good.

Then in discussing with my therapist what I was going through, I made the connection that what I had just experienced is the pattern of my life: struggle, fight, suffer, and plough forward to success . . . and then collapse—give up the ghost to death. I was amazed at the clarity, and obviousness of the connections.

"So," you say, "that's all nice, but what does that get you?"

The short of it, in Janov's language, is that when those feelings come up at times when they are restimulated, the valence will be reduced. (Here I should add that this Primal was not a one shot deal. After some years I am still having to relive that scene or related scenes. This is because I can only tolerate such excruciating pain from 10 to 30 seconds at a shot; my birth, as I know now, was besought with this agony over a course of hours or days. That's a lot of pain to feel in order to free myself of it.) In addition when those feelings come up, I know what they really are, and I can separate those historical feelings from my present life.

But let me elaborate to give you a more concrete context. After about a year and a half of reliving those birth scenes repeatedly, I realized that I was not close to death, and had a brand new life to live. I decided to go to graduate school and get my master's degree in marriage and family therapy. Applying and getting accepted is no easy chore, especially for an old man. California State University, in San Bernardino, gets a lot of applications, but they only accept twelve students a year. From the get-go all those old birth feelings came up. I felt weak and helpless, convinced my efforts would be for naught. I told my therapist, "What's the use. Even if I got accepted, which I probably won't, I'll be 70 when I graduate." And he said, "Yes, and you will be 70 if you don't." Every time I thought about all I had to do just to apply made my arms feel weak, and I found myself thinking, what's the use? I had to get references, and it had been so long since I was in college, most of my old professors were already dead. I had to write a letter of intent, which meant the best pitch letter I've ever written in my life. But, as push came to shove, I could do all that because I had felt so much of my pain in its proper context. I knew the enemy, and had sufficiently weakened it by reliving those ruinous events of my history to where they no longer had complete control over what I did. I didn't have to fail. I had real choice.

case history

I have had a hard time focusing on one subject at a time. At this point I am literally driven to distraction. When I try to focus I feel a great agitation inside; I cannot sit still, and I need to move. I get bored almost immediately and I want to bang my head against the wall. I need something exciting to keep my attention. I need a high level of stimulation in order to focus:

something that matches the amount of stimulation and distraction from inside. This stimulation comes from my whole life, but no doubt started while my mother was carrying me. She did not want me, and I was at best an inconvenience.

All of the rage and anxiety has stayed inside and kept me agitated. That overrides everything. I am obliged to keep focusing on the past because I know I have to resolve the pain, and I simply cannot. It is everywhere inside me, and that is why I cannot relax. That agitation inside has the feeling and the valence of a life-and-death event. It is therefore urgent and demands attention.

I could never get my father and mother to care about me and to feel they wanted me, so I could feel wanted. In my Primals, I would try to make them love me and then feel that it was me (and my ADD) that they didn't like. "Can't they see that I have a good heart and that I am a good person?" They never recognized my existence from the beginning because I was a terrible intrusion into their lives. My mother would never let me sit on her lap. All my need for affection was thwarted and those needs just stayed inside.

I felt in my birth that I could not move forward, could not get anywhere, and was frustrated with no outlet. In my Primals, as I try to get out, my breathing becomes erratic and I feel that I have to push harder, and then panic sets in and I become agitated and overwhelmed. I feel stuck and doom sets in; I am going to die and there is nothing I can do about it. Helpless and hopeless. Whenever I am blocked and helpless, I always have to push harder to keep that feeling away. Again, I am in constant tumult. I feel I am being crushed. The only device left to me to move forward was to try to breathe out. Here my throat seized on me and I could no longer breathe; I could not get any air in. I was terrified and that feeling stayed all of my life. So it is no wonder I could not concentrate. And there is the ADD, which is now leaving bit by bit.

19

the root cause of Alzheimer's and deep depression

There is more and more evidence pointing to one key aspect in the development of Alzheimer's disease, namely, too little oxygen at the very start of life. Researchers believe that the brain, in constant adaptation to the early imprint of reduced oxygen, may gradually lose its ability to retrieve information. It is saying, in effect, "I am lacking supplies," as it struggles to adjust to an inhospitable environment. If an adequate supply of oxygen is not delivered to the fetus in the critical window during gestation and at birth, problems may continue throughout the life cycle. Over time we find a deterioration of cognitive functioning, including a change in the amount and strength of certain synapses. When the oxygen deprivation occurs at certain times in the pregnancy (and we are still learning when these are), the adaptation may become almost immutable.

One striking example of this effect is found in the recent work of Weihong Song, Canada's research chair in Alzheimer's disease and a professor of psychiatry at the University of British Columbia, in Vancouver.[1] Song put young mice engineered to develop amyloid, an Alzheimer's-like plaque, in reduced oxygen chambers for one month. Six months later the oxygen-deprived mice had developed twice as many amyloidal plaques as similar animals raised normally. It turns out that one major culprit in Alzheimer's disease is the increased clumping of these plaques, which ultimately turn into the disease itself. In Song's study, not only were these plaques larger than normal, but also the

hypoxic mice had a hard time navigating the maze—a task which depends on normal memory processes. (More technically, beta amyloid
is formed when a gene known as BACE1 produces an enzyme that cuts
long strands of harmless amyloid protein into the harmful plaques.)
This ultimately can result in the type of cell death we find in Alzheimer's patients.

More information is coming forth all the time on this subject. A
study published in the journal *Neurobiology of Aging* used monkeys,
some with adequate cages and others with far-too-small cages, to see
what that kind of stress did to the animals later on.[2] Those animals
with no room to move around or exercise were more stressed, with
higher levels of stress hormones; they also had more of the amyloid
plagues. In another study, reported in *Science Daily*, scientists at the
Max Planck Institute of Psychiatry found that fewer than ten percent of
Alzheimer's cases have a genetic basis. "Our findings show that stress
hormones and stress can cause changes in the tau protein like those
that arise in Alzheimer's disease," notes Osborne Almeida.[3] In short,
life experience alters our propensity for disease.

What I want to underline is how early all this occurs. Here again
the experiences with the greatest impact, those that endure and alter
our neurobiology, seem to happen while we are being carried. There is
an allusion in the article to the role of stress in Parkinson's disease, as
well, and other recent studies have tied early experience to the later development of psychosis. As I've said, all roads lead to Rome. It is logical
that experience while the brain and physiologic system are developing
has a major influence on our lives, for our maturing organs and tissues
are incredibly sensitive during this time.

The connection between oxygen deprivation and memory loss may
derive from what is, in essence, a neural fuel shortage. Much like an
automobile needs gasoline to fuel the engine, a brain needs oxygen to
do its work. When the brain is hyper-stimulated it expends oxygen at
a high rate. There is a corresponding increase in the manufacture of
amyloid plaque, particularly in the region dealing with memory retrieval. The brain can tolerate only so much of this pain, it seems, before amyloid plaque accumulates and memory is jeopardized. In our
therapy, we've managed to lower the frequency and amplitude of pa-

tients' brainwaves so that, over time, the brain expends less oxygen. We think that eventually this might curtail the damaging effects of amyloid plaque on the memory system.

Another encouraging sign for patients with memory loss is the success we've had, in therapy, in normalizing patients' body temperatures. Changes in readings taken at intake from those at exit may indicate that we are reaching early imprints where memory loss originates. To understand how this works, one needs to keep in mind that there are a series of oxygen-conservation measures that an organism employs as a response to hypoxia. First, there is a constriction of blood vessels, accompanied by constricted breathing and radically reduced physical movement. There is also a significant reduction in vital signs—blood pressure, heart rate, and body temperature; the system basically slows down to survive. Body temperature, which appears to be an accurate index of how much oxygen we had at birth, is one of the main ways we know our patients are suffering. The more oxygen-deprivation trauma at birth, the more likely there will be lowered body temperature later on. When we return to origins in primal therapy, we can possibly re-route the brain and re-circuit our physiologic responses so that we are no longer prisoners of our hypoxic histories.

Important research in this area is now being done by Gary Lynch, a well-known neurobiologist at the University of California, Irving. Lynch found that with very early trauma there was a later likelihood of memory problems.[4] After years of suppressing feelings there seems to be a "caving in" of the externally oriented prefrontal area as neurons under constant pressure from the early imprint begin to die. In studies of rodents, Lynch found that the hippocampus, an area of the brain known to be concerned with memory, tends to diminish in size when the animals are exposed to stress. In addition, mice that have their hippocampi surgically tampered with are much more excitable and prone to anxiety states; they do not adapt well. In short, one's neurophysiologic responses to very early events may be integral to the later development of Alzheimer's.

As I've suggested, heavy anesthesia or painkillers given to the pregnant mother at birth can seriously diminish the oxygen levels in the newborn, as can strangulation on the umbilical cord, or being blocked from egress. Worse, this oxygen deficiency may be imprinted into the entire physiologic system, thereby damaging the brain and, perhaps, affecting the part of the limbic system that deals with memory: the hippocampus. In other words, low oxygen during birth may set up a template that gradually diminishes memory over a span of decades. The imprint progressively gnaws away at limbic structures until the appearance of the full-blown disease around the age of seventy. Even after the onset of Alzheimer's, the imprint continues to do damage because it remains an active and unresolved force, a reminder to the brain that there is not enough oxygen; and there very well may not be.

There are two key ways this affliction can be addressed. One is to actually increase the oxygen supply to the brain through oxygen drops taken daily or hyperbaric oxygen treatments done over weeks. The other strategy, preferable in my view, is to relive the lack of oxygen when it really mattered—at birth. I want to reiterate a key point here, even if a bit repetitive. When we relive oxygen deprivation at birth or before we reopen the channels for oxygen delivery—that is, we return to the occasion of trauma and experience the event again, this time with a mature brain, such that breathing normalizes and resting oxygen levels stabilize. Reliving the exact event—from possibly four or five decades earlier—enables the victim to finally incorporate the event into consciousness at the uppermost cortical levels. That is an extraordinary breakthrough, for it means that afflictions such as Alzheimer's can perhaps be alleviated. If we dampen the force of the imprint, we may be able to reset the clock, restoring the natural balance in the brain.

Of course more research will be needed to validate these theories, and what I've enumerated here is merely a starting point. For those who wish to test this framework in a more rigorous scientific fashion, a simple project would be to compare those patients with Alzheimer's against a control group in good health and see if the dementia group had a troubled birth or gestational history. At the Primal Center we plan to test this basic hypothesis in the near future. We want to look at a history of the painkillers and anesthetics taken by pregnant mothers. We believe we'll find a correlation between Alzheimer's diagnosis and exposure to painkillers that reduce oxygen to the fetus. This is not to say that hypoxia at birth is the only cause of Alzheimer's disease, but it may be a key factor that has been ignored.

Apart from Alzheimer's disease, all of this also underlies much of the deep depression I have seen (see *Janov Solution* for a full discussion), in which a drop in core body temperature accompanies a personality of constant exhaustion and helplessness. Once again, what appears to be happening is that body, in response to hypoxia, is momentarily running on the earlier temperature conditions preset in the womb; the system is doing its best to avoid a mismatch between supply and demand.[5] In a sense, the whole personality seems to shrivel up, constricting rather than expanding, and not just metaphorically. When the depressed person speaks he exhales less air; his words hardly escape his mouth, and there is an air of fatigue about him. During primal therapy, as such patients get close to deep early feelings of womb-life and birth, their body temperature can fall three degrees in minutes as the experience of asphyxiation is being relived. The low oxygen imprint may also explain why neonates born to smoking mothers are frequently born at lower birth weights.

An experiment reported by G. Bonsignore and his team investigated what happens to rats born with reduced oxygen.[6] Those females who were born with limited oxygen were less loving to their offspring; they were slow to retrieve pups and less likely to lick their offspring with frequency. The author believes that hypoxia at birth results later in "arousal deficit." It seems that the animals had less energy and that, possibly, there were reduced dopamine levels in their systems; they were simply not as aggressive or energetic. Clearly the study has implications for humans. According to some studies, as many as 50 percent of us are born without adequate amounts of oxygen. Depletion of energy, then, is one way that hypoxia at or near birth shows its effects.

In some respects, depression can be as fatal a condition as heavy smoking. It is not a benign affliction that we can eradicate with pills. A survey of more than 60,000 individuals by King's College, in London, and the University of Bergen, in Norway, for instance, found that the early mortality rate for depressives and smokers was about the same.[7] This, indeed, supports my notion that one of the great risk factors for terminal illness is repression. We need to understand how deep "deep" is because otherwise we shall be skimming the surface of depression, leaving the root cause to continue its destruction.

As therapists, we must be cautious about deciding what key feelings a patient should or is feeling. However, after observing thousands of sessions over decades, I believe that hopelessness and helplessness lie at the base of numerous other feelings. These are the feelings that usually accompany life-and-death gestational or birth traumas, and what so many patients report to me in describing their reliving. Part of this, of course, may be tied to the massive physiologic effort it requires to prevent gestational trauma from surfacing. Repression of womb-life events is nearly always a life-and-death matter.

PART FOUR: TOWARD A FEELING THERAPY

20

the role of evolution in psychotherapy

When scientists were polled recently about the greatest discovery in science, the majority chose Darwin's theory of evolution. That is not terribly surprising. It explains so much in so many fields of scientific endeavor. Yet the concept of evolution is rarely applied to psychotherapy, particularly when it comes to the treatment of emotional problems, and in fact it may be essential to improving our mental health.

The brain develops in three major cycles, first described by the American physician and neuroscientist Paul MacLean.[1] I describe them as instinct, feeling, and thinking. As discussed earlier, each evolved and was itself a major part of the brain of our animal forebearers. To summarize this simply, and perhaps a bit crudely, we inherited our instinctual brain from reptiles and our feeling brain from primates. Those animals are alive inside of us: their brains are still functional, otherwise we would not see in humans many of the primitive responses we see in animals. It is necessary to take the evolution of the brain into account to understand how and when ideas arrive and what neural soil they grow out of. It may seem fatuous to claim that psychoanalysts, cognitive behavioral therapists, and other insight therapists are anti-evolutionists, but when one addresses ideas in therapy without regard to their evolution or history, that is the only conclusion I can come to. In some respects, current approaches to psychotherapy are equivalent to geological studies examining the earth and, without ever looking at the fossil evidence, concluding it is just a few thousand years old. We are skimming the surface and missing the substrata.

I have often called my therapy "evolution in reverse," because we must treat the areas of the brain in reverse order to how they developed in human evolution. Thoughts bereft of feelings are, in essence, homeless; they have no roots. Any proper psychotherapy must adhere to the laws of biology and evolution; we need to find our emotional roots, the basis for so many of our thoughts and beliefs. In therapy, when we follow our history in reverse it must adhere to the natural order of things. Many approaches that contain elements similar to primal therapy are ineffective and damaging because they violate this order. Rebirthing therapy, for instance, defies evolutionary principles by attacking the most remote and early imprints first. We must start by addressing problems in the present, giving ourselves a good foundation in regard to our current lives and associated feelings before arriving much later at the deeper, instinctive brain.

Any ploy or mechanism by a therapist that defies evolution will end in failure because evolution is merciless and unrelenting; it is how we survived, and will not allow us to cheat its principles. If evolution is neglected it will perforce end in abreaction: the release of feeling without connection and resolution. Bioenergetics, for instance, which focuses on the patient's body and muscles, violates that law. Likewise, trying to achieve bodily release through the mantra of Gestalt therapy, "act like an ape!" is inadequate. LSD and hallucinogens completely disregard the neurologic order of the nervous system and spray feelings everywhere, eliminating any chance of possible connection. A Primal, however, teaches us about our evolution because it follows the neuraxis precisely, telling us where and how that evolution took place.

Some years ago my colleague, neurologist Michael Holden, and I did a study of ten subjects who each had been through more than ten LSD trips. They all had a similar brain pattern—low-voltage, fast signals; and they all had sleep problems due to leaky gates. One temporary positive effect of their weakened gating system was that they had more access to their feelings. The downside was that the leaky gates persisted and caused all kinds of problems later on; I mean years later on. In an electroencephalograph (EEG), voltage can be a measure of how many neurons are recruited in the service of repression; as pain mounts, amplitude goes up in an effort to hold back the upsweeping pain. But for

subjects exposed to multiple doses of LSD we see lower voltage amplitude, indicating, presumably, that the brain cannot manage to gather
enough neurons to repress. This happens in some drug psychothera-
pies that blast the gating system wide open in a hurry to get to the unconscious. What we have is instantaneous primal therapy with all its
inherent dangers: a therapy that violates evolution.

Perhaps the easiest way to understand all this is by revisiting Darwin's theory, taking the core principles of species' survival and applying them to the brain. Each new brain level in evolution helps out
with survival; otherwise it would not be there. As discussed earlier, the
brainstem and early limbic system have everything to do with survival.
They control our breathing, blood pressure, heart rate, and body temperature. The neocortex, last in the evolutionary line, detects not only
external enemies but also maladaptive feelings. In so doing, it helps us
survive by disconnecting us from the source of our pain. At the bottom of all this lies a self we will never meet again until we have access
to deep brain structures. That may be never; imprinted pain may kill
us prematurely if we don't exercise the right method to combat it—and
that method is a therapy rooted in feelings.

Ideas cannot trump feelings, neither in insight therapy nor through
stubborn efforts to talk ourselves out of our obsessions and phobias.
The reason is this: ideas developed later in evolution and are less essential to our survival. That's not to say the neocortex is unimportant
to survival—it is very important but its concerns are less immediately
dire. When someone is in a coma without a functional neocortex his
survival functions (heart rate, blood pressure, etc.) are still operation-
al. Animals, too, survive very well without a complex neocortex. They
won't survive, however, if the brainstem is damaged: breathing is a pre-
condition for life.

Each lower level of brain function is designed to keep us alive.
Lower levels may modify higher ones but the process does not work in
reverse. Imagine if the higher-level neocortex could permanently modify brainstem functions, could tell the lower brain to stop breathing,
for instance. We survive because it cannot. Feelings can certainly sway
ideas but ideas can only suppress feelings, not eradicate them. We see
in our therapy how physiology and limbic feelings directly affect ideas

and beliefs. A very rapid heart rate can push someone to be active, yet no matter how hard we try we often cannot permanently alter the heart rate—especially when the rate is accompanied by high anxiety. Ideas are hundreds of millions years away from physiological and emotional functions. Before we can address them, we must target the lower brain impulses that drive us.

If we understand what happens to us in the womb and later is re-represented on higher brain levels, then when traumas affect the more primitive levels (a smoking or drug-using mother who diminishes oxygen levels to the fetus, for instance) we may treat them accordingly. Often therapy aims, mistakenly in my view, to correct distorted ideas by adjusting a patient's patterns of thought: her ability, through upper-level cortical structures, to re-script a current situation. "After all your husband is not that bad," the therapist says. "Why not try to accept him as he is?" But if the underpinnings of ideas are not first addressed, the ideas themselves will not be altered in an organic and lasting way.

pain's neurological evolution

One might say we are prisoners of the brain's evolution; we come out of antiquity into modern life, having been conducted through centuries of neurological development, always in the proper order. We can no more change that order than we do in sleep, where, if we do not spend enough time dreaming—attaining a state of second-line limbic consciousness in the process—we suffer. When that happens psychosis lurks; we develop physical and mental symptoms. As with sleep, which follows a regular, sequential progression, primal therapy must strictly obey evolutionary edicts, meaning it must enter the deep unconscious slowly and progressively. Down on that deep level lie many of our remote, life-and-death pains. These show themselves in nightmares associated with terrible anxiety states. When the pain inside a nightmare surges upward into consciousness, what happens? Psychotic ideation. It is as though the pain and emotional content rise unabated, in pure form, into our thinking apparatus.

We do not take patients into birth traumas in the first weeks of therapy for the same reason that in dream sleep we do not go directly into deep sleep. Evolution is an ordered affair. We must not superimpose our theory or techniques on patients. The rule is that it is not up to us to decide for the patient. It is always the patient and his readiness that dictates our approach.

Some patients are skeptical of this autonomy, or embrace it in a way that contradicts what more than forty years of research has taught us. I remember seeing a patient who had just started therapy; he told me that since hc had forgiven his parents he felt much better: proof, in his mind, that ideas can trump feelings. Yet when he was measured his stress hormone levels had not changed. Although he thought he was better, the empirical evidence suggested otherwise.

In truth, the neocortex is quite adept at deceiving itself. It produces the thought of being well without actually making us well. But what's the difference? At some point, doesn't the thought that we are well amount to the same thing as actually being well? Not really: the higher-order brain looks at itself subjectively and misinterprets what it sees. In therapy, we don't want to be anesthetized in order to get well because that leaves us cut off from our feelings, disconnected from the source of our joy and sorrow. The same is true if we are constantly trying to convince ourselves we feel fine when we don't feel fine.

The brain is complex and multilayered. To stay on any one level in therapy to the exclusion of the others means that any progress made is partial. If we stay only on the emotional level and cry and cry without higher-level connection there will be no progress. If, instead, we focus exclusively on the top level and discuss feelings without their profound experience, then we will fail, as well. Using neurofeedback or bieofeedback to reprogram the brain is also deficient. In this case, the therapist establishes the norm to which the patient must adhere, and the patient is imprisoned by the dictates of so-called "normal brainwaves." To bring these approaches together in a meaningful way, we must take a closer look at evolution.

Scientists from several countries recently convened to discuss the possible evolution of dinosaurs.[2] There were many explanations, few satisfying. One, however, seemed credible. The question was which came first: dinosaurs or birds? Since fossils were found of feathered dinosaurs, scientists theorized that dinosaurs predated birds in evolution. They studied filmed footage of birds found near an excavation site and discovered that the birds had similar appendages to dinosaurs. In analyzing the birds' behavior, the scientists discovered that the birds were born knowing only how to run. It was only later, as their personal evolution continued, that the birds began to fly. This evidence added credibility to the notion that birds came second, not first; that birds evolved from dinosaurs, not the reverse. It remains a moot question but it has led me to think about our own therapy: how current observation can be a powerful tool in which to test the validity of evolutionary hypotheses.

When we observe a primal session we are really exploring evolution: both the individual's personal history (ontogeny) and the history of the human species (phylogeny). It is my position, as I've said, that unless the system is allowed to follow evolution exactly there will only be abreaction and not a connected, resolved feeling; that's why we need to pay close attention to evolution. During a reliving of birth, where we *will* find skyrocketing vital signs, we *will not* find crying like we see in a two-year-old, nor will we find radical movements of the legs and arms, nor any words whatsoever. All these come later in personal evolution. To summon these reactions at the wrong time is to defy evolution and violate biology and how it progresses.

The minute a patient who is reliving something from early childhood uses words like entertaining, satisfactory, disappointing, we know he is not in the feeling brain and the experience is not authentic. A five-year-old does not normally use sophisticated words to describe feelings, and so we can be fairly certain that the reliving is an adult's fabrication. One's cognitive ability, in other words, is a check on the reality of what the patient shows us in therapy. If we don't know how the brain develops, at least minimally, then we might err in therapy; worse, we might push the patient beyond his tolerance level: where evolution allows him to go for the moment. That will accomplish nothing but to overload the system and encourage symbolic acting-out.

When we observe progress during a session we are seeing how the brain works: what functions it uses to protect us and how it recruits thoughts in a way that can make us, at once, safe and neurotic. We learn the laws of fetal and infant evolution: what the critical needs are during early development and how they can be fulfilled, so as to avoid later neurosis. We learn that it is virtually impossible to satisfy needs that are long past their due date. Most of all, we learn what biologic laws not to violate, so that we can proceed in a therapeutic sequence that leads to healing.

Applying an evolutionary perspective also means departing from some of my earlier descriptions of primal therapy in *The Primal Scream*. When we place therapy in an evolutionary context we know, for instance, that screams follow grunts in evolution. On the way out of the womb, but not fully out, a child does not have the capacity to scream. Thus, if we force screaming in therapy, we may be defying the course of evolution. If we try to make something dramatic happen to prove how smart and effective we are, then the patient will suffer. If we are patient and trust evolution, we'll be on the right track.

therapy as a time machine: stem cells, cancer, and Darwin revisited

Is therapy nothing more than a time machine, a means to revisit our history, to turn back the clock to previously neutral, non-neurotic states? It may sound far-fetched, but more and more evidence suggests it's true. As I discussed earlier, scientists are now learning how to wind back the developmental clock on the microscopic level—taking a current skin cell, for example, and treating it so that it returns to a previously neutral, uncommitted state: an embryonic state. Once that is done, the cell can be reprogrammed to become another kind of cell.

During this critical window certain needs must be fulfilled and, if they are not, cells may become imprinted in adverse ways. As I pointed out earlier, gestational stress may leave its mark on genes through the process of methylation, producing alterations in hippocampal cells that affect later memory. The assumption by some researchers is that the process of methylation may be altered. Their thinking is that when the patient goes back to the neurophysiologic state where the imprint occurred, the imprint can be adjusted, leading to a normalization of the cell. Here's another way to put it: once a mark is made on the cell we are psychologically and physiologically affected for life, until, and only until, the inciting event is revisited and relived. And it can be relived unconsciously; it can be re-experienced without a specific awareness of it once we are locked into the memory circuit.

What happens in our therapy, I believe, is a sort of neural time warp: when patients relive traumatic events that preceded and caused a neurotic deviation, they return to a neutral state of internal harmony. That harmony is not only what the patient reports but what his brainwaves, immune system, vital functions, and neurophysiology indicate. Again, it is evolution in reverse: we go back to the brain originally involved in laying down the experience. But we cannot do that if the therapist and patient are engaged in psychic badinage regarding present-day events.

So what does devolution in therapy really entail? It means, first and foremost, not to skip evolutionary steps. It means a therapeutic setting that encourages reflection and introspection: a right-brain, lower-level therapy versus a left-brain, cortical-level approach. It means beginning in therapy with the most recent traumas and letting the vehicle of feeling carry us back in history to related earlier events. We target the late brain neocortex first and work back in time to preverbal life. Unlike rebirthers, who lead patients into birth traumas long before the system can integrate them, we do not reach infancy and pre-birth events until far into therapy. As I've suggested, that results in abreaction: going through the emotions of feeling without its full physiologic content.

A proper therapy begins with a basic understanding of neurophysiology so that the therapist knows what to expect on each evolutionary level visited by the patient. That means not provoking a patient to express in words a preverbal feeling. It means knowing when a patient is ready for the experience of a deep early feeling, carefully titrating vital signs and seeing how they are affecting the whole person, not pushing patients to go somewhere before they are ready. Most important, it means recognizing what a birth imprint looks like and what a reliving looks like. Sometimes reliving birth trauma and pre-birth trauma is not necessary in therapy, but when it is needed we don't arrive there until late in the course of treatment. Deeply depressed patients usually begin therapy exhibiting deep hopelessness and very low body temperature. Before delving too far into the origins of that deep-level despair, we need to understand how to normalize vital signs and consider what kind of feelings the patient can accept.

When we finally arrive at birth events late in therapy we are more able to live in the present. This is what is meant by revisiting the past to ensure the present: the deeper we go in history, the less it has its grip on our current life and the closer we get to wellness. Ultimately, we are discussing the meaning of freedom—to be liberated from our history; to be free from the prison of our past.

When we wonder whether we can call a therapy scientific or not we have only to ask, "Does it elucidate and clarify the properties of nature?" We cannot ask whether it works because that is subjective; it depends on the criterion we use. If behavior changes for a time do we have a cure? Is there still a gnawing tension in the body? Elevated cortisol readings? Is the blood pressure too high? The important differences inherent in these questions distinguish scientific questions from those that require a moral perspective alone. Science relies on quantifiable assessment, but it also relies on qualitative human results. Do we know more about humanity in this therapy, or are we only after some sort of pragmatic, mechanical solution that "works"? Are we doing deep breathing because it happens to be in vogue? Are we matching our brainwaves to some empirical ideal? Absolutely not. Here the focus is on the technique, not the patient, nor their evolution, alone. That is the major difference. When we focus on how the patient evolves we learn; when we decide on how we treat him beforehand we don't. It is not a matter of defying evolution, but rather of harnessing it for the good of mankind. That is Darwin's legacy.

21

on the corrective emotional experience

In the era of Freud and psychoanalysis the linchpin of therapy was the analysis of transference: how the patient responded to the doctor and, in turn, how the doctor responded to the patient. The whole idea was to change the patient through a corrective emotional relationship, help him to be more independent, rely less on the doctor for advice, love, and guidance. Decades later, the notion of the corrective emotional experience has gained many adherents. The present-day theory is that it is not enough to relive early trauma, the therapist must follow the reliving with a corrective experience that will allow the patient to make progress and change. Allowing the patient to wallow in his pain, the thinking goes, only reinforces neurosis.

So why not create a new ending to a traumatic memory? Why not replace painful feelings associated with early events with healthier, more empowering modes of thought? At first glance this strategy may seem appealing, but it is a concocted science that defies the patient's reality. It is not our job to rewrite history. It is enough to help patients learn about themselves and their history. Once that happens patients can heal by themselves.

But isn't it true that patients who relive without rewriting the ending to their early experiences continue to suffer and be neurotic? One only comes to that conclusion in the absence of clinical experience. What we have seen year after year is that reliving, in and of itself, leads to profound changes in the neurologic, psychologic, and physiologic systems through integration. Over and over in double-blind studies there have

LIFE BEFORE BIRTH

been changes in brain functioning, hormone secretion and, above all, changes in how the patient feels about himself and his world. There is a systemic decrease in body temperature and blood pressure, which does not happen in those who abreact and fail to connect their early feelings to conscious awareness. What I call abreaction, the discharge of the feeling in the third-line brain, is a random event that does not follow neurologic functioning.

Many clinics and mental health professionals claim to be doing primal therapy, yet the results show that the patient continues to suffer; hence, the notion that patients, after a reliving, wallow in pain. If only the higher level, the frontal cortex, is addressed—even if issues are resolved on that level—it will indeed look as though the patient is in inordinate pain. Lacking the theory and techniques to go deeper into early developing brain structures, it is easy for therapists to misinterpret what is happening.

Providing a different ending to a traumatic memory depends, in too many cases, on the imagination of the doctor supplying it. Clearly this is not an organic affair. And what happens when each doctor provides the corrective narrative in a different way? Are there several different scenarios for a single patient? Implicit in this approach is that the doctor knows best. Wrong, it is the patient and his unconscious who knows best. If there were no connection we would not see the systematic physiological changes we find in our therapy.

Reliving is sufficient for healing, but it must be a true reliving; when we provide a script for the patient any reliving that results is a fabrication. Our job is not to cheerlead the patient away from reality, nor to help him lead a symbolic life. In fact, it is that pseudo-reality which has been driving the patient to act-out, have fits of rage, suffer from diminished sexuality, and remain unable to relax. It is that reality, too, that makes a patient exhibit deviant behavior, revealing himself in public or shying away from human contact. Where does it come from? A history beginning before birth, or in the critical first years, when emotional contact was so painful as to remain an enduring biologic memory.

When a doctor prescribes Zoloft for a patient, he is producing a happy ending. Instead of feeling pain the patient has become, à la Candide, egregiously sanguine. He is happy now, or is he? His stress hormone level is still very high, and although he's convinced himself he's content, the body's operating systems indicate otherwise. That delusion will make him prey to serious disease, possibly death, too early in life. Many drugs that function on upper levels of the brain work this way: they aid repression, a socially accepted but dangerous way to handle one's problems. We all want to put on a happy face. So we do, and then try to develop a rationale for our choice, aided by drugs that disguise persistent symptoms.

When a therapist offers a "good" ending for the patient, he is simply offering a defense against feeling. The one thing that would resolve and integrate the unconscious has been ignored by a well-meaning doctor who does not want his patient or himself to feel any more pain. Yet healing involves full immersion in our feelings. Nothing else. It is only when the therapist does not know how to get a patient to feel fully that mood altering medications or, worse, an invented ending to the trauma, needs to be provided for the patient.

Left to his own solutions, the patient who has felt completely most likely will rewrite his own scenario as time goes on. He will lead a different life, one based on his desires rather than the imprint. The exhibitionist will stop showing himself. The man with erectile dysfunction, a brain-based problem, will see relief from his sexual difficulty. The neurotic will be able to cope with routine stress. In each case, reliving the deep experience of a feeling will lead the patient, automatically, to the third-line awareness of it which corrective emotional experience targets.

There are so many levels to pain that a person can relive higher-level representations of it and still have enough pain stored down below to continue to experience dysfunctional moods and behaviors. It is not that the therapy itself is faulty; it is because the road is longer than we thought. Problems arise when a therapist has not acknowledged the depth of pain, nor produced the techniques necessary to probe deeply into the early developing brain. It took years for us to develop primal therapy, and I do not wish to spend time judging therapists, yet I do wish to preserve the integrity of our approach. When one of my students shows a tape of primal therapy (which we do systematically), we know immediately when a mistake has taken place and why integration has not occurred. Put simply, there are two different ways to go amiss: (1) to believe what is not there or (2) to refuse to believe what is there. It is when the doctor forces the patient into too much pain, too soon, that the patient suffers unnecessarily and must be supplied with a concocted ending to their traumatic history. Therapists must receive careful training: if they have not seen and studied what connection can do, then they may be compelled to resort to a "happy-ending" script based on rationalization or medication; however, if the doctor does not force the issue and escalate pain out of sequence, there is no need for a different ending. Connection says and does it all.

awareness versus consciousness

One of the major confusions in the field of psychology arises in equating awareness and consciousness. They are not the same, at least not from the standpoint of primal therapy, and the difference between them has major implications for treatment. Consciousness requires that all levels of the brain work together in harmony, whereas awareness is largely the domain of the prefrontal cortex. Thus, there may be those who are acutely aware—of politics or the environment, for example—but are functionally unconscious. We can go to seminar after seminar, studying neurology, or Chinese history, or marketing, or anything else, but never have any internal access to feelings. It is like we are operating with some of our marbles missing and, indeed, those marbles—or neurons, more precisely—may be absent from duty. The universal goal in a profound psychotherapy should be to restore an individual to consciousness: that means the full integration and function of all three levels of the brain, including our earliest and most remote feelings.

There is an interesting research project on this subject reported out of the University of Tel Aviv. Researchers there studied sleep patterns during gestation and found that differences in taste, smell, and responses to other factors were associated with differences in the placental environment. Because consciousness requires the various levels of the brain to work together in synchrony, events that occur before birth when the brain is undergoing rapid development become extremely significant. If the fetus is disturbed, through lack of sleep, secondhand tobacco smoke, poor nutrition, high levels of cortisol, or other intrauterine trauma, the proper integration of our feelings and thought processes may also be disrupted.

In the last weeks of gestation there is already in place, in inchoate fashion, the connection between the thalamus (the relay station of our feelings) and the top-level prefrontal cortex, which eventually makes us aware of our feelings. This connection is what brings certain emotional content to consciousness, so that we can begin to understand it on higher levels of the brain. Thus, the template for emotions is in place before we arrive on earth and, generally, it becomes evermore functional as the years go on.

However, when the intrauterine environment is disrupted through maternal trauma, particularly when trauma occurs late in gestation, integration may not proceed as it should. What investigators have found is that the fetal brain has two gears—fast and slow—reflected in the brainwave frequencies associated with different levels of consciousness and different kinds of sleep stages (active and quiet). After the seventh month of gestation there is generally a kind of synchrony of the left and right hemispheres signaling, perhaps, the beginning of integration. In this period of synchrony we find an enhanced complicity between feelings and thoughts, and a greater harmony between external and internal awareness. Serious trauma during this period, however, can prevent integration from taking place, and result in changes to consciousness that persist across the lifespan.

The reason awareness is not synonymous with consciousness is that it deals only with the last evolutionary neuronal development: the prefrontal cortex. Once we are conscious we have words to explain our feelings, but words about feelings are not the same as the feelings themselves; in fact, our verbal explanations about the things we feel are conceived in a different area of the brain than the first-order feelings. Certainly, some types of awareness are important for our survival. Being aware of the components of a healthy diet, for example, is crucial to our longevity regardless of whether we have an emotional response to eating broccoli. But a therapy of awareness versus one of consciousness has an important difference in terms of systemic impact it may have on the body and mind.

In science we are after the universal so that we can apply our knowledge to many patients, not a select few. A therapy of ideas usually can only apply to a specific patient; a therapy of needs, on the other hand, can apply to many individuals because biologically we all have similar needs. When we try to convince a patient to believe different ideas ("people actually do like you"), we generate no universal laws; the approach is idiosyncratic. But if we address the feelings underneath, we can generate universal propositions: for instance, that pain unleashed from the brainstem can produce paranoid ideas, or that the frontal cortex can transform early unmet needs into complex unrealities.

There are really two types of awareness: one is left prefrontal awareness of our external surroundings; the second is right orbitofrontal awareness, which gives us access to our inner milieu. When they are merged, we are finally conscious. There is then a radical neuro-physiological and psychological change: a qualitative leap from an incomplete state to a more comprehensive one.

In short, what we achieve in our therapy is a greater harmony between the right and left hemispheres, implying better communication between various areas of the brain. It also means that we are less driven by unconscious forces and, further, that our behavior does not proceed in robotic fashion. Arriving at that sort of integration requires a therapeutic approach that takes patients back to the womb, both physiologically and neurologically, to relive early experiences. This last point is absolutely critical. If there is no room for gestational development in therapy, then there can be no claim of profound consciousness. For it is during this period that events create an imprint that follows us throughout our lives.

memory and reliving: in search of lost time

Research reported in a September 26, 2000 briefing of the *Proceedings of the National Academy of Sciences*,[1] indicates that when a visual memory is activated the visual cortex is busy. Likewise an auditory memory, when aroused, will light up the auditory cortex. The report goes on to say that those memories with heavy emotional content activate limbic structures as parts of the frontal cortex recruit information from these areas to construct the total memory. In other words, memory affects multiple areas of the brain, and we need to arouse all relevant areas when we help patients go back and visit their past. Too often recall is an intellectual exercise bereft of the emotional connection which would make for personality change. When this connection takes place (through what I've earlier called "integration") disparate aspects of our history assemble in the brain to become whole. If one goal of psychotherapy is to make a person whole, then memory must be complete and connected.

Without proper cortical connection, the energy associated with our memories is not dissipated but, instead, rerouted back into the system. That can create symptoms from hypothyroidism to asthma; though these may have a genetic basis, I submit that they frequently will not become manifest without a residue of trauma. There a number of reasons I believe this to be true, one of which is that the process of reliving often eliminates troubling symptoms.

As I've suggested, one of the most important by-products of the connection made through reliving is that stress hormone levels are reduced permanently. When we consider that high stress hormone levels impact so many symptoms, from nightmares to depression, from palpitations to hypertension, this finding is of great importance. Cortisol levels do not drop over time without deep feeling (see *Primal Healing* for a full discussion).

In short, what is curative about reliving is that repression is lifted and the system is reacting as it should have originally. The pain is finally traveling to its proper destination, connecting with frontal cortical structures, and producing conscious awareness. We must be careful here to draw distinction between cortical awareness bereft of feeling and conscious awareness derived from feeling. As I've said, a purely cortical response to pain is equivalent to repression: an automatic process that masks but does not heal.

In the course of our therapy, as patients' defenses weaken, pain begins its march to the frontal cortex. When the feelings lock-in and connect the system can finally relax. All vital signs fall below baseline readings. Until there is this lock-in, however, the cortex may continually ruminate about various dangers, making sleep difficult or impossible. Low-lying imprinted terror in the brainstem can activate cortical centers, creating paroxysms of bizarre thoughts: "There's no space for me" or, "I am stuck and no one is helping." Often these are residual feelings from birth, emanating from an imprint unbeknownst to the patient. The latest evolving cortex must deal with the input in some fashion or another. It must make it "ego-syntonic": comfortable and not alien to the self.

What we do in our therapy is take away the symbolism, "I am stuck—in my job, in my marriage," and help the patient place it in direct context: "I am stuck in the canal and in danger of dying." As I write this, I am aware of how strange and perhaps unbelievable all of it seems. But this is not an intellectual proposition stemming from some ideas of mine, an *a priori*, or *partis pris*. Rather it is the result of careful observation and measurement over thirty years.

Recently, we carried out research at the UCLA Pulmonary Laboratory with a young man in his thirties. After reliving a birth sequence, he suddenly went into apnea and stopped breathing for a full minute. This was not a voluntary act. He replicated what happened to him at birth. It was a wordless reliving which achieved some kind of awareness that was not totally verbal. In fact, it was a connected sensation that heretofore played out in his sleep where he suffered from periodic apnea. Even if we don't have words to wrap around it, when we relive terror from the beginning of life, the experience may still be a connected event. It has entered awareness. Afterward, what we suffer from is no longer a vague, inexplicable anxiety. It is what it was: terror.

Early in life terror is enormous because there is not, as yet, a sufficient damping system in place. When patients relive the terror, it is exactly the same as it was originally, unmitigated by any defenses. The patient is now in the same state as she was as a fetus or infant. For the first time, he understands the power of what is driving him. For the first time, he understands why he needs constant painkillers and tranquilizers. Does the infant feel terror? The fetus? Of course. They simply do not have the emotional equipment as yet to express it, so it is expressed biologically.

22

pregnancy: the new critical window

I know it sounds like an oxymoron for me to give advice since I am not by profession nor intention an aficionado of advice. But let us not minimize what a carrying mother can do for the good or bad of her child. I am supposed to say here, in the spirit of optimism, that under no circumstances should you feel guilty, that no matter what you do during your pregnancy, the chances are good your baby will turn out fine. But if guilt helps make your baby better, why not? Look, a few cigarettes, a dose of tranquilizers, or a few glasses of wine is not benign. During pregnancy the baby's nerve cells are rapidly forming. Anything you do to compromise that growth and development can produce an effect for a lifetime. If there is anything our research points to it is this: What you do to yourself while carrying has a lifelong effect. For nine months, the baby is a tag-a-long; he gets what you get, only worse. If you get temporarily drunk, the baby gets compromised brain cells. Not in every case, but enough not to take chances. I've been told by my editor not to make you feel guilty, but don't ignore what I say: go on feeling a little extra cautious; second-guess yourself if it is good for your baby. Anything that keeps you aware of the importance of pregnancy can be lifesaving for the child.

Okay, now a bit of advice: watch your stress. There is no way to eliminate stress entirely, but there are certainly ways to manage it. Don't plan a new business or start a series of complicated projects that put you under stress while pregnant. The baby will feel this anxiety and suffer. Try to work out problems with your spouse before you get pregnant. Once you are pregnant, it is largely too late. That doesn't mean you should never argue or fight again; but try to resolve the more serious difficulties before you introduce a new life on this planet. The baby deserves his or her best chance at life, and what you do during pregnancy to manage your stress is important, in that regard.

Needless to say, it is important to eat right—meaning, above all, getting enough calories into your diet: plenty of protein, calcium, folic acid, and fiber, because you are feeding the baby. He must eat right for the healthy development of his brain and immune system. It is not just a temporary diet for him; it is a matter of health and longevity. Any vanity you might have concerning body image—dieting that deprives the child of key vitamins and minerals, for instance—might mean a life of adversity for the child: poor school performance, broken relationships, attention problems, not to mention a weakened immune system and greater risk of mental illness.

As for whether it's a good idea to take tranquilizers and painkillers to relieve anxiety, I'm not sure. Either way, anxiety or pills, the baby suffers. From a professional standpoint, I always opt for no drugs, as we've seen that they alter the fetus's physiology. Listen, if up till now you have done something not so hot for the baby and you feel bad, that's okay. The pictures won't fall off the walls, and your fridge won't melt. You just made a mistake. Now change.

I know how much I had to change when my wife was pregnant, and to this day I regret how poorly I did. Before the birth of our child we enlisted in a new program at our hospital where, for the doctor's convenience and for our own, the baby was kept in a drawer except on occasions we wanted to hold her. If I had known then what I know now, it never would have happened. It imprinted terror into her physiology and led to a variety of problems I will not get into here. I will say, however, that I know where my daughter's decisions came from and why she chose the drugs she did. But we are all stupid until we have good information.

That is why I write: to change birth practices, to discourage the use of anesthetics such as fentanyl and Demerol that may pose a risk to the child. Oh yes, it is easy for me to say, a man who will never be pregnant. But a degree of suffering for the mother means a lifetime of ease for the baby. It is a trade-off. From what we've observed, even epidurals may have adverse effects: the baby is weaker and less aggressive when it comes to rooting for the breast right after birth.

Don't just take my word for it. Read French obstetrician Frederic Leboyer, who popularized the practice of immersing the newborn in a warm water bath, without drugs and without bright lights. Leboyer recommends that the baby be held right away and for a long time. He advises against cutting the umbilical cord too soon as the child's attachment with his mother is vital at the start of life. Of course I have every reason to sing Leboyer's praises. When he came to visit me and saw our work he stood up and shouted, "I am vindicated!" Of course the reason I respect his work has nothing to do with ego.

You cannot leave a baby untouched for weeks or days and expect no damage; it may show up as a lifelong fear of enclosed spaces, or as anxiety attacks or depression. In some cases, it may emerge in the sex addict who constantly needs to be touched. I know this may sound ridiculous, but I assure you it is not. The birth process is one of the most perilous journeys we will make during our lifetime. We come so close to death, perhaps the closest we will ever come (short of taking our last breath), and this occurs at the very start of our lives: it is imprinted. It is no wonder some of us go on fearing death for a lifetime: the near-death experience continues to dog us and makes us anxious. We are afraid because this early fear, if not met with love, remains near the surface all the time. I see the results every day in my patients.

The baby, in the womb and as a newly born infant, has the most wide-open emotional window he is ever going to have. Everything has a great impact. One cigarette can constitute an imprint, producing a choking and a bronchial constriction that can become a prototype as to how the child will respond to later trauma. How do we know? Because we have measured the after-effects. More important, we have measured the "during-effects." When the body temperature goes up or down three degrees in minutes during primal therapy, we know how true it is. When the patient's permanent level of blood pressure drops continuously over a year of therapy, we see again what early imprints have done and what reliving can do. When stress hormone levels drop we have yet more confirmation. Yes, statistical studies are important, but so is experience. How many studies do we need to know that we should pick up a crying baby in her crib?

Don't plan a cesarean at anyone's convenience. It interrupts natural biologic processes, and that can be damaging. My patients who were delivered through cesarean are often passive, waiting for something to magically happen. When they get themselves in a jam, they expect someone to intercede and help out. They are prone to fall behind, preparing for events that have already happened; they abhor surprises and plan obsessively so that they won't be caught off guard. These effects are not universal for cesarean patients, but they happen often enough that I can make this generalization: Do not rush into a cesarean birth merely for the sake of the doctor's schedule. This is a human life you are bringing into the world, and any delivery by cesarean should be done with careful deliberation and discussion and only as a last resort.

For pregnant mothers, there is no greater advice I can give than this: be open, expressive, and feeling with your children. A caring mother gives her baby the best chance for long-term well-being. Yes, even if you don't eat those carrots and tomatoes when you should, love will help.

Your child is part of you and feels what you feel, even though he doesn't have words to express it. He will have the words in twenty years when he says, "I don't know how or why I got into drugs," or, "I don't know why I keep moving around and cannot stay in one place. Something inside moves me." The better possibility, of course, is that your child will have the words to thank you for having given him love when he most needed it. All I ask is awareness. The research is there; we don't have to guess anymore.

23

feeling emotional pain: can it be a matter of life and death?

The question is, why am I writing all of this? What difference will it make? Without appearing too dramatic, I think a child's development in the womb can be a matter of life and death. At the very least it is something every pregnant woman should consider. During pregnancy she is constructing a new being on this earth, and what happens during these nine months will profoundly affect her child throughout his life. From what we've seen, it may indeed determine how long that child lives.

Lack of love kills. I have been writing about this for decades, but too often my warning cries have fallen on deaf ears. With the abundance of new evidence that has emerged—including the work of distinguished fetal scientists, geneticists, and neurologists from Sweden to New Zealand—perhaps that will begin to change. As further validation for my theory, an article published in *Science Daily*[1] indicates that those who experienced trauma while being carried and in childhood died, on average, twenty years earlier than those who did not have those risk factors. The title, aptly enough, was "Traumatic Childhood Might Take Years Off Adult Life." The average age of death, according to the Centers for Disease Control and Prevention,[2] was sixty—not close enough to the average age of the non-risk group (seventy-nine), to be easily discounted.

What the study found was that those children exposed to six or more risk factors were at "double the risk of premature death." More evidence of what I've been saying all along: lack of love can indeed be fatal. Risk factors cited in the study included living in a household with substance abuse, domestic violence, growing in the womb of a battered mother, verbal and physical abuse, mental illness in the home, and parental separation or divorce. Any one of these, it appears, is powerful enough to create lifelong damage.

Just as soberly, the two most common ways to exit this planet are heart attack and cancer. It is now fairly well established that womb-life affects heart function, and there is emerging evidence from the University of Toronto showing a possible link between early physical abuse and the occurrence of cancer. In interpreting the results, researchers hypothesized that one key factor in the occurrence of cancer was a deregulation of cortisol production. What the researchers didn't study were the more subtle abuses originating during our time in the womb. For now, these can only be inferred. But based on our experience this kind of trauma may be just as shattering as that which occurs in the first years of life. Our research has found that incoming patients at the Primal Center are generally quite high in the stress hormone cortisol and typically normalize after one year of the therapy; in addition, they seem to have a lower-than-average incidence of cancer after completing therapy.

What I have repeatedly noted is that first-line pain, emanating from low in the brain, is almost always a matter of life and death. What is critical here is that the valence—or force of the pain—provokes a commensurate amount of repression. And it is that repression that may account for many serious diseases, including cancer, since it is holding down enormous force. I propose a study in cancer patients (and controls without cancer) to see what kind of womb-life and birth trauma those individuals experienced, and how this time may or may not have contributed to the disease.

Another line of study, as hinted above, should attempt to verify early evidence that experience in the womb can affect heart function years later. Dementia also warrants examination since some forms of late-stage memory loss may have fetal origins. Further, womb-life may have a significant effect on the development of our personality, resulting in different kinds of postures (defeated vs. upright), modes of expression (timid vs. garrulous), gaits (hesitant vs. purposeful), and emotions (fearful vs. self-assured). In other words, adverse early experience in the developing fetus or infant is possibly transmuted into mistrust, fear, or other later aberration in personality—all different avenues for expressing the same early feeling. It is a truncated language but it emanates from specific kinds of imprints and is predicated, in many cases, by a mother who during pregnancy smokes, has birth complications, uses drugs, or is under high levels of stress. Connected through feelings these early events form a gestalt. That is why when patients go back and relive their origins, all of the disparate reactions may become linked and resolved.

All of this bears influence on what is called our "basic character structure." It is widely believed that our psychological disposition derives from heredity; most likely, however, a substantial portion of it does not. The tendency toward depression, for example, is often predicted by the mother's emotional state while carrying. It has been found, as well, that traumatic birth can account for a majority of the causes of attention deficit disorder. This is to say nothing of the tendency to suicide, which has already been well documented by the child psychologist Lee Salk and others. When the early environment is dangerous, the mother excessively agitated, the newborn will search for clues from the outside as to how to behave. He will be hyper-alert to clues from others to direct his behavior. In addition, if the mother drinks or takes drugs she will not only calm herself but the fetus, as well. With high enough levels of exposure this may set up a later tendency for heavy drinking or drug use; when life gets tough there will be a resort to alcohol—an association set up during womb-life.

Again, my aim is not to alarm expectant mothers, nor to encourage legislative efforts to regulate a mother's decision-making process during childbirth. Rather it is to alert us all as to the profound influence of gestational life. We need to pay heed. This research may prove no less important than what concerned Louis Pasteur, the great French scientist of the mid-nineteenth century. If Pasteur had not looked beyond conventional causes, if he had not proposed that boiling wine could kill harmful bacteria, or injected chickens with cholera to study the progression of the disease, our knowledge of vaccination would be nowhere near where it is today. Science and medicine require new and extraordinary methods. If we omit key epochs in our lives that play an important role in the development of neurosis, we will never arrive at cures.

What most of medicine and psychotherapy involves today is the treatment of fragments of a human being, pieces of an original memory that has lost its connection to the whole. So we have coughing spells, frequent colds, anxiety, and phobias—all pieces of an original imprint. We then go about treating the varied offshoots from a central imprint rather than the imprint itself; treatment becomes interminable. What we get is a fragment of progress—a change in aspects of an early experience, rather than a holistic recalibration of neural and physiologic mechanisms connected with the experience. As I noted earlier, in primal therapy we treat the phobias, the high blood pressure and palpitations, sometimes all with the same therapeutic techniques or medication. And the reason our treatment is effective is because these various symptoms are all of a piece, all aspects of the same early experience.

It is critical to be forewarned about early trauma and later disease. That way we can address our pain, relive aspects of it, and prevent later manifestation in mental illness and disease. When we unload some of the energy utilized in repressing very early trauma, we release pressure on the system that often results in the emergence of health problems. To attack remote pains (which due to their early life-endangering imprint are often catastrophic), is to attack encased memories that are terribly painful and damaging to the system. Of course it is one thing to describe their effects, even to fully understand them; it is quite another to be able to eliminate their source and force.

We have had good success with attention deficit disorder (ADD) because we've been able to resolve some of the incredible pressure on the system, which keeps one from focusing and concentrating. ADD is really an example of poor gating: underlying pain surges upward, interferes with the neocortex, and keeps the brain from disciplined cohesion. I often use the example of a puzzle barely put together. Disruption at or before birth often upsets the brain's organization and is then compounded by more childhood pain until the gating system becomes ineffective. So much pain is coming up from the limbic system, in other words, that the mind loses cohesion; it becomes fractured and unable to control the force of lower-level feelings.

So what should a therapy be and do? First of all, it needs to focus on history. Any therapy without a "why" in it cannot work on a deep level. Any time a therapy ushers patients through a mechanical process, requiring them to pray, meditate, think new thoughts, undergo biofeedback, and so forth, it cannot succeed. We are the results of our histories, yet almost every therapy extant ignores those histories and takes the symptom for the problem: crushes it with words and ideas, drugs it with medication, punishes it with exhortations or the invocation of a deity, pleads with it to be more wholesome, or analyzes it to death with some kind of guess about its causes. Let me be clear: No therapist can ever know what is in your unconscious; the unconscious contains a record of events long before we had words, and linguistic approaches offer little hope for ascertaining what is going on in those lower regions of the brain.

Understand, there is a qualitative difference between events that happened to us while being carried in mother's womb, and those events that happened during birth and after. It is a matter of irreversibility—what happens to us during gestation imprints a "now-print" memory that endures as if that were our genetic legacy. Our physiology and later psychology revolve around this imprint. When trauma occurs while we are in the womb, there are little or no compensating mechanisms that will right the ship. We adjust to the imbalance and go on from there. If the imprint includes an orientation toward passivity, then our vital signs, body temperature, and blood pressure will accommodate themselves to that new state; it is all of a piece, an ensemble of reactions.

Shortly after birth there may be the brief possibility to correct the imbalance. For example, although high stress levels in the carrying mother can produce practically the same configuration in the offspring, and although this can and does alter the sex hormone secretions, events that play out against this background may determine whether the imprint becomes fixed. In other words, the pre-birth imprint is in place, but it is the embarrassment and hurt caused, for instance, by a tyrannical father who shows no love to his son that compounds the imprint and alters the son's sexual proclivities. Thus, altered sex hormone balance plus key painful events in early childhood may contribute to the appearance of homosexuality.

When all this happens before the age of six months, chances are increased that homosexuality will be made manifest. In this case the imprint is set down, in part, during gestational life, making it more or less permanent and seemingly genetic; the physiologic system believes it is genetic, and makes accommodations to it. Such imprints begin in the womb and may affect not only our sexual disposition but also the performance of our immune system. That is why chronic conditions such as allergies, which are generally thought of genetic (because they begin so early and remain such an active force), may also indicate something harmful that occurred during pregnancy. Are we born with allergies? Are we born gay? Yes and no. It seems to me that as we prepare to be born we gather all our genetic assets and abilities together to go on throughout life. Who we become, however, is largely shaped by what is engraved on our system during our nine months in the womb.

Despite the new evidence that is emerging every day in this field, intellectuals continue to doubt and refute the importance of addressing gestational imprints in psychotherapy. At least one prominent psychologist says that the imprint is unimportant or even non-existent, citing a number of concentration camp internees who have later made a very good adjustment after being mistreated at the hands of the Nazis. These researchers don't speak the right language. They are bound by a brain that is apparent and observable, by left-brain therapy approaches which are taken as gospel. When truths are offered beyond facts and statistics, truths that involve a different kind of language, they are abjured as lacking precision and "objectivity." It doesn't surprise me that our therapy is slow to gain acceptance in these circles: Left-brainers want and relate to statistical truths when mostly what we offer are biologic ones. But I fear that if we continue to leave the body out of our assessment of mental health, we will make little progress in psychotherapy.

For too long, we have been talking to the wrong brain. The correct brain is one that contains our history, our pain, and our feelings: the limbic brain that stores and processes our deepest feelings, which can finally liberate us. This area of the brain does understand our early afflictions; we need to speak that language—one without words. At the same time we have to convince the upper brain—the neocortex that spouts words and ideas—that it is necessary to go back to early life and relive that original lack of love, to experience anew feelings that were too physiologically stressful to bear at the time. We have to convince that thinking brain to let go and let the lower brain systems emerge and breathe the air of freedom. It can be done.

In the early days of primal therapy, to help patients access their deep feelings, I would have two patients kneel face-to-face and express their feelings while "talking in tongues." This is not that different from an old Holy Roller religious exercise that parishioners engaged in. At the time many thought I was crazy—and, of course, a number of them still do. But what the exercise did, though I didn't fully understand it at the time, was take away all *verbal* language so that only pure feeling could be expressed. Without the ability to speak in their native language, patients were forced to revert to the expression of primal feelings, feelings laid down in the womb and the critical the first years of life.

Unfortunately, the brain we need to address doesn't talk, doesn't understand English, and, as a matter of fact, doesn't understand words. In fact, the term "understand" is a bit of a misnomer. We are not after understanding in the intellectual sense of the term; we are after integration that can happen without cerebral understanding. Yes, understanding helps, but it must not be confused with resolving, connecting, and integrating. When a therapist tries to get a patient to report on his feelings all may be lost, for those feelings may be wordless. Trying to express them verbally distances us from the origins of our pain in the lower brain. And since one layer of brain tissue cannot do the work of another, we have effectively trumped our efforts. Once we get away from words we can focus on what is curative. Understanding came last in human evolution, long after feeling, and it will not lead us to the type of long-term healing we are after. None of this requires abstract or esoteric methods. We can make major changes in society just by paying attention to gestation and changing our birth practices.

In the last years of Albert Einstein's life he was searching for a unified theory that would explain so much of the complex world of the heavens. He wanted to explain all of nature's forces as they pertain to the stars, the moons, the sun, and all of the events in the cosmos. In a way, I, too, have been looking for such a theory. I believe we have come some way into explaining a good deal of human behavior, its deviations, symptoms, and perversions. There is always more to learn, but perhaps we have charted the beginnings of a unified field theory in psychology. I'll say it once again, in the hope that scientists, doctors, psychotherapists, psychologists, and expectant mothers everywhere are ready to listen: feeling isn't just another psychological approach; it is a *sine qua non* for mental health.

appendix a:
manifesto for a new psychotherapy

Having had a long practice in psychotherapy, and having read so many journal articles in our field and seen how difficult it is to get approvals, I want to state a few thrusts that have influenced my viewpoints in this book:

1. To insist that biologic truths must be considered primary;
2. That statistical truths are secondary;
3. That the field of psychotherapy needs to change into an experiential therapy;
4. That this new psychotherapy, has to be able to reach back into the time before birth and address the generating sources of so many physical and psychological problems;
5. That evolution dictates how any therapy is practiced and must not be neglected in favor of pragmatism. (Currently, only six sessions for patients of psychologists are approved for insurance payments);
6. That we must adopt a new definition of memory that encompasses non-verbal and preverbal times;
7. That the psychological must be considered as that layer lying above the emotional and is part and parcel of it;
8. That insights and cognitive approaches fail to distinguish the role of thoughts in the human psyche, treating the psyche as something independent of the rest of us;

9. That thoughts cannot change imprinted feelings, but imprinted feelings can and do change thoughts;

10. That the goal of psychotherapy must be to restore feelings to human beings so that when they leave treatment they can love and live fully;

11. That measuring progress in psychotherapy must take into consideration the neurophysiologic aspects of the human condition, and not be satisfied with patient reports;

12. That there needs to be a place for new ideas in psychology.

appendix b: research questionnaire

Arthur Janov is currently conducting research with a German medical clinic. The following questionnaire is being used as part of that research. If you'd like to take part in this research project, please answer the following questions to the best of your ability and send them to Dr. Arthur Janov at The Primal Center, 209 Ashland Ave., Santa Monica, CA, 90405.

1. Can you describe your birth? Drugs, anesthesia, natural, breech, cesarean? Pre-term birth or late birth? Home birth or hospital? Was there breastfeeding or bottle feeding? For how long? Did your mother have adequate milk?

2. Can you describe your gestation period? Was your mother and the household calm and not under stress? Was there marital discord if any kind? Was the father in the home throughout your being carried? Any talk of separation or divorce? Was there a recognized marriage before your birth?

3. Was the external environment benevolent? Were there poverty, wars, strikes or disasters in the environment?

4. Were one or both parents under stress? For what reasons?

5. Did your mother regularly take medication or tranquilizers or pain killers? Did she drink alcohol?

6. Did your mother consume unhealthy during gestation? Was she on an unhealthy diet?

7. Would you describe the family while mother was carrying as loving? As unloving?

8. Was your mother chronically anxious or depressed? For how long? Was she exceptionally tense?

9. Were you an accident or a wanted baby? Were you born after a long delay between your older sibling and you?

10. Were you held immediately after birth? Were you sickly as a newborn? Describe.

For more information, please contact us at

Primal Center
209 Ashland Ave.
Santa Monica, California 90405

e-mail: primalctr@mac.com
website: www.primaltherapy.com
blog: arthurjanov.com
telephone: (310) 392-2003

endnotes

PART ONE: WOMB-LIFE, A NEW PARADIGM

Chapter One: How Love Sculpts the Brain

1 Hamzelou J., "It pays to remember what made you sad," *New Scientist*, April 17, 2010, http://www.newscientist.com/article/dn18763-it-pays-to-remember-what-made-you-sad.html, as reported in *Proceedings of the National Academy of Sciences* (accessed June 16, 2011).

2 Meaney M., et al., "The effects of postnatal handling on the development of the glucocorticoid receptor systems and stress recovery in the rat," *Progress in Neuro-Psychopharmacology Proceedings and Biological Psychiatry* 9, no. 5-6(1985): 731-34.

Chapter Two: Are We Already Who We Are at Birth?

1 Condron B., Daubert E., Heffron D., Mandell J., "Serotonergic dystrophy induced by excess serotonin," *Molecular and Cellular Neuroscience* 44(2010): 297-306.

2 Segerstrale M., Juuri J., Lanore F., Piepponen P., Lauri S., Mulle C., Taira T., "High Firing of Neonatal Hippocampal Interneurons is Caused by Attenuation of Potassium Currents by Afterhyperpolarizing Active Kainite Receptors Tonically," *Journal of Neuroscience* 30, no. 19 (2010): 6507 and *Science Daily*, May 10, 2010.

3 Hollenbeck, A., et al., "Neonates prenatally exposed to anesthetics: Four-year follow-up," *Child Psychiatry and Human Development* 17, no. 1 (1986): 66-70.

4 Nyberg K. et al., "Perinatal medication as a potential risk factor for adult drug use in North American cohort," *Epidemiology* 11(2000): 715-16.

5 Gaidos S., "A pregnant question," *Science News*, 177, no. 12, June 5, 2010:22-25.

6 See note 1.

7 Alwan S., Reefhuis J., Botto L., Rasmussen S., Onley R., Friedman J., "Selective serotonin-reuptake inhibitors in pregnancy and the risk for birth defects," *New England Journal of Medicine* 356(2007): 2684-92.

8 Breton C., et al., "Variation in the GST mu Locus and Tobacco Smoke as Determinants of Childhood Lung Function," *American Journal of Respiratory Care and Critical Care Medicine* 179(2009): 601-7.

9 *Science Daily*, "Link between childhood physical abuse and heart disease," July 23, 2010, http://www.sciencedaily.com/releases/2010/07/100722102043.htm (accessed June 14, 2012).

10 Gluckman P., *The Fetal Matrix: Evolution, Development, and Disease* (Cambridge, UK: Cambridge University Press, 2004).

11 Wright R., et al. "Prenatal Maternal Stress and Cord Blood Innate and Adaptive Cytokine Responses in an Inner-city Cohort," *American Journal of Respiratory and Critical Care Medicine* 182, no. 1 (2010): 25-33.

Chapter Three: Searching for a Universal Psychology

1 Medina J., "Molecules of Mind," *Psychiatric Times*, July 2007, http://www.psychiatrictimes.com/molecules.

2 Connor, Steve. "Premature babies may feel pain more as adults," *The Independent,* July 28, 2000, http://www.independent.co.uk/news/science/premature-babies-may-feel-pain-more-as-adults-706250.html (accessed June 16, 2011).

3 Reijmers L., et al., "Localization of a Stable Neural Correlate of Associative Memory," *Science* 317, no. 1230(2007): doi:10.1126/science.1143839 (accessed June 16, 2011).

4 *Science Daily,* "Researchers Know What You Were About to Say; fMRI Used to Detect Memory Storage and Retrieval," Dec. 25, 2005, http://www.sciencedaily.com /releases/2005/12/051224095748.htm (accessed June 16, 2011.

Chapter Four: How the Brain Talks to Itself

1 Herrick, C., *The Brain of the Tiger Salamander: Amby stoma tigrinum* (Chicago: University of Chicago Press, 1948).

2 Lowery C., Hardman M., Manning N., Hall R., Anand K., Clancy B., "Neurodevelopmental changes of fetal pain," *Semin Perinatol* 31 no. 5(2007): 275-82.

3 LeDoux J., et al., "Preventing the return of fear in humans using reconsolidation of update mechanisms," *Nature* 463 (2010): 49-53.

Chapter Five: The Womb as a Black Box

1 Schacter D., *Science,* 235, no. 4786 (1987): 373-4.

2 Eisenberg N., et al., "Rejection Really Hurts," *Science,* Oct. 10, 2003.

3 Parry, Vivienne. "How emotional pain can really hurt," BBC News, July 21, http://news.bbc.co.uk/2/hi/7512107.stm (accessed June 16, 2011).

PART TWO: THE SCIENCE OF EARLY HUMAN DEVELOPMENT

Chapter Six: How We Internalize our External World: Telomores as a Predictor of Life Expectancy

1 Tyrka A., et al., "Childhood Maltreatment Biological Psychiatry and Telomere Shortening: Preliminary Support for an Effect of Early Stress on Cellular Aging," *Biological Psychiatry* 67, no. 6 (2010).

2 Ibid.

3 Kananen L., et al., "Childhood adversities are associated with shorter telomere length at adult age both in individuals with an anxiety disorder and controls," *Plos One* 5, no. 5 (2010).

4 Carey B., "Too Much Stress May Give Genes Gray Hair," *New York Times*, Nov. 30, 2004; Epel E., et al., "Accelerated telomore shortening in response to stress," *Proceedings of the National Academy of Sciences* 101, no. 49 (2004): 171312-17315.

5 Okuda K. et al., "Telomore length in newborn," *Pediatr Res* 52, no.3 (2002):(abstract).

Chapter Seven: How Repression Works

Chapter Eight: Epigenetics: The Inheritance of Acquired Characteristics

1 Sarkar P., Bergman K., Fisk N., O'Connor T., Glover V., "Ontogeny of fetal exposure to maternal cortisol using midtrimester amniotic fluid as a biomarker," *Clinical Endocrinology*, 66, no. 5 (2007): 636-40.

2 Bielski Z., "Stress During Pregnancy May Lower Baby's IQ," *The Globe and Mail*, July 5, 2009.

3 Field T., et al., "Prenatal depression effects on the fetus and new-born," *Infant Behavior Development* 27(2004): 216-29.

4 I think this means that the right (feeling) brain is forced to be hyper-active to deal with emotional push. It is, after all, the right prefrontal brain (orbitofrontal area) that maintains a history of our feelings and has an internal focus.

5 Geddes L., "Bit of a crybaby? Blame your serotonin levels," *New Scientist*, July 15, 2010.

6 *Healthday News*, "C-Section Stress Could Alter Baby's Immune Cells," July 9, 2009.

7 Linus Pauling Institute at Oregon State University, "Epigenetic concepts offer new approach to degenerative disease," Experimental Biology Conference; Anaheim, California, April 29, 2010, as reported in *Science Daily*, http://www.sciencedaily.com/releases/2010/04/100428081836.htm (accessed June 16, 2011).

8 *Science Daily*, "Good parenting triumphs over prenatal stress," Feb. 26, 2010, http://www.sciencedaily.com/releases/2010/02/100225140906.htm (accessed June 16, 2011).

9 See the index for a questionnaire devised to measure the effects of early experience on later disease.

10 See chapter 1; note 2.

11 We will need to carry out research on demethylation when we can. Our hypothesis is that if we take a certain sample (lymphoblasts) from the bone marrow and see how it grows into white blood cells, we can measure demethylation. It is a preliminary theory, but there may be a way, in the near future, to see what effects our therapy or other chemicals may have on methylation.

12 Garcia R., Vouimba R-M., Baudry M., Thompson R., "The amygdala modulates prefrontal activity relative to conditioned fear," *Nature* 402(1999): 294-96.

13 Anand K., Hickey P., "Pain and its Effects in the Human Neonate and Fetus," *New England Journal of Medicine* 317(1987): 1321-9.

14 McGowan P., et al., "Epigenetic regulation of the glucocorticoid receptor in human brain associates with childhood abuse," *Nature Neuroscience* 12(2009): 342-48.

15 Lesham M., Schulkin J., Shachar-Dadon, A., "Adversity before conception will affect adult progency in rats," *Developmental Psychology* 45, no. 1 (2009): 9.

16 Bucay H., et al., "Endorphins, personality, and inheritance: Establishing the biochemical bases of inheritance," *Bioscience Hypothesis* 2, no. 3 (2009): 170-71.

17 Laybutt, D., et al., "Chronic high-fat diet in fathers programs β-cell dysfunction in female rat offspring," *Nature* 467 (2010): 963-966.

Chapter Nine: Oxytocin: The Hormone of Love

1 Harmon K., "A Phone Call from Mom Reduces Stress as Well As a Hug," *Scientific American*, May 11, 2010; Seltzer L., Ziegler T., Pollak S., "Social vocalizations can release oxytocin in humans," *Proceedings of the Royal Society* (2010). ePub ahead of print. May 12, 2010. doi, http://rspb.royalsocietypublishing.org/content/early/2010/05/06/rspb.2010.0567.full#cited-by (accessed June 17, 2011).

2 Insel T., "A Neurological Basis of Social Attachment," *Am J Psychiatry* 154 (1997): 726-35.

3 Carmichael M., Humbert R., Dixen J., Palmisano G., Greenleaf W., Davidson J., "Plasma oxytocin increases in the human sexual response," *J Clin Endocrinol Metab* 64(1987): 27-31; Carmichael M., Warburton V.,

Dixen J., Davidson J., "Relationship among cardiovascular, muscular, and oxytocin responses during human sexual activity," *Archives of Sexual Behavior* 23(1994): 59–79.

4 Devarajan K, Rusak B., "Oxytocin levels in plasma and cerecrospinal fluid of male rats: effects of circadian phase, light and stress," *Neuorsci Lett* 367, no. 2 (2004): 144-47.

5 Murphy M., Seckl J., Burton S., Checkley S., Lightman S. "Changes in oxytocin and vasopressin secretion during sexual activity in men," *Journal of Clinical Endocrinology and Metabolism* 65(1987): 738–741.

Chapter Ten: Womb-life and Serotonin Output: The Origin For Later Mental Life

1 Ranalli P., "The Emerging Reality of Fetal Pain in Late Abortion," http://www.nrlc.org/news/2000/NRL09/ranalli.html (accessed June 17, 2011).

2 van Aerts L., "Toxicity of Ecstacy," [sic] Ecstacy.org, http://www. ectsacy.org/info/leon.html (accessed July 17, 2011).

3 Cote F., et al., "Maternal serotonin is crucial for murine embryonic development," *Proceedings of the National Academy of Sciences* 104, no. 1 (2006): 329-34.

Chapter Eleven: Early Trauma and Epilepsy

Chapter Twelve: Imipramine Binding Study

Chapter Thirteen: How Addiction Gets its Start in Our Lives

1 Schaal B., et al., "Human fetuses learn odors from their pregnant mother's diet," *Chemical Senses 25, no. 6 (2000): 729-37.*

Chapter Fourteen: The Birth Trauma

1 Duncan J., et al., "Brainstem serotonergic deficiency in sudden infant death syndrome," *Journal of The American Medical Association* 303, no. 5 (2010): 430-37.

2 Steriade, M., "Coherent oscillations and short-term plasticity in corticothalamic networks," *Trends in Neuroscience* 22, no. 8 (1999): 337-45.

3 Korosi A., et al., "The pathways from mother's love to baby's future," *Frontiers In Behavioral Neuroscience* 3, no. 27 (2009), http://www.ncbi. nlm.nih.gov/pmc/articles/PMC2759360/ (accessed June 17, 2011).

4 Anand K., et al., "Can Adverse Neonatal Experiences Alter Brain Development and Subsequent Behavior?" *Biology of the Neonate* 77, no. 2 (2000): 69-82.

5 Ibid: p 70.

6 Ibid: p 70.

PART THREE: EXPLAINING ADULT MENTAL ILLNESS AND DISEASE

Chapter Fifteen: Anoxia, Reduced Oxygen at Birth, and Adult Behavior

1 Fendt M., et al., "Behavioral Alterations in Rats Following Neonatal Hypoxia and Effects of Clozapine," *Pharmacopsychiatry* 41, no.4 (2008): 138-45; Cannon, T.D., et al., "Decreased Neurotrophic Response to Birth Hypozia in the Etiology of Schizophrenia," *Biological Psychiatry* 64, no. (2008): 797-802.

2 Minkel J., "Putting Madness in its Place," *Scientific American*, November 2009, http://www.scientificamerican.com/article.cfm?id=putting-madness-in-its-place (accessed June 16, 2011).

3 Malaspina D., et al., "Acute maternal stress in pregnancy and schizophrenia in offspring: a cohort prospective study," *BMC Psychiatry* 8 (2008): 71.

4 *Science Daily,* "Severe Stressful Events Early in Pregnancy May be Associated with Schizophrenia Among Offspring," Feb. 5, 2008, Kashan A., et al., "Higher Risk of Offspring Schizophrenia Following Antenatal Maternal Exposure to Severe Adverse Life Events," *Archives of General Psychiatry* 65, no. 2 (2008): 146-52.

5 *Science Daily,* "Mother's Prenatal Stress Predisposes Their Babies to Asthma and Allergy, Study Shows," May 19, 2008, http://www.sciencedaily.com/releases/2008/05/080518122143.htm (accessed June 17, 2011); Wright, R., et al., "Maternal Stress and Perinatal Programming in the Expression of Atopy," *Expert Review of Clinical Immunology* 4, no. 5 (2008): 535-8.

6 Seckl J., "Glucorticoid Programming and PTSD Risk," *Annals of the N.Y. Academy of Science* 1071(2008): 351-378.

7 Cottrell E., et al., "Prenatal Stress, Glucocorticoids, and the Programming of Adult Disease," *Behavioral Neuroscience* 3, no. 19 (2009), http://www.ncbi.nlm.nih.gov/pmc/articles/PMC2759372/ (accessed June 16, 2011).

8 Hoffman E., et al., "Hemispheric Quantitative EEG Changes Following Emotional Reactions in Neurotic Patients," *Acta Psychiatrica Scandinavica* 63, no. 2 (1981): 153-64.

9 Shirtcliff E., et al., "Early Childhood Stress Is Associated With Elevated Antibody Levels to Herpes Simplex Virus Type 1," *Proceedings of the National Academy of Sciences of the United States of America* 106, no. 80 (2009): 2963-7.

10 Singer D., "Metabolic adaptation to hypoxia: cost and benefit of being small," *Respiratory Physiology and Neurobiology* 141, no. 3 (2004): 215-28.

11 Huot R., et al., "Negative Affect in Offspring of Depressed Mothers is Predicted by Infant Levels at 6 Months, and Maternal Depression during Pregnancy but Not Post-Partum," *Annals of the New York Academy of Science* 1032 (2004): 234-6.

12 Thomson P., "'Down Will Come Baby': Prenatal Stress, Primitive Defenses and Gestational Dysregulation," *Journal of Trauma and Dissociation* 8, no. 3 (2007): 85-113.

13 Ibid.

14 Kaplan L., et al., "Effects of Mother's Prenatal Psychiatric Status and Postnatal Caregiving on Infant Biobehavioral Regulation: Can Prenatal Programming Be Modified?" *Early Human Development* 84, no. 4 (2008): 249-56.

15 Jacobson B., et al., "Obstetic Care and Proneness of Offspring to Suicide as Adults," *British Medical Journal* 317, no. 7169(1998): 1346-9.

16 Ibid: p 1346.

17 Dobbs D., "A Depression Switch?" *New York Times*, April 2, 2006.

Chapter Sixteen: On the Nature of Anxiety

1 See chapter eight; note 1.

2 Murgatroyd C., et al., "Dynamic DNA Methylation Programs Persistent Adverse Effects of Early-Life Stress," *Nature Neuroscience* 12 (2009): 1559-66.

3 Ibid.

Chapter Seventeen: On Psychopathology

1 Kiehl, K., "Inside the Mind of a Psychopath," *Scientific American Mind*, Sept. 2010, 22.

2 Craig, M., et al., "Altered Connections on the Road to Psychopathy," *Molecular Psychiatry* 14, no. 10 (2009): 946-53.

3 Chesterton, G. K., Orthodoxy (Chicago: Moody, 2009) 34.

Chapter Eighteen: On Attention Deficit Disorder
1 Radiohead, *OK Computer*, compact disc, Capitol, July 1, 1997

2 Spinney, L., "Stressed Out? It Could Be In Your Genes," *The Independent*, December 2, 2010, http://www.independent.co.uk/news/science/stressed-out-it-could-be-in-your-genes-2148653.html (accessed June 16, 2010).

Chapter Nineteen: The Root Cause of Alzheimer's and Deep Depression
1 Song, W., et al., "Hypoxia facilitates Alzheimer's disease pathogenesis by up-regulating BACE1 gene expression," *Proceedings of the National Academy of Sciences of the United States of America* 103, no. 49 (2006): 18727-32.

2 Merril D., et al., "Association of Early Experience with Neurodegeneration in Aged Primates," *Neurobiology of Aging* 32, no. 1 (2011): 151-56.

3 *Science Daily*, "Stress may increase risk for Alzheimer's disease," May 27, 2011, http://www.sciencedaily.com/releases/2011/05/110526114535.htm; Sotiropoulos I., Osborne F. et al., "Stress Acts Cumulatively to Precipitate Alzheimer's Disease-Like Tau Pathology and Cognitive Deficits," *Journal of Neuroscience* 31, no. 21 (2011) 7840-7.

4 Lynch, G., et al., "Hypoxia facilitates Alzheimer's disease pathogenesis by up-regulating BACE1 gene expression," *Proceedings of the National Academy of Sciences of the United States of America* 107, no. 29 (2010): 13123-8.

5 Singer D., "Neonatal Tolerance to Hypoxia," *Comparative Biochemistry and Physiology. Part A, Molecular & Integrative Physiology* 123, no. 3 (1999): 221-34.

6 Bonsignore G., et al., "Long-term Effects of Acute Perinatal Asphyxia on Rat Maternal Behavior," *Neurotoxicol Teratol* 25, no. 5 (2003): 571-8.

7 Mykletun A., et al., "Levels of anxiety and depression as predictors of mortality: the HUNT study," *The British Journal of Psychiatry* 195, no. 2 (2009): 118-25.

PART FOUR: TOWARD A FEELING THERAPY

Chapter Twenty: The Role of Evolution in Primal Therapy

1 MacLean P., *The Triune Brain in Evolution: Role in Paleocerebral Functions* (New York: Springer, 1990).

2 Harmon K., "Colorizing Dinosaurs: Feather Pigments Reveal Appearance of Extinct Animals," *Scientific American*, January 27, 2010.

Chapter Twenty-one: On the Corrective Emotional Experience

1 Wheeler M., Peterson S., Buckner R. "Memory's echo: vivid remembering reactivates sensory-specific cortex," *Proceedings of the National Academy of Sciences* 97, no. 20 2000:11125-9.

Chapter Twenty-two: Pregnancy: The New Critical Window

Chapter Twenty-three: Conclusion: Feeling Emotional Pain—Can it Be a Matter of Life and Death?

1 *Science Daily*, "Traumatic Childhood Might Take Years Off Adult Life," October 7, 2009, http://www.sciencedaily.com/releases/2009/10/091006115140.htm (accessed June 16, 2011); Brown D., et

al., "Adverse Childhood Experiences and The Risk of Premature Mortality," *American Journal of Preventative Medicine* 37, no. 5 (2009).

2   Ibid.

index